Freedom of Information

Mediating American History

David Copeland
General Editor

Vol. 1

PETER LANG
New York • Washington, D.C./Baltimore • Bern
Frankfurt am Main • Berlin • Brussels • Vienna • Oxford

Shannon E. Martin

FREEDOM
OF INFORMATION

The News the Media Use

PETER LANG
New York • Washington, D.C./Baltimore • Bern
Frankfurt am Main • Berlin • Brussels • Vienna • Oxford

180576593

Library of Congress Cataloging-in-Publication Data

Martin, Shannon E.
Freedom of information: the news the media use /
Shannon E. Martin.
p. cm. —(Mediating American history; v. 1)
Includes bibliographical references and index.
1. Government and the press—United States.
2. Freedom of information—United States.
3. Government information—United States. I. Title.
PN4745.M37 323.44'50973—dc22 2007045059
ISBN 978-0-8204-8634-5 (hardcover)
ISBN 978-0-8204-8181-4 (paperback)
ISSN 0085-2473

Bibliographic information published by **Die Deutsche Bibliothek**.
Die Deutsche Bibliothek lists this publication in the "Deutsche
Nationalbibliografie"; detailed bibliographic data is available
on the Internet at http://dnb.ddb.de/.

Cover design by Joni Holst
Cover image, "Wanted" (1983), courtesy of Edwin A. Martin, Jr.

The paper in this book meets the guidelines for permanence and durability
of the Committee on Production Guidelines for Book Longevity
of the Council of Library Resources.

Contents

Acknowledgments   vii

Preface   ix

Part One. Government Information and News: Introduction   1

CHAPTER 1   Information and Government   7

CHAPTER 2   Government and News Media   17

CHAPTER 3   How News Media Report About Government-held Information   31

CHAPTER 4   Government Housekeeping   41

CHAPTER 5   The Paper Curtain   49

CHAPTER 6   The Freedom of Information Act   59

Part Two. Freedom of Information Act in Practice: Introduction   77

CHAPTER 7   Federal Agencies through the Lens of FOIA   83

CHAPTER 8   The Famous, the Not-So-Famous, and FOIA   97

CHAPTER 9   The Business of Government, Consumers, and FOIA   113

CHAPTER 10   States and Freedom of Information   131

Part Three. Freedom of Information Act Tomorrow: Introduction   151

CHAPTER 11   Enthusiasm, Awards, and FOIA   153

CHAPTER 12   Is Less Really More?   161

APPENDIX A   Title 5. Government Organization and Employees
              Part I. The Agencies Generally Chapter 5. Administrative
              Procedure SubChapter II. Administrative Procedure 5
              Uscs § 552   171

APPENDIX B   Contact Information for FOIA Offices
              of Federal Offices, Departments and Agencies   189

Notes   211
Bibliography   239
Index   247

Acknowledgments

Any book of scholarship owes a large debt to all the researchers and authors who came before the work at hand. This author's attempt to thank them all could never be adequate for the gratitude owed. To those who provided immediate opportunity, guidance, energy and support for this author, and this book in particular, I say thanks with a heartiness that I hope will be felt across time and distance.

David Copeland, editor and historian, allowed me to dream and then realize that dream on the pages that follow here. He should always hold a special place in the constellation of those who care about access to government-held information.

My colleagues at the University of Maine also generously allowed me a sabbatical leave to work on the manuscript while they taught my courses and covered my service obligations. The librarians at the university's Fogler Library Special Collections patiently worked around me, providing copy service and quiet time for my review of the James Russell Wiggins papers housed there. Paige Lilly, special collections librarian, was not only helpful but encouraged me.

My family, particularly my husband, never complained about my negligence of our home life when I, instead, focused exclusively on research, contemplation, and writing to complete the project. They patiently read drafts and provided both comments and edits with good will and clarity.

Humble gratitude also goes to the many organizations, both private and public, that watch over our rights of access to government information. Many of them are noted in the pages of the book, but many remain unnamed, to be sure. The generous patrons who support the work of state-level and local empowerment groups are the sustainers of FOIA. In counterpoint, the government agency FOIA officers and dedicated staff members, who not only respond to requests but also help novice information seekers find success, can never be adequately thanked here.

There are so many journalists, editors, social activities, and government employees who have given their lives to establish and protect our information access rights that the shortcomings observed here may seem to be the petty complaints of the comfortable. This book is dedicated to keeping their work ever present as we continue their best efforts.

Preface

Those of us who care about the relationship of journalism and government in this country often write about a mythical world. Many of us believe in the ideals of democracy and civil liberties, and tend to forget we live in a representative democracy where liberties exist for some more than others. We often preach that good journalism is necessary for an informed citizenry and conveniently ignore than neither our journalism nor our citizen's commitment to being informed measure up to the mythology. In fact, neither does the impact of the average informed citizen in our government or economy live up what we often preach or teach or write about.

The book that follows, *Freedom of Information: News the Media Use*, helps us face many of the realities of the relationship between journalism and government in this country. It helps us know the historical context of the interaction between journalists and public officials, and the development of much of the law that controls that relationship. For example, Prof. Shannon Martin, a trained historian, provides a good basic legislative history of the Freedom of Information Act through the adoption of the Homeland Security Act. She reminds us of important facts, including that journalists use freedom of information laws less often than businesses, convicted criminals, and citizen interest groups.

However, the book's strength is the summaries of hundreds of successful efforts of journalists and activists to obtain information from the federal government, and particularly the CIA and the FBI. I have waited most of my professional life for this kind of compilation of stories generated by use of the federal Freedom of Information Act. Thanks to Prof. Martin, a former reporter, we can read about the FBI's attention to student activists in the 1960s, the relationship between Chief Justice Earl Warren and FBI Director J. Edgar Hoover, and more about the secrecy of the current Bush Administration. We gain insights into the FBI surveillance of Princess Diana, Col. Oliver North, U.S. Supreme Court justices, Jack Abramoff, and of course Dr. Martin Luther King.

Prof. Martin tells us of dozens of media reports of waste in government spending, federal agency mismanagement, and influence peddling. Then there were times federal agencies treated similar requests differently. She reports on fights to get access to drinking water safety reports, tests of over-the-counter medicines, and risks to health by nuclear waste. Prof. Martin doesn't hesitate to critique the many problems with how the Freedom of Information Act works. She talks about the delays in getting records and the use of the FOIA by a convicted bomber who filed 1,000 suits from prison seeking information from agencies such as the Drug Enforcement Administration with the funding of "grateful clients."

In addition, unlike many books of its kind, the following book pays attention to state access to records. She summarizes state access issues and provides dozens of examples of the state access issues and problems. She writes of access to data about the Exxon Mobile oil spill, fights over access to personal information held by a public utility, and the battle by a former member of the National Guard to get the documents she needed in order to successfully bring a paternity suit after the guardsman's who fathered the baby committed suicide before the child was born.

At least part of Prof. Martin's book should be read by all serious journalists, teachers of reporting and teachers of media law. It should be assigned and discussed in classes considering the role of journalism and the relationship between government and media. It should be assigned to reporting students everywhere. I would hope the political science professionals would pay attention to the realities of political life portrayed in the book. Citizen activists, policy makers, and teachers of civics need to read Prof. Martin's book.

Far too little has been written about one of the most important subjects in our country—the role of information in our republic. We need to pay more attention to what information is and is not available, and who uses it and for what. We need to get more involved in a public discussion of what should and should not be available, and why.

One of the many reasons the role of information in our republic does not have the featured role in our body politic that it deserves is that too many of us pay homage to the myths about media and government without trying to reconcile our dreams with political and journalistic realties. Prof. Martin's book is an important contribution to the research and discussion we need.

Bill F. Chamberlin
November 2007

Part One
Government Information and News: Introduction

Heightened attention to information collection, storage, and retrieval became something of a public pastime at the end of the twentieth century. Document shredding, for example, used to be a part of life only among agencies and organizations that dealt in top secret materials. But shredders are now commonplace in many American households. Information technology software and hardware advances also gave us the benefits of knowing whatever interested us at the moment, wherever we might be, with no more effort than the touch of a button. "Cellphones," for example, not only let us reach out to others at our convenience but also provide music, Web browsing, and movie viewing. Rapidly expanding use of personal computers and digital libraries, the general acceptance of the World Wide Web as a pervasive information resource, and the increased reliance on PINs and bar codes gave everyone both the freedom to be anywhere and at the same time in constant communication with everyone else. With this increased use of digitization, some people began to feel overwhelmed with data resources and the expectation that if we could be all and know all, then we should.

In 1989, Richard Wurman wrote about "information anxiety," which he claimed many were suffering as they found ever-changing technologies difficult to learn, and day-to-day inventories of knowledge more difficult to master.[1] Anne Branscomb took a slightly different tact in understanding the world of zeros and ones by describing the shifting of legal rights and controls over some common types of information as it moved from paper formats to digital records. In her 1994 book, *Who Owns Information: From Privacy to Public Access*, Branscomb began her discussion with the following observation:

> Collections of data that had once been dispersed to cubbyholes and file drawers now wend their way as patterns of electronic impulses into vast databases where, by virtue of their comprehensive nature and instant cross-accessibility, they become commodities more valuable than the sum of their independent parts.[2]

The U.S. government is thought to be the largest data collector in the world, and the loss or misuse of large government databases can wreak havoc on the lives of those with personal information contained within the data collections and files.

A case in point was the reported theft of a single laptop computer from a U.S. Department of Veteran Affairs employee's home in early 2006. An estimated 26.4 million veterans and about 2.2 million active-duty service members had their social security numbers and other personal identifiers exposed by way of the lost laptop which contained a copy of a comprehensive database. A follow-up study at the Department of Veteran Affairs, after the laptop loss, revealed that the office could not provide the total number of laptops owned and used by the agency, could neither say where the laptops were, nor what was stored on those laptops.

The privacy breach from this particular database mishandling was serious enough that veterans' groups almost immediately filed lawsuits asking for nearly $30 billion.[3] The public learned of this security lapse, in part, because reporters and special interest groups pushed the Veteran Affairs information office to provide details as a civic duty.

In May 2006 other news headlines also declared that the U.S. government's National Security Agency (NSA) had secretly collected the telephone call activities of millions of Americans who were not suspects in criminal investigations. "It's the largest database ever assembled in the world," according to at least one source who preferred to remain anonymous.[4] The call records database was said to contain billions of domestic calls supplied by three of the major telecommunications companies.

The practice of reviewing phone routing records had traditionally been confined to those under law enforcement agency scrutiny, but this particular sweep of data sent cries of outrage and concern across the country. "If [the reports] are true, we are talking about the single largest, the most massive, invasion of privacy in American history," Barry Steinhardt, director of the American Civil Liberties Union's Technology and Liberty Project, told a reporter from the *Boston Globe*.[5]

This data collection project was reported to have begun in 2001 shortly after the September 11 attacks that occurred on the Pentagon near Washington, D.C., and the World Trade towers in New York City. Though this phone records database is said not to include customers' names and street addresses, it was widely speculated that NSA could easily merge the information with existing databases that do contain personal identifiers.

Federal laws that prohibit telephone companies from providing subscriber activity information have existed since the 1934 Communications Act, with fines reaching more than a $1 million per violation. So the decision to accede to the government's request was not lightly made. In fact, one large telecommunications company decided not to comply with the request and now faces the prospect of lost government service contracts as a result.[6] Again, the public learned of this data-mining activity because contracts between government and private companies where public monies are spent must be made available for review.

These calling records were not the only information-sweep operation initiated by the government. The Government Accounting Office (GAO), an agency established to monitor government spending of tax dollars and disclose to the public what government is doing on behalf of constituents, reported that at least fifty-two government agencies had, or planned, nearly 200 data-mining projects since 2004, according to the *Washington Post*.[7]

Assessing the cost of collecting and using all this information is another question examined by the GAO annually. In a 2006 report on that budget year's information technologies investments, twenty-nine projects at five federal agencies were found to have failed performance analysis and documentation to support the expenditures. These projects totaled $65 billion among the Departments of Agriculture, Commerce, Energy, Transportation and Treasury.[8] It probably was no comfort to the American voters, either, when a congressional committee reported in March 2006 that the federal government rated only a D+ on computer security across the executive branch offices. Their assessment was part of the Federal Information Security Management Act that required annual review of information controls since 2002.

The act requires all agencies to provide information technologies inventories, and test their systems for security vulnerability, as well as to develop plans for system outages and attacks. In the 2005 report there were eight agencies out of twenty-four that were considered complete failures. These included the Departments of Homeland Security, Defense, State, Energy, Interior, Agriculture, Veterans Affairs, and Health and Human Services.[9]

The concerns about how government is collecting, using, storing, and reusing the information it collects is not a recent development initiated by widespread computer use alone. These concerns were raised by the first congress of the newly formed United States in 1789.[10] As soon as President George Washington took office, the executive and legislative branches fought over which state documents and activities could be protected from scrutiny by those not directly part of the agencies empowered to be doing that work.[11]

The struggle for information control among government bodies and with members of the public and press has risen and fallen with the necessities of other concerns about national security in times of war as well as law and order during times of domestic unrest. It was not until the middle of the twentieth century that an overt and pointed legislative act insisted that government-held information would be publicly available.

The passage of the Freedom of Information Act (FOIA) in 1966 stipulated that all government information would be available to the public with the exception of nine categories of documents. These particular groups of information would be exempt from public review unless court ordered. While the usefulness of the FOIA legislation has been debated for almost fifty years, the need for transparency in government information holdings has not.

There are many examples of government-held information, once brought to light, that proved invaluable to community members who were trying to understand why their particular community suffered higher-than-average cancer rates, or soldiers concerned about health risks to themselves or their children after serving in a particular war arena, or to learn what some members of the government were willing to do in order to retain their personal powers in government.

Part One of the book examines the government's historical responsibilities for the management of public information and the news media's interests in access to that store of documents. These chapters review and examine the criteria established to provide or exclude information to those requesters or interest groups that might seek clearer understanding of government activities, or who simply like to check up on what those in powerful agency positions are doing.

Several chapters will first identify what constitutes government information, how it is defined in the law, and where that definition originates. Next, a historical review will highlight how it has come to be that news media spend so much time reporting on government. Particularly noted will be the news norms in handling government activities and government news sources. The long history of the news media, sometimes dubbed the "fourth estate" by those both supportive and disgruntled with the members of the press, indicates the love/hate relationship that both the public and the government have with reporters. The final chapter in this section will review the ways in which news media report information about government and will provide some of the subsequent uses of those reports. Though special attention here is given to news media reporting on government information it should not be thought that news media have sole responsibility for investigating and providing government data. Instead, these examples are provided because media reports are how many Americans learn about what they may later decide was pretty important to have known.

Part Two focuses on the wealth of information that dozens of government agencies gather, store, and manage since the formalized reporting system of the FOIA legislation. Many of these caches of documents and databases were revealed by news organizations and activist groups interested in learning about the system of data collection, the norms of storage and uses of those stores. The chapters in this section are organized by point of view in order to highlight the variation in attitudes about government management of certain kinds of information.

Part Three looks forward to the ways in which FOIA advocates assess the application of the law, celebrate their access success, and work toward expanding those opportunities. At the conclusion of this section, however, the sobering questions about the sustainability of a twentieth-century FOIA in a climate of information terrorism, heightened security concerns and public wariness as the country seek twenty-first-century answers.

1

Information and Government

During the two centuries since the U.S. Constitution was ratified, the federal government has enacted tens of thousands of laws that require Americans to provide information about themselves. The regular U.S. census of who we are and where we are was an early government data collection tool.[1] Inventors and businesses are required to provide information about their creative products in order to be issued patents and trademarks.[2] Licensing of all manner of practice was part of the government's efforts to regulate trade but also to keep track of what Americans' were doing with and for each other.

While government was habitually asking for information from Americans, it was less ardent about writing laws that required government to provide information to its citizens. The best known of these information disclosure laws is the 1966 Freedom of Information Act (FOIA) which will be discussed at length in the following chapters. The first effort, however, by the federal legislature not only entailed that the executive branch provide information when asked for but also distribute government-held information during the first session of the first congress.[3] That section said in part,

> The Secretary of State shall publish in at least three of the public newspapers printed within the United States ... every bill, order, resolution and vote of the houses of Congress, as well as presidential objections of those actions. ...

This inclusion among the early laws of the country followed a tradition among many forms of government—democracies, republics, and oligarchies—around the world. Since the days of the Greek city states and the Chinese dynasties of the second century BCE, the legislative acts or the edicts of the government leaders were often officially distributed either by publishing handbills that were available at postal offices, nailed to placards, or repeated by criers at public gathering places for all to hear.[4]

Information Controls

These efforts—nascent mass communication—at keeping the general population apprised of government activity were never perfect. In times of civil unrest or unilateral war, government was often selective about what it told anyone about itself. Concerns about national security and protecting the country were usually the rationale both offered and accepted. Historians have chronicled these curtailed government self-reports as well as some of the criticism from the public that followed, and we are reminded afresh of the discordant views about government transparency each time there is conflict between the executive branch, the legislative branch, and the courts.[5] National security interests, as a deterrent for public access to government-held information, will be discussed at greater length in later chapters of Part II.

Another reason for denying public access to government-held information, beyond national security, has been the perceived right of privacy that most Americans believe is theirs. Though not explicitly part of the Bill of Rights, the Supreme Court has, during the twentieth century, given voice to an implied right. Privacy, the absence or avoidance of publicity or display, was recognized as desirable at least as early as William Shakespeare's 1598 play *The Merry Wives of Windsor*. Though privacy may have been sought by Americans since the founding of the nation, it was not legally specified at the federal level until the Privacy Act of 1974. The U.S. Supreme Court, however, has interpreted at least half of the Bill of Rights to guarantee a "right of privacy." These include the First, Third, Fourth, Fifth, and Ninth Amendments, in addition to the post–Civil War Fourteenth Amendment and English Common Law tradition.

There are counter social interests, according to court decisions, that prevent privacy from reaching the status of an absolute right. These include the public's right to know about government, government officials and government business, national defense and military necessity, criminal law enforcement, public health and safety, and fiduciary values such as trust, accountability, or loyalty. It is common, therefore, to balance privacy with these other social concerns, and though the courts have declared privacy a fundamental right, this right has also been superseded in court opinions by compelling state interests.

During the nineteenth century, several influential articles were published that supported the explicit legal recognition of a right of privacy. Judge Thomas

M. Cooley's 1880 *A Treatise on the Law of Torts* reported on the right of personal immunity and a right to be let alone. That phrase, a "right to be let alone," was repeated in the often-cited Samuel D. Warren and Louis D. Brandeis' 1890 *Harvard Law Review* article, "The Right to Privacy." In that work the authors described the right to enjoy life, which was central to the *Declaration of Independence* and the *Constitution*, as not only the right to liberty but also the right to be let alone. While unwanted public scrutiny was often the result of media attention in the nineteenth century, the modern regulations that protect privacy frequently concern government activities.

The range of privacy laws enacted by the federal government in the twentieth century include not only the 1974 Privacy Act, but also the Fair Credit Reporting Act of 1970, the Family Educational Rights and Privacy Act of 1974, the Right to Financial Privacy Act of 1978, the 1980 Privacy Protection Act, the Cable Communications Policy Act of 1984, the 1986 Electronic Communications Privacy Act, the Video Privacy Protection Act of 1988, the 1991 Telephone Consumer Protection Act, the Drivers' Privacy Protection Act of 1994, the 1996 Electronic Freedom of Information Act Amendments, and in 2000 the Children's Online Privacy Protection Act, the 1999 Financial Services Modernization Act, and the 1996 Health Insurance Portability and Accountability Act.

Depository Library Program

To counteract this tendency of government to minimize self-reports, in the interest of national security or privacy rights, Congress did provide, for anyone who could get to a public library, the opportunity to know about the kinds of things government programs were doing and more importantly how the government was working for all its citizens. An early effort to put government activity reports in the hands of anyone interested in reading about them was the enactment of the depository library system.

The Continental Congress passed resolutions at least twice that directed the publication and distribution of copies of the Congress' *Journals*, which detailed the results of the legislature's deliberations, as well as the new laws.[6] The distribution was directed primarily to the states' legislative and executive branch offices as well as to the delegates who would in turn distribute the reports to other appropriate locations within their states. In addition, the Continental Congress specifically noted in 1784 that complete copies of congressional material be provided to the Library Company of Philadelphia.[7] Congress regularly directed, as well, that its "state papers" be printed and distributed for public review.[8]

Despite the rising cost of publishing these materials as the population expanded away from the original colonies, the legislature continued to allocate money for this endeavor.[9] Noted in the legislature's records was the observation that "in a country so extensive as America, and where the people are so widely scattered, it was a work of immense difficulty to have a regular and accurate account of the measures of Government communicated through every part of the Union."[10]

The rather straightforward but costly difficulties of publishing and distributing government information were soon joined by the more troublesome problem of defining what information should be considered worthy of government publication.[11]

It is important to note here that the presumption among congressional members was that public access to government material was a responsibility of the government. The cost and difficulty of preparation, publication, and distribution were the burden of government bodies, not of the citizens desiring to be informed.

The many resolutions that provided for publication of, and thus public access to, government-held information enumerated no direct cost to the recipient for receiving the pamphlets, reports, and journals. The expectation, instead, was that the government shouldered the printing costs because it should. During the nearly one hundred years of this system, where Congress had to act on each occasion for printing as a special resolution, the laws became so complicated and confusing that in 1895 The Printing Act[12] was passed to provide for a single government publishing office and all-encompassing directive on the distribution of those publications to designated offices and public facilities, which included depository libraries.[13] Revisions of the law pertaining to library distribution of government information became referred to as the Depository Library Act (DLA) during the latter half of the 1960s.[14]

Modifications to the DLA occurred at regular intervals in Congress, but the intent of the original legislation codified in U.S. Codes, Title 44, remains the same. Provisions of Title 44 of the U.S. Code, Chapter 19, designate the establishment and operation of depository libraries under the direction of the Superintendent of Documents. Documents are to include journals of the Senate and House of Representatives; all publications, not confidential in character, printed upon the requisition of a congressional committee; Senate and House public bills and resolutions; and reports on private bills, concurrent or simple resolutions.[15]

The DLA was founded on three principles: (1) With certain specified exceptions, all government publications shall be made available to depository libraries; (2) Depository libraries shall be located in each state and congressional district in order to make government publications widely available; and (3) These government publications shall be available for the free use of the general public. More than one depository library may be located in each congressional district and there are about 1,400 designated libraries across the country. Usually these libraries are not stand-alone facilities but are housed in an existing library, like a university, technical college, or public library "where it [the library] can best serve the public need."[16]

Clearly the intention of the law is to provide free and convenient access to government information through a program of libraries established throughout the United States. While the bulk of the material for publication emanates specifically from the legislature, also included are documents about other branches of government that often come in the form of reports and hearings material.

Government Information Defined

This brings us back, however, to defining what it is that is intended for the public to have available for its own inspection. One might have thought that logically prior to framing laws about public access to, control over, and storage of government information would be the task of characterizing information. Unfortunately, however, the term "information" is rarely, and inconsistently, defined in the law. In the area of the law that will be described at greater length in a following chapter, the FOIA signed into law in 1966 does not define information, but rather details the format of the information documents to be administered under that law.

While these laws in particular, the DLA and the FOIA, provide testament to the intentions of Congress to support a free flow of information, it is difficult to know by the language of the law and under any given administration what content is likely to be excluded from public access. Defining "information" has, sadly, not been clearly accomplished under the law.

The U.S. federal government is reported to be the single largest consumer and distributor of information in the world.[17] The definition and management of all that information is under the jurisdiction of dozens of agencies in a variety of government branches and has evolved in response to the particular offices or agencies.[18] Sometimes the statutory language seems to be referring to information content, and at other times seems to be referring to the means of storage or carrier of data.

A review of the ways in which the word "information" is used in the federal statutes draws sharp attention to the variety of understandings of that concept. If, for example, the language of a statute seems to refer to information no matter what form it is in—computer database or paper—the access controls pose very different problems than if the language of the statute seems to refer to a specific kind of information content—tax records or birth certificates.

The search for a clear and precise understanding of information might naturally turn to the English language dictionaries. The word "information" has a long history in the English language. The *Oxford English Dictionary*, for example, identifies a Latin root, informare [to inform, in the scholastic sense],[19] and cites literary references dating as early as Chaucer's *Melibee*.[20] The definitions include (1) The action of informing; formation or molding of the mind or character, training, instruction, teaching; and communication of instructive knowledge. (2) The action of informing; communication of the knowledge or news of some fact or occurrence; and the action of telling or the fact of being told of something. (3) Knowledge communicated concerning some particular fact, subject, or event; intelligence, news. (4) The action of informing against, charging, or accusing.

Clearly the common use of the word suggests both the action of communicating knowledge and the "stuff" that creates or shapes instruction. "Information" then, might easily be considered both message and messenger, content and carrier, to some further goal. A review of definitions occasionally provided in the law is no less confusing.

Dozens of federal statutes direct the collection, management, and dissemination of information. Many of these statutes defer the definition of "information" to another statute. For instance, Title 5's Authority for Employment[21] and Title 13's Census Administration[22] refer to Title 26's Internal Revenue Code[23] for a definition of "information." Similarly, Title 15's Consumer Product Safety[24] refers to Title 5's FOIA[25] for a definition of "information." Unfortunately, neither the Internal Revenue Code nor the FOIA define "information" per se, but instead, define the parameters of jurisdiction over information and what kind of information is excluded.

These parameters cluster around concerns of content more often than form, and generally ignore both the action of informing described in the *Oxford English Dictionary* and the accusatory context cited in *Black's Law Dictionary*, considered the reference standard for legal documents.[26] The Internal Revenue Code defines "information" only in terms of what is exempt from public disclosure. In this case, "information" may refer to almost any of the conceptual frames already described here.

The legislative language also fails to succinctly define "information," and instead describes what is not public information, or which content is exempt from public disclosure. These parameters can be, on their face, very far-reaching exemptions. For example, in the tax code "qualified confidential information" is any information that is subject to the non-disclosure provision of any local law of the beneficiary[27] or that which is determined would seriously impair assessment, collection, or enforcement under the internal revenue laws.[28]

The implied definition of "information" cited in the FOIA, as another example, applies only to the specific needs of the law and not to a more general concept of information. "Information" is again described in its relation only to what is public and what is not, rather than what constitutes "information." Public information is described as "descriptions of its [agency's] central and field organization; … statements of general course and method; … rules of procedure; … final opinions; … statements of policy; … administrative manuals and instructions."[29]

While non-public information is described as the information that is "specifically authorized under … Executive order to be kept secret in the interest of national defense or foreign policy;…related solely to the internal personal rules and practices of an agency; … trade secrets; … inter-agency or intra-agency memorandums; … personnel files; … records or information compiled for law enforcement purposes; … financial institutions' reports; … geological and geophysical data."[30]

These few examples are simply to provide contrasts in the variations and characteristics of legal definitions of what is government information. The FOIA description of information predominantly relates to content rather than form—that is, what the information is about, rather than in what way it is carried—like trade secrets or geological and geophysical data. But within that same act, "information" is also defined in terms of its specific forms, like memorandums,—information that is conveyed in "x"—rather than "information" simpliciter. Then, just to complete the confusion, these content descriptions of information do not reflect the definitions relative to process found in either the *Oxford English Dictionary* [the action of …] or *Black's Law Dictionary* [an accusation against …].

Other examples of "information" definitions that relate specifically to content rather than form or carrier, and least of all to process or action, include the following:

> "Information" means facts obtained or solicited by the use of written report forms, application forms, schedules, questionnaires, or other similar methods calling either for answers to identical questions from ten or more persons other than agencies, instrumentalities, or employees of the United States … 44 U.S.C. sec.3502.

> The term "energy information" includes (a) all information in whatever form on (i) fuel reserves, exploration, extraction, and energy resources … (b) matters relating to energy and fuels … 15 U.S.C. sec.796(e).

The term "proprietary information" means (a) information contained in a bid or proposal; (b) cost or pricing data; or (c) any other information submitted to the government by a contractor and designated as proprietary. 41 U.S.C. sec.423(p)(6).

These definitions point to a variety of understandings about the nature of government information, and are obviously inconsistent with any one concept of information. They separately focus either on form or format of data, or on the content itself. They also illustrate the differences among legislative definitions of "information" as well as differences with authoritative dictionaries.

The range of concerns, and the confusion about the definition of "information" in federal legislation, is most evident in the fact that there is such a large body of court decisions surrounding the definition and parameters of content available under the FOIA. Thousands of suits and challenges are brought each year to the Justice Department for appeals. The confusion over defining government information, or just what constitutes "information," however, is certainly not confined to that single piece of legislation or the federal government.

Uses of "Information" as a Term of Art Beyond the Legal Definitions

Even the academic discipline of information science is less than transparent in defining that which it studies. Information scientists offer a host of definitions—all of which may be in part useful and accurate—but are certainly not cohesive. Fritz Machlup, a twentieth-century linguist, provided a short list of some of these varying definitions in his compilation, "Semantic Quirks in Studies of Information."[31]

For instance, in linguistics, "information" might be said to define word meaning or content" while in logic or philosophy, Machlup said, it might refer to what he calls "exclusive statements." Genetic engineers use the word to describe the messages encoded by nucleotide bases, and in cybernetics, the word "information" may refer to activity where there is no human interaction at all.

As information science emerged as an academic discipline in the mid-twentieth century[32] during the post–World War II era and the initial cold war era, government information was at the heart of the concern. In an article widely circulated in the late 1940s, Vannevar Bush challenged the scientific community to reevaluate common perceptions of "information" as the government struggled with massive amounts of data generated during the world wars, the burgeoning population growth and the uptick of industrial innovation.[33] The need now, he wrote, was for a new way of thinking about this information and new systems to store and retrieve the collected materials to launch us all into a more efficient and knowledgeable society.

Among the more recent scholarship on the definition of "information" is a work of Gordon Miller. Miller notes that there are a multitude of meanings, "both in ordinary usage and in scholarly discourse."[34] He asserts that the concept of information includes *process* as well as *form* with the "deepest etymological and philosophical roots of the concept ... nourished by the Pythagorean emphasis on form and the Heraclitean emphasis on process."[35]

Miller traces the concept, starting with uses by both Plato and Aristotle. Plato's theory of forms and the possibility of attaining true knowledge of the world through stable, permanent, and independently existing forms, ideas, or universals (to inform) is contrasted with Aristotle's theory of forms posited primarily as essential particulars discovered through a series of questions about a thing's responsible factors—material, efficient, final, and formal types.

These concepts were subsequently Christianized by Augustine and Thomas Aquinas during the Middle Ages. The essential difference among the concept elements remains one of process and form. During this period, however, the concept elements focused on "the sense that the locus of the information is not primarily [a process—in-forming] within the person informed, but rather in the thing [or substance] communicated—the message or subject matter."[36]

Miller writes that with the advance of modern scientific methods and the thrust toward quantifying, the concept of information changed to one of process rather than instruction that molded. And the outcome in modern language is that both machine and human "information processing" are apparently often envisioned in something of a factory metaphor, in that pieces of raw data are thought to be taken in by the mechanical or human "factory" and processed into some sort of finished product, such as lists, reports, and analyses for machines, and percepts, concepts, and memories for humans.[37] Miller concludes that the longtime dissociation of information and in-formation makes the reassociation problematic for information scientists. This detailed analysis helped information scientists but seems to have done little toward framing legal concerns with information.

Any review of congressional policy for public access to information suggests that Congress has occasionally taken on the role of protector in this area of citizens' rights. But a review of the kinds of material that might be included or excluded in statutory definitions of "information" suggests that the protected right of access may be undermined by a host of distinctions in terminology by legislators.

The constant review and assessment of public access to government-held information is unabated. With the events of September 11, 2001, the concerns of the nation changed once more toward exclusion from access, withholding and reclassification of what had previously been easily available. For example, the Environmental Protection Agency web site was quickly shut down to prevent voyeurs from divining "soft targets" for further damage.[38] Information that had previously been available through the Department of Defense and the Justice Department was scrutinized for "sensitive information."[39] Even the National Transportation Services and National Parks were more careful about the kinds of information they routinely gave to requesters.[40]

Concern over defining the term "information" is not unreasonable. As the Supreme Court's understanding and interpretation of the single word "person" determined the applicability of certain fee waivers under FOIA, so, too, might the usefulness of FOIA hinge on the Supreme Court's interpretation of the single word "information" where free-flowing government information content runs head-on into government security and controlled information carriers and conduits. The next chapter will report the history of the desirability of access to information about government activities, and how newspapers came to be an agent of that component in governance structure. Subsequent parts of the book will focus on specific examples of one avenue to government information—the FOIA. The examples chosen relate to specific agencies and periods of political change in the U.S. government. All the examples, however, are part of a larger collection of important work carried on day after day by regular citizens who are acting on behalf of the greater public good by demanding that government agencies respond to the constituencies for whom they are supposed to be working.

2

Government
and News Media

Government information can be as inclusive as every patent ever issued for every invention ever created in the United States and as exclusive as the travel route for the president as he toured the site of the 2005 Katrina hurricane damage in the Mississippi River region. As was discussed in the previous chapter, there has been both a tradition of openness and of selective closure about which and what kind of government information is available for public inspection and what should be kept from those who may ask for a particular document, record, or dataset.

Since that difference will continue long after this book has served its purpose, let's turn our attention to why the news media have on some occasions had a special relationship with government officers who provide and protect the production, storage, and distribution of government-held information. That special relationship sometimes meant that news reporters were given documents that would not have been available to any others who might ask, and on other occasions the media were denied access to government-held records that were more freely available to other citizens who asked for the information.

Clearly the news media, whether the format is print on paper, broadcast over the air, cable, or Web, have a larger voice than almost any other entity in society. That presence makes media attention to government—another unusually large presence in society—a voice to be reckoned with. As any public relations professional knows, the quickest way to get a client noticed among the blur of a day's activities is to hold a news event, timed for media deadlines and broadcast schedules. By the same token, the best way to shield a client from notice is to time the client's exposure for the end of the day's news cycle.

Government officers and those responsive to the public are required by the nature of their jobs to answer questions about government activities, and news representatives have often been the most persistent about asking and expecting those answers. Why this is common has as much to do with the routines of reporting as it has to do with the presumptions of a representative democracy.

Public Need for News About Government

Government and news media have been linked since the citizens of Rome who lived in far-flung regions of that Empire received subscription reports of what government was doing back in the capital. It wasn't just idle curiosity that spurred Romans to keep up with government activities. It was a requirement of citizenship that Romans everywhere stay abreast of the law and act within those rights and responsibilities conferred by the senate.

In colonial America, newspapers carried not only amusements and diversions; they also "addressed items of local concern, items of intercolonial interest and transatlantic matters that affected colonial life or the world situation."[1] In his twentieth-century review of colonial newspapers, historian David Copeland characterized the various news items published in these fledgling broadsheets, reminding the modern student that newspapers during that period were still "taking shape" and "in their infancy."[2] He found, however, that many of the news reports were about government activity of one sort or another.

During the 1720s, for example, crime and the courts were a relatively small proportion of the news—about 4 percent. But ten years later and with twice the number of newspapers, that category of information comprised three times the space in the newspapers.[3] Copeland asserts that "Crime and court news served a vital function in colonial newspapers. ... [N]ewspapers let colonists know that American governments meant business when dealing with criminals ... to deter crime."[4]

The newspaper's role alongside government, however, was not the primary function of a good newspaper, which "ought to be the Register of the times."[5] Instead, historian Charles E. Clark argues that colonial newspapers were more often simply concerned with the items of interest to their readers. If that included government news, politics, and international commerce, then the publishers were happy to print items on those topics.[6] Since newspapers were often the product of a publisher's venture into a subscriber-supported project that conveniently gathered some content from the publisher's other job— that of community postmaster—so much the better.

Newspapers and Government News

John Campbell, Boston postmaster and publisher of the *Boston News–Letter*, on April 24, 1704, was expanding a practice begun by his father, Duncan Campbell, several years earlier when he introduced his printed newspaper. Handwritten newsletters were often exchanged between colonial postmasters and government officials in other cities. The missives included some local news as well as reports of government activities in distant ports.[7] Soon after son John took over the duties of the newsletter, it went to press rather than pen to paper, and was distributed not only to those far away but also to his fellow Bostonians. "Campbell's role as simple intelligencer became expanded instantly to the role of one who creates, produces and markets a product," Clark explained.[8]

The quantity of government news carried in the colonial papers was dependent on the demands for space in any given issue of the newspaper. Colonists were not only concerned with government and politics but also with activities in the royal courts, the shipping industry, advances in agriculture and science, as well as the latest literature. When Andrew Bradford published the first magazine in the American colonies, *The American Magazine or a Monthly View of the Political State of the British Colonies,*[9] nearly half the content was devoted to the proceedings of governing assemblies in Maryland, New Jersey, New York, and Pennsylvania.[10] Though the venture did not survive past the third issue, government news continued to be carried in other publications.

By 1757 Andrew Bradford's nephew, William, tried again to publish a magazine for and about the colonies. *The American Magazine and Monthly Chronicle* continued publication until late in 1774 because "we shall think it our duty to give our readers such an authentic account of every thing relating to their own happiness and safety, as a *free people* have a right to expect. … [The articles published shall] tend to promote *peace and good government, industry,* and *public spirit, a love* of LIBERTY and our excellent constitution. …"[11]

As the revolution and a federal constitution brought the American colonists out from under Great Britain's rule, some presumptions about a just society held sway on both sides of the Atlantic. Thomas Jefferson, writing from Paris while the Federal Convention was meeting in Philadelphia, famously urged Edward Carrington to provide open access to public inquiry about government activity. In his letter dated January 16, 1787, Jefferson wrote:

> The way to prevent these irregular interpositions of the people [into Congress' actions] is to give them full information of their affairs thro' the channel of the public papers & to contrive that those papers should penetrate the whole mass

of the people. ... I should mean that every man should receive those papers & be capable of reading them.[12]

Newspapers were seen by many of the founding framers as both the blessing of a vigorous democracy and the bane of leadership. Although Jefferson in the above mentioned letter voiced his preference for newspapers,[13] others had been less enthusiastic. The governor of New York, Sir William Cosby, was not pleased with the anti-administration stories that Peter Zenger published in the 1733 *New York Weekly Journal* and had Zenger arrested in 1734. The Peter Zenger case was just the beginning of a testy relationship between government and the press in what would eventually be the United States.[14]

Newspapers and Society

The role that newspapers held in American society and in the revolution, founding, and successful launching of the nation has been chronicled and examined by many historians.[15] As an unofficial spokesperson, the community newspaper often found itself either as champion of the underdog—or the underdog itself—when some aspect of government threatened to overwhelm community sensibilities. Some historians credit the development of this relationship to parallel growth and prosperity of towns with their local newspapers.

Others suggest that in order for the communities to blend and build working state governments, the newspapers provided a necessary social bond of information and dialogue. In either case, the newspapers were inexpensive, plentiful, and comprehendible so that many households during the late eighteenth, nineteenth, and twentieth centuries could read and subscribe to multiple publications and did so.

Why was it, then, that in times of frustration with, or fear of government, newspapers were leaders in calling officials to task? Where was it written that the "people have a right to know a few things" about what government was doing, and why was it the media's responsibility to get that sort of information?[16] The answer to these questions may be found by piecing together many small incidents and large traditions that grew as the country was growing.

Thomas C. Leonard suggested in his 1995 book *News for All: America's Coming-of-Age with the Press* that newspaper audiences were created by the sharing of news at a very local level. Editors and publishers were neighbors and accessible. "Americans have been talking back to their press and editing it in their own ways since the days of Benjamin Franklin," Leonard wrote.[17] And it is this conversation that created a sense that newspapers represented not only public views but a consortium of voices that spoke more loudly than any individual might hope to muster. As the newspapers grew more commercially stable and economically powerful, they began more independent crusades that shaped local as well as national politics on many occasions.[18]

Government News and the Newspapers Business in the Twentieth Century

Newspapers in the twentieth century found that they were not only a business concern but were in the business of being concerned about the politics that shaped their communities. As an entity that began to find itself referred to as the "fourth estate" tried to balance itself against the explicit three branches of government, newspapers looked on their responsibilities more formally. And the Hutchins Commission of the 1940s explicitly warned that if newspapers did not provide policies and standards to warrant public trust, then government might well have to step in and do the job for them.[19]

Herbert Brucker echoes this warning in his 1949 book, *Freedom of Information*. There, he details the origin of both the term the "fourth estate" and the need for another voice in the political life of representative democracies that newspapers had come to represent.[20] And, he reminds readers that newspapers have limited responsibilities when he quotes Walter Lippmann:

> The press ... is like the beam of a searchlight that moves restless about, bringing one episode and then another out of darkness into vision. ...
>
> [T]he troubles of the press, like the troubles of representative government ... go back to a common source: to the failure of self-governing people to transcend their casual experience and their prejudice. ... It is because they are compelled to act without reliable pictures of the world that governments ... make such small headway against the more obvious failings of democracy.[21]

Brucker makes his plea for a modern free press by quoting liberally from previous centuries, including eighteenth-century writer Thomas Erskine who noted that "a free press has examined and detected [government's] errors, and the people have from time to time reformed them. This freedom alone has made our Government what it is; this freedom alone can preserve it."[22] Brucker closes the argument by saying that "we cannot approach the faults of contemporary journalism without first accepting the major premise that, no matter what else is done, we cannot have democracy with a Fourth Estate, sheltered behind the principle of a free press."[23]

Too Many Stories and Not Enough News

As newspaper advocates and media professionals debated the role and responsibilities of mass communication in the twentieth century, other constituencies weighed in on how much news was *too* much news and when the people *did* have a right to know a few things about government activities.

The seminal 1890 *Harvard Law Review* article by Louis Brandeis and Samuel Warren provided an argument from law about why Americans might need to know about what government was doing, but they certainly did not have to know everything about what their neighbors were doing.[24] Their concern was for protecting the privacy rights of citizens against invasion by those who might try to suggest that all forms of exposure were a public service. This argument continues today with the line dividing those who want more and those who want less, moving as regularly as the tides.

Battle lines were not drawn entirely by news organizations and the public alone. Some frustrations had been brewing for decades between state and federal agencies that were unwilling to share information with each other. A review of the laws in October 1951 revealed that statutes, agency regulations, and executive orders all presented barriers preventing public access to government records.[25]

Among statutes were those directed at national security, confidential information acquired from private citizens under compulsion of law, information acquired from persons who avail themselves of benefits or services offered by the government, and information whose premature disclosure would give unfair advantage to recipients.

These sorts of prohibitions were contrasted with the general Administrative Procedure Act section 3 (c) "Save as otherwise required by statute, matters of official record shall in accordance with published rule be made available to persons properly and directly concerned except information held confidential for good cause found."[26] The agency rules, however, were said to be the broadest and most restrictive, and the most sweeping controls were reported to have been part of the presidential orders and directives.[27]

The result of this kind of authority review led to the October 2, 1951, Senate Bill 2190, to "Prohibit Unreasonable Suppression of Information by the Executive Branch of the Government (Repeal of Executive Order No. 10290)." The executive order in question prescribed the standards for classification of documents within the executive branch. Ultimately the bill failed, but review of its legal premise—that Congress could overturn or supersede an executive order of this sort—changed the tenor of the conversation about what legislatures could do if they found agencies and executives unwilling to respond to queries about their offices' records.[28]

By the early 1950s the state attorneys general, too, were so tired of playing catch-up with the Federal Internal Revenue, the Federal Alcohol Administration, and the Federal Department of Justice that they passed a resolution at their December 1952 meeting recommending to Congress that drastic changes be made. In their "Resolution 1: Settlement of Criminal and Civil Charges of Federal Administrative Agencies" they asked that

> [T]he powers of secret administrative settlement, now possessed by the Secretary of the Treasury and his agents and the Attorney General and his agents be terminated, and in lieu thereof that procedures be adopted whereby each and every civil or criminal settlement involving the internal revenue and the Federal Alcohol Administration Act be submitted to the federal district courts for approval by the federal judiciary, and thereafter the record of such settlement be maintained as a public record in the file of the clerks of the various federal district courts.[29]

Whereas this concern focused on the news at home, another issue drew some attention from the news editors abroad. The Department of Defense issued a memorandum on clearance protocols for public relations materials. On a copy of the "Armed Forces Medical Library, A-9" page that James Russell Wiggins kept in his files are the notes in pencil "?Thought Control?" above the following instructions:

1. All papers, speeches, interviews, and public utterances prepared by any member of the staff will be submitted to the Director for clearance prior to publication or utterance.
2. "… civilian personnel employed by the Army Establishment will submit their writings and public statements to the appropriate security review authority when the material concerns military subjects. In non instance should the materials be submitted to a publisher prior to clearance." … "military subjects" will be construed to include papers covering the policies or activities … as well as those areas of medicine which are of special importance or special interest to the military services. [quotation marks in original text]

Newspapers Champion Access to Government Information

During the 1950s, too, many news organizations were wrestling with the best way to move the conflict out of small skirmishes and into a frontal attack for change.

Committees had looked at state-level efforts but found them fractured and lacking the force for change that seemed to be needed. To gather strength on this larger scale the Associated Press Managing Editors (APME) appointed a group of their editors to get the discussion focused on a national effort.

James Russell Wiggins, editor at the *Washington Post*, was named chairman of APME's Freedom of Information Committee in 1952. Committee members were from across the United Sates, and included Walter Lister, *Philadelphia Bulletin*; Raymond L. Crowley, *St. Louis Post-Dispatch*; James Pope, *Louisville Courier-Journals & Times*; Robert P. Early, *Indianapolis Star*; Frank A. Knight, Charlestown W.Va. *Gazette*; G.H. Salisbury, Albany *Knickerbocker News*, and Howard C. Cleavinger, Spokane *Chronicle*.[30]

APME members emphasized the FOIA fight as one fought on behalf of all citizens. V.M. Newton, Jr., the managing editor of the *Tampa Morning Tribune* put it succinctly when he wrote to Wiggins, "We are fighting for [everyone's] right to know and not for the selfish aims in the newspaper business."[31]

In a rather longer version of the same argument, George E. Clapp, managing editor of the *New London Day*, wrote to the Associated Press's Victor Hackler on March 12, 1952, expressing dismay at the lack of understanding among some news professionals:

> I have encountered some newspapermen, one or two of them editors, who seem to have but the foggiest notion of that all-important point—that the newspapers, fighting for access to news, especially news on the public record, are not simply trying to promote more hot news stories for their pages, but on the contrary are acting *in behalf of the public. [Clapp's emphasis]*...
>
> There is, undoubtedly, an increasing tendency on the part of some public officials, elective or appointive, to tell the public to go to hell on essential basic information about their government. ... Of course the reporter is after the story; but the result he gets is often vital to the background information of the taxpayer and voter, who certainly will never learn of the doings of his governmental agencies unless newsmen gather the facts for him.
>
> I have a sneaking suspicion that the public *does not begin* to understand this situation, and that it is almost impossible to overemphasize the factor of acting on behalf of the public, and giving the public something that it is *entitled* to have, namely, straight facts on the operation of various agencies of government. *[Clapp's emphasis]*[32]

James S. Pope, managing editor of the *Louisville Courier-Journal & Times*, said it all again in a letter to William W. Vosburgh, Jr., of the *Waterbury*

Republican & American in Connecticut when asked about newspapers issuing a general statement about public access to government information:

> Take off the curse of its being a newspaper statement first of all, clearly. I said in one case that "all the newspaper loses (when a story is concealed) is a story, but the people lose touch with and understanding of their government and public officials, and cannot properly perform their duty of controlling government."
>
>   In other words, we must combat a general reaction that the newspapers are just promoting a vested interest, just trying to obtain, and sell more news ... All information about government and its workers belongs to the public itself in a democracy. If all citizens had time to look at records and attend meetings themselves, that would be fine, for the right to do so is theirs, not ours. However, they obviously can't keep up with things that way, so we become an agency for the reception of information they require.[33]

An example of the kind of image the news industry was trying to combat is evident by the comments of Pope in a letter to Charles F. Brannan, Secretary of Agriculture in Washington D.C., March 7, 1952, over the dismissal of an agency staff member.

Brannan said he brushed off reporters' questions about the dismissal because he had no intention of giving the public any information on personnel matters. Pope wrote to Brannan:

> We certainly never expected you to discuss possible criminal actions before formal charges could be made. ... It still is not clear to me why the regulation under which he was discharged could not be cited. I presume there is no regulation which requires discharge of a man simply because he is suspected. I wonder what reason you gave Mr. Cowart for his dismissal, whether the same reason could not have been given the public.
>
>   We believe it is implicit in our political philosophy that a man has a right to a fair hearing when ousted from public office, just as he has in court. Cowart was [at that time] accused of nothing, and the statement to which we objected assumed, for the Department of Agriculture, the right to withhold any reasons in all such cases, not just the reason that governed this particular one. ... We have become convinced of a fundamental law: secrecy breeds corruption. ... I believe the policy is at odds with our concept of democratic rule.[34]

Wiggins later in that same year wrote a similar sentiment to the Associated Press General Manager Frank J. Starzel, quoting the *London Magazine* of 1747:

> Every subject not only has the right, but is duty bound, to enquire into the publick measures pursued; because by such inquiry he may discover that some

of the publick measures tend toward over-turning the liberties of his country; and by making such a discovery in time, and acting strenuously according to his state, against them, he may disappoint their effect. This enquiry ought always be made with great deference to our superiors in power, but it ought to be made with freedom and even with jealousy. [35]

In Wiggins' 1956 book, *Freedom or Secrecy*, he compares the progress toward open government in England and the United States as a way of suggesting that there is a natural progression or evolution to self-governance that is historic rather than a political anomaly. He writes:

In the United Sates, the struggle against the sixteenth-century restrictions proceeded along the same lines it followed in England. Licensing of the press was abandoned. Doors of legislatures and of Congress were opened. Court proceedings were made public. Laws of seditious libel were moderated and the defenses against libel made available. At local, state and federal levels it was conceded that the people had a right to information.

After three centuries of progress, events seem now to be moving in another direction. There is abroad, in this country, and in the rest of the world, an impulse to secrecy. It is an impulse which will alter and curb our governmental institutions if it is not itself altered and curbed.[36]

Case Law of Newspapers' Challenges to Government

The seeds for this growth of distrusting government that developed among newspaper professionals can be found among the earliest American sources of rebellion. As early as the 1765 Stamp Act which placed a heavy tax on paper used for publishing, government has been seen as no friend to mass communication, albeit, it was the British government at that time.

Though the 1791 U.S. Constitution's first amendment prohibited laws against free speech, the press, practice of religion, assembly, and petitioning the government for redress of grievances, the federal courts did not even take a freedom of the press case until the 1930s. Discriminatory tax raised its head again when Louisiana passed a special income tax for advertising in newspapers with more than 20,000 circulation.

The law was directed at about a dozen publications that might pose political problems for the current administration, and the Supreme Court again denied the state this levy.[37] Nearly two hundred years after the Stamp Act, another state law tried again to impose a newsprint-and-ink tax on large circulation newspapers, which was again rejected by the court.[38]

Discriminatory tax, however, was just one issue among many that the publishers found to be a vexing government attempt at information control. Direct prior restraint on news publication was first heard in the Supreme Court nearly 150 years after the ratification of the first amendment's prohibition on press restraints. In *Near v. Minnesota* the Supreme Court struck down the enforcement of gag laws, or prepublication restrictions.[39]

This kind of sweeping prior restraint on the press was a greater social harm, the court said, than the damage done to an individual or special social group by whatever outrageous statement might be published. Again in 1971 the court acted in emergency sessions to reverse a prepublication restraining order sought by President Richard M. Nixon when, first, the *New York Times* and then the *Washington Post* began publishing portions of the "History of the U.S. Decision-Making Process on Vietnam Policy," referred to as the Pentagon Papers.

There were no military secrets contained in the published portion, but the political fallout was expected to be an avalanche. For fifteen days the restraining order was in place while the court heard oral arguments and prepared its opinion. The 6–3 per curiam verdict rendered by the court was not reached on first amendment grounds but rather on national security standards.[40]

Each member of the court also issued individual opinions of the legal arguments used to reach the overarching outcome, suggesting there were deep divisions about the merits of any particular argument. In many ways there were no winners in the case. The court had not reached its verdict with a clear legal statement of principles; the newspapers had not quashed prior restraint on publication, and the executive branch had not won a lasting victory in protecting once-classified work papers.

Newspaper publishers and government officials again locked horns two years later when the *Washington Post* and the *New York Times* began publishing a series of stories that were based on public records and anonymous sources linking political dirty tricks to the White House. There were many small skirmishes in court with no clear winners over the control of office memoranda and the proprieties of political party funding.

Ultimately, President Nixon resigned from office and left many questions about what had actually occurred at his direction or with his blessing before and after the 1972 break-in at the Watergate Building office of the Democrat National Headquarters.

Newspaper publishers had learned, however, to continue their careful consideration of publish and perish should they cross an ill-defined line between public interest and national security when government-held information is the source of disclosure. The right of the people to know what government officials were doing was still a nebulous concept.

Right to Know Principles Tested

In Wiggins' 1956 book, *Freedom or Secrecy*, he outlined the boundaries of what he believed the right to know ought to include:

> (1) the right to get information; (2) the right to print without prior restraint; (3) the right to print without fear of reprisal not under due process; (4) the right of access to facilities and material essential to communication; and (5) the right to distribute information without interference by government acting under law or by citizens acting in defiance of the law.[41]

Clearly, even a generation later some branches of the government were still a long way from sharing this view. Beyond the court cases there were many instances of direct interference by the executive branch in providing information, or allowing information gathering.

Reporting war efforts always provided grounds for differences of opinion about what should or should not be covered by the news organizations. During conflicts in the eighteenth and nineteenth centuries, the tactical problems of coordinating both, who offered and exactly what was in the government report, were continuing problems for the executive branch and its military officers.

Soldiers in the field were often at liberty to speak to anyone asking questions because military minders were not part of the retinue. As for the reporters, getting accurate and newsworthy information was just part of the task. Relaying that information intact, to the news organization presented an entirely different and difficult set of problems for the field reporter. When the military excluded reporters from their ranks, the reporters got information, accurate or not, flattering or not, any way they could, and often the results were deplorable.

During the initial launch of American troops during the Spanish-American war of 1898 journalists were pointedly told not to write stories about the ships leaving for Cuba. Reporters went ahead and hired their own transportation so that they could relay, first hand, what the Navy was doing. When military censors tried to intervene in the journalists' relays, one correspondent for the *New York Sun* wrote, "the writer...found himself held down to ...only the facts as had been reported to Washington [already], and whose publication would not hurt the country's interests."[42]

When the military tried to include reporters as part of their ranks, the results were still somewhat mixed. General Dwight D. Eisenhower was reported to have said, "Public opinion wins war."[43] While reporters often had designated or informal military minders who controlled the stories and specific content, the realization that the reports that resulted from either model of information management were sometimes false led the public to change its mind about the success of a conflict.[44]

The U.S. involvement in Vietnam remains a sore spot for many military strategists.[45] And as the U.S. involvement in Iraq and Afghanistan continued into the 2006 elections, there were many calls for a reevaluation of media reporting on casualties, military initiatives, and day-to-day combat.

Reports on military action are usually the most sensitive kind of government information to relay. It often brings to boil the best and worst in political thinking because the public and the government are hyper-engaged in a victory. But it is this very kind of flash point that offers the best indication that all is not well in government transparency.

Many Americans were sickened and disappointed with the evidence of prisoner abuse both in Iraq and Guantanamo camps. Some retaliated by suggesting the media should not have provided the information about these situations to the public at large. Abuses and misuse, however, are the very concerns that the founding framers wanted exposed when they created a three-branch government and a Bill of Rights.

The next chapter will briefly review the sources of news media reports on government-held information, with subsequent chapters discussing specific examples of these reports. The deeper look at what kinds of changes resulted from the scrutiny on government activity will provide readers with a broader understanding of both the long and short term benefits of news media efforts toward government transparency.

3

How News Media Report About Government-held Information

Newspapers took up the task of reporting on government activities because their readers expected *that* news alongside all the other events of the day. As Francis Williams wrote in his 1969 book, *The Right to Know: The Rise of the World Press*, the news media have traditionally had three linked responsibilities, among others, which include "to collect and publish the news, to interpret and comment on it, [and] to act as a guard dog of the public interest in areas of public concern where executive power may be arbitrarily used."[1]

The details about how those responsibilities have been shouldered become the history of the media in any society. In the United States, reporters quickly developed strategies for collecting and writing about government news that were streamlined and efficient because deadlines were omnipresent and because many reporters were paid per story or by the inch. The number of stories or the length of the stories determined the salary for the week. Speed and efficiency, as a result, played some role in the development of news-gathering norms and subsequently in the kinds of news that made it to the daily papers.

Any modern journalism education textbook reflects those norms, even today. For example, the Missouri Group's *News Reporting and Writing* book not only instructs students in the computation of tax rates, budgets, and poll data, but also devotes whole chapters to gathering information about and reporting on the courts and police as well as "beats" that include city and county governments. "Beat" reporting, according to these authors, is a reporter's assignment area of responsibility. A beat may be an institution, such as the courthouse; a geographical area, such as a small town; a subject, such as crime.[2]

Similarly, entire textbooks have been devoted to journalism education on government reporting. In *Advanced Reporting: Beyond News Events*, the authors provide chapters on covering "beats" as well as a chapter on freedom of information laws that include public records, open meetings, and the courts.[3] *Investigative Reporting for Print and Broadcast* dedicates entire chapters to special problems and concerns with reporting on government.[4]

Henry H. Schulte's *Reporting Public Affairs* textbook contains separate chapters describing journalists' routines[5] for covering municipal government, county government, state government, and federal government, as well as chapters on the judiciary and law enforcement. And then there is the sequence of Investigative Reporters and Editors' books that are devoted to the use of public documents and government information to report community stories.

The Reporter's Handbook: An Investigator's Guide to Documents and Techniques is several hundred pages of "how to" find and get government information in pursuit of understanding what government is doing. In the foreword to the first edition, Robert W. Greene wrote, "No pointless war stories here. ... It is our handbook."[6]

In all of these textbook examples, the Freedom of Information Act (FOIA) plays a large role in how reporters might seek background or data for their news stories. FOIA is not the only, nor even the first, strategy suggested by the book authors. But it is always included as a means to the desired end of reporting on government activities, and it is always referenced in the success stories.[7]

Government Reports as Part of News-Gathering Routines

Some government reports have always been publicly available. Census reports, for example, have been part of the public record since their origination, as required by the Constitution. Apart from super-sleuthing and FOIA requests, some agencies routinely provide reports and agency materials to depository libraries. These reports come from federal regulatory agencies, advisory committees and commissions, as well as state-level government agencies.

Perhaps the largest and richest source of government information can be found in congressional hearings, House and Senate reports, and the General Accounting Office (GAO) reports. The GAO was created in 1921 to investigate, on behalf of Congress, those federal government departments and programs that the House and the Senate both allocate money for and upon which they depend for administering federal initiatives. Thousands of these reports are assembled annually and can be found in depository libraries across the country or online at government Web sites.[8]

It is estimated that tens of thousands of government-generated reports containing hundreds of thousands of government-held data items are released each year. So why is there demand by FOIA requestors for even more government documents? The answer to that question most frequently has to do with availability. Until late in the twentieth century, the Government Printing Office (GPO) was charged with publishing almost all of the government documents and reports to be made public.

Following the Paperwork Reduction Act of 1980 and amendments in 1995,[9] the Office of Management and Budget (OMB) Circular No. A-130 established the secession of many paper-printed government materials in favor of electronic formats for distribution and storage. Robert W. Houk, who served as the head of GPO as Public Printer, offered a plan for this shift in his white paper, "GPO/2001: Vision for a New Millennium." Dissemination efforts, he wrote, should include FIND, SEND, and INTERACT. FIND was a federal information directory to locate the original government document; SEND was a satellite network used to actually distribute the requested documents; and INTERACT was a system for online communication that provided the conduit within which FIND and SEND could connect government documents with public requests.[10]

Congress did not move forward with this vision but did continue to limit funding for paper printing of government documents, much to the concern of depository librarians.[11] The result for many information seekers was to ask particular agencies for particular documents, and FOIA was usually the means to that end. One initiative by the Clinton administration to stem the flow of requests through agencies' FOIA offices was to establish FirstGov.gov, which was intended to offer routinely requested information at a single Web portal for easy access.

FirstGov.gov was launched in September 2000, boasting that it offered more than 47 million Web pages for searching by topic, rather than housed solely by agency confinements. Within a year the site also offered simultaneous searches in all fifty states' documents as well. The Government Services Administration (GSA) was named administrator of the project, and soon found itself overwhelmed with the demands of millions of hits per month after the September 11, 2001, terrorist acts that left many Americans scrambling for information sources that were available from home.[12]

Information Classification Designations

The search for ways to learn about what government-held information might contain and then finding ways to view that information plagues not only the information seeker but also the administrators given the task of collecting, organizing, storing, and retrieving so much data at every level of government. When President Harry Truman instituted the information classification system "in order to protect the security of the United States," he claimed he was forced to the action because world conditions made it necessary for him to protect "official information the unauthorized disclosure of which would or could harm, tend to impair, or otherwise threaten the security of the nation."[13]

Each successive president has issued an executive order detailing the use of information classification categories and duration of those designations.[14] The effects on information availability rise and fall with each administration. For example, under President George W. Bush, the security of government documents resulted in more than doubling the number of items classified as secret. Under the Clinton administration, between 5 and 8 million new documents, letters, and email messages were classified each year of 1996 through 1999 with about 200 million pages declassified each year.

During the initial years of the Bush administration, that number jumped to more than 11 million in 2000. The tide of classification dropped to more than 8 million items in 2001. By 2004, though, about 15.6 million items were classified and only 28 million pages were declassified.[15]

Congress was relatively unfazed by Truman's 1950s' classification order, but members of the media were outraged and vocal. There were several cases-in-point that angered reporters trying to cover government activity. Among these was the government's pursuit of atomic energy testing and development. The establishment of the Atomic Energy Commission (AEC) was seen as a barrier to reporting what was under way because all employees were sworn to secrecy, allowing only designated agency members to act as spokespersons and to release only that information not designated as "restricted."[16]

By the early 1950s Congress joined the news media's concerns about getting AEC information and began organizing subcommittee reviews of instances of the executive branch denying them access to information necessary for congressional investigations. Eventually these investigations led to the establishment of Moss' Committee, described more fully in Chapter 6.

APME and Information Access

Outside of government offices, the Associated Press Managing Editors (APME) organized a special committee to do an "extensive check of every case wherein President Truman's executive censorship order has deprived the people of the right to know about their government without endangering national security."[17] Though the federal agencies were featured most frequently among news media profession-als who talked about information access, the state and local governments received much attention and raised considerable ire as well.

"Red" Newton, managing editor at the *Tampa Morning Tribune*, pushed the committee to keep an accurate account of every instance when reporters were barred from non-security news reporting. "I do not think we should be content with four or five cases. ... The people ... will understand concrete cases ... show-ing where the President's order has robbed them of their rightful information about their government."[18]

APME began compiling examples to share with other members and created a series for publication, as newspapers found space for them. Though the pieces offered by Associated Press and datelined New York did not carry a byline when published in many newspapers, the series was written by James Devlin. Among the examples collected were the following:

Supreme Court Backs Up Papers' Right To Report, Hiding of Facts by Executive or Administrative Agencies Hit, Boston, February 19, 1952. A freedom-of-informa-tion battle between the Massachusetts Senate and the State Commissioner of Labor and Industries late in the 1951 established the right of the public's elected representatives to data held by the administrative department. The struggle stemmed from newspaper quests for a withheld report. Governor Paul A. Dever had backed up John J. DelMonte, commission of labor and industries, when he refused to turn over to the Senate a survey of Massachusetts's industrial out-look—financed with $11,500 of the taxpayers' money. A State Supreme Court Advisory opinion on November 14 told the senators they were entitled to such data to enable them to carry out their duties.

Censorship Continues in Pawtucket, Pawtucket, R.I., February 20, 1952. A tight clamp on all details of city finances and financing was a conspicuous feature of the 1951 news censorship in the city of Pawtucket. Even the mayor—much less the newsmen—didn't know the details. And the censorship continues. City payrolls were withheld for more than half the years, until Mayor Lawrence A. McCarthy made an issue of the secrecy about financial affairs. He went into Superior Court with a taxpayer's suit.

It Can Happen Here And It Has, New York, March 12, 1952. The Associated Press conducted a nation-wide survey of official suppression of news and what is being done about it. The survey showed that newspapers are sometimes able to prove that news of crime and accidents are censored to conceal circumstances embarrassing to the department or to protect prominent persons or political friends from unfavorable publicity. ... A county employee handling public money stole marriage license fees. County officials went into secret session, decided he wouldn't do it again and kept him on the job. The matter was kept quiet. Taxpayers learned of it six years later when the thefts mounted to $18,000 and they were called upon to make up the loss. ...

Officials of one town knew for 15 years that the federal public health service had condemned its drinking water. The newspapers didn't know. Neither did the people. A reporter for the *Lacrosse (Wis.) Tribune* learned that railroad trains did not take on water at Lacrosse. He found that the U.S. public health service had reported it had a high bacterial count. The reporter also found that the first report on the poor condition of the water had been filed 15 years before and repeated every year since. The former city engineer and some members of the city council had known about it, but never made it public. ...

In North Carolina, editors found that in some local courts, judgments were changed after regular court hours, warrants were withhold from public scrutiny, and prominent citizens were allowed to enter pleased without public appearances. ...

The Biddeford (Maine) Journal reported the local board of education holds public meetings but the board withholds information on when they will be held.

Military Security, New York, March 13, 1952, Military censorship poses the question of where security ends and the cover-up of mistakes begins, particularly on the home front. ... A reporter wanted to know why maps showing atomic installations were hung on airport bulletin boards. The President [Truman] rebuked the reporter. He said such questions only attracted attention to the maps. The maps are intended to guide pilots so they won't fly over such installations. Was security jeopardized in hanging the maps on the bulletin boards in the first place, or in asking how come?

State Government and Information Access

Each state developed information access laws on independent initiatives, and as is evident from the reports noted above among the news stories, each state had very different views about what should be made public. Some states included open records language in their constitutions while others came along soon after the federal government began its pursuit of public records laws. The history of Maine's public records laws is emblematic of many states, though unique in its particular evolution of the laws.

Maine as an Example

Though a New England state, Maine did not declare statehood, separate from Massachusetts, until about fifty years after the American Revolution. Maine's Freedom of Access Act (FOAA), signed into law in 1975, declared that public proceedings exist to aid in the conduct of the people's business.[19] The section goes on to note that government action should be "taken openly and that the records of their actions be open to pubic inspection and their deliberations be conducted openly." Maine's FOAA specifically says that public records are defined as

> any written, printed or graphic matter or any mechanical or electronic data compilation from which information can be obtained, directly or after translation into a form susceptible of visual or aural comprehension, that is in the possession or custody of an agency or public official of this State or any of its political subdivisions, or is in the possession or custody of an association, the membership of which is composed exclusively of one or more of any of these entities, and has been received or prepared for use in connection with the transaction of public or governmental business or contains information relating to the transaction of public or governmental business, except. ...[20]

This section is followed by nineteen listed exemptions with the most recent being social security numbers held by the Department of Inland Fisheries and Wildlife when issuing licenses.

During the intervening years between the initial legislation and the end of the twentieth century, that body and the state courts have provided hundreds of exceptions to the general principle articulated in Maine's FOAA.[21] These exemptions have ranged from provisions of the Maine Dairy and Nutrition Council:

> All meetings and records of the council are subject to the provisions of Title 1, chapter 13, subchapter I, except that by majority vote of those members present records and meetings of the board may be closed to the public when public disclosure of the subject matter of the records or meetings would adversely affect the competitive position of the milk industry of the State or segments of that industry. The Commissioner of Agriculture, Food and Rural Resources and those members of the Legislature appointed to serve on the joint standing committee of the Legislature having jurisdiction over agricultural, conservation and forestry matters have access to all material designated confidential by the council[22]

to the data collection and dissemination of toxic use and hazardous waste reports generated by the Toxics Use, Toxics Release and Hazardous Waste Reduction Program where the commissioner shall ensure the confidentiality of any information designated as confidential or a trade secret.[23]

All States

Many state governments struggled with the problem of public access to government-held information that may not have been envisioned by lawmakers as public information. For example, The Alaska Attorney General was asked in the 1980s to issue an opinion on whether the Alyeska Pipeline Service Company documents filed with the State Pipeline Coordinator's Office should be available as public documents to the competing Northwest Pipeline Company. The attorney general's opinion said that these documents should probably be considered public records.[24] That same year the Kansas Court of Appeals was asked to consider whether Southwestern Bell Telephone could protect from FOAA those documents, submitted for review on the question of a rate increase, as trade secrets.[25]

Every state in the nation has similar examples that specifically affect business and industry. Washington State allows exemptions for information about the specifics of financing life sciences research.[26] Another similar example is found in South Carolina where university foundations that receive public funds in the form of federal grants for research must also respond to requests for public information,[27] while Oregon courts question the fees imposed for access to logs kept by the university for animal research facilities.[28]

In a slightly different perspective, the Louisiana courts found that a committee concerned with the purchase and use of experimental animals by the university was not governed by state information access laws.[29] The lists of exemptions are unique to each state, as are the eligible public reviewers. Several states, for example, require that information access is made available only to state residents or citizens.[30]

The effort across the country to provide a statutory avenue to government information was uneven but persistent, as is evident from the range of dates for state adoption of access laws. The uses of the laws have varied just as widely and are not restricted to geographic markers even when inquiries begin at a very local level. For example, the 1963 explosion at a Birmingham, Alabama, Baptist church that killed four young women led to multiple hearings and mistrials.

At the close of the twentieth century, one of the accused bombers was still trying to use information access laws to get his Federal Bureau of Investigation (FBI) file so that he could prove his innocence,[31] and the family of one of the victims was also filing FOIA requests for the FBI's aerial photos of her burial in order to locate the true grave, mistakenly marked for more than thirty years.[32]

At the federal level, the evidence that information access laws are used for a variety of investigations is often more pronounced just because the attention is more wide-spread. In a 2006 *New York Times* story, it was reported that a FOIA request of records from the Centers for Disease Control and Prevention revealed that a disproportionate amount of salary bonuses went to the highest ranking officials in the agency during the past four years rather than to the scientists.[33]

Denials, however, were just as likely when media requests were made. In 2004 Miles Moore reported that the National Highway Traffic Safety Administration (NHTSA) was withdrawing its earlier statements that it would release tire safety data as quickly as possible, when a *Detroit Free Press* request through FOIA revealed that the NHTSA had never released such a report.[34]

In Baltimore it was reported that the United States Postal Service was correct to deny a FOIA request for redacted portions of a contract with Hallmark Cards, who was supplying packaging materials to them. "Congress spoke loudly through the Postal Reorganization Act," according to Judge Roger L. Gregory who heard an appeal of the denial. "The postal service may withhold information of a commercial nature which would not normally be disclosed under good business practices," the court said.[35]

What follows in the next part of this book is a closer look at the history and evolution of the laws that directly affect government information access. An initial chapter will be devoted to the executive branch's "housekeeping" regulations. These executive orders permit those agencies under the direct authority of the president to protect from outside review those memos, lists and files that are part of the day-to-day running of an arm of the government, but that do not rise to the level of public scrutiny because they are considered so mundane. Next comes a review of the historical events that led up to the congressional activities that resulted in the FOIA.

A chapter will be devoted to the immediate history around the FOIA adoption, and then several of the most expansive and revealing investigations of the executive branch will be discussed. The aim of all this review, the discussions, and ultimately the analysis is to understand the many reasons that the media pursued government information on behalf of the public in general, as well as the concomitant benefits for itself. With that understanding it ought to be possible at the end of the book to decide for ourselves if this incessant effort to learn what government is doing actually has a place in a democracy and if that place is best served by the laws now in effect.

4

Government Housekeeping

Among the early statutes promulgated by Congress was "[a]n Act to provide for the safe-keeping of the Acts, Records and Seal of the United States, and for other purposes."[1] The statute is often referred to as the "Housekeeping Statute" because it details the handing of official documents in Congress, and by extension, the executive branch's handling of those documents, and authorizations administered as a result of congressional acts.

Section 2 of the statute said:

> That whenever a bill, order, resolution, or vote of the Senate and House of Representatives, having been approved and signed by the President of the United States, or not having been returned by him with his objections, shall become a law or take effect, it shall forthwith thereafter be received by the said Secretary from the President; and whenever a bill, order, resolution or vote, shall be returned by the President with his objections, and shall, on two-thirds of both Houses of Congress, and thereby become a law or take effect, it shall, in such cases be received by the said Secretary from the President of the Senate, or the Speaker of the House of Representatives, in whichsoever House it shall last have been so approved; and the said Secretary shall, as soon as conveniently may be, after he shall receive the same, cause every such law, order resolution, and vote, to be published in at least three of the public newspapers printed within the United States, and shall also cause one printed copy to be delivered to each Senator and Representative of the United States, and two printed copies duly authenticated to be sent to the Executive authority of each state; and he shall carefully preserve the originals, and shall cause the same to be recorded in books to be provided for the purpose.

Section 7 also instructs the executive branch:

> That the said Secretary shall forthwith after his appointment be entitled to have the custody and charge of the said seal of the United States, and also of

all books, records and papers, remaining in the office of the last Secretary of the United States in Congress assembled; and such of the said books, records and papers, as may appertain to the Treasury department, or War department, shall be delivered over to the principal officers in the said departments respectively, as the President of the United States shall direct.

Though the work papers of the executive branch were clearly designated by this statute to remain with the office, rather than with the temporary holder of that office, it is less clear what rights Congress thought it had to access those work papers. The "Housekeeping Statute" provided for public access to enacted resolutions, orders and votes, as well as the president's refusal to enact and his reasons for so doing. In fact, the statute requires that all of these materials not only be made public, but that they be distributed, and not just be available for inspection. How much of this effort toward government transparency can be found in executive branch work products has been a point of dispute since the first presidency.[2]

Tension about sharing information existed between the executive branch and the legislature since the very first president and Congress. Though the U.S. Constitution directs that the president "shall from time to time give to the Congress information of the State of the Union,"[3] there were instances when legislators wanted more than summary statements from the executive branch. As treaties were formalized and investigations pursued, the president's cabinet members often had detailed information about preliminary activities. Legislators occasionally wanted anything that might be useful in the deliberative process required by Congress before ratifying initiatives or allocating funds for government activities.

The Constitution does not grant Congress the power to demand and receive information at will from the executive branch, but the framers seemed to expect the president and cabinet members to be forthcoming when asked about specific details. As early in the nation's history as 1792, Congress launched an investigation into a military defeat at the hands of the Wabash Indians in November 1791. The review committee requested "persons, papers and records, as may be necessary to assist their inquiries."[4]

President George Washington conferred with his cabinet. Secretary of State Thomas Jefferson responded that the congressional committee had the right to review the actions of the executive branch, the right to make the request for information, and that the "executive ought to communicate such papers as the public good would permit, and ought to refuse those, the disclosure of which would injure the public … to exercise discretion."[5]

The exercise of discretion prescribed by the executive branch, sometimes referred to as "executive privilege," was tested almost immediately. In 1794 the

House of Representatives requested that the executive branch supply to them a letter, sent to the British Minister on the subject of Anglo-American relations, that had been omitted from materials previously requested.[6] The issue arose more pointedly the same year when the Senate began asking for details about the evolution of Jay's Treaty. Many members of the legislature were unhappy with the trade relationship outlined in the treaty and did not want to ratify the document.

The president eventually provided most of what was requested except "those particulars which, in my judgment, for public considerations, ought not to be communicated."[7] Public outcry about the terms of the treaty and Washington's refusal to provide Congress with all details was so great that the president felt pressed to defend himself not only with a personal address to the legislature but also in the newspapers.[8]

Frustration over the executive branch's handling of work information erupted again in 1798 during the "XYZ Affair" of John Adam's presidency. Code-encrypted messages that had been sent to Adams by U.S. negotiators in France were not included in the materials supplied to Congress when Adams asked for permission to prepare for war with that country. Some members of Congress suspected that the missing letters would not support Adams' war interests and so demanded to see them.

Adams claimed that the documents were withheld to protect the life and safety of his informants who were so far from home and essentially in soon-to-be enemy territory. When he finally did release the materials, he asked that the letters "be considered in confidence," during the congressional deliberations, and to consider the "consequences of their publication."[9] Congress decided that the encrypted messages held clear evidence of French malfeasance, hastening American attitudes in support of war with France.

When Thomas Jefferson became president, there was an expectation that more information from the executive branch would flow to Congress than had been the case in the Washington and Adams administrations. There is evidence, however, of just the opposite. Jefferson was said to have increased the use of codes in his presidential correspondence and established a parallel set of state and personal papers. The official letters went into the State Department's files, but he withheld diplomatic correspondence that he deemed was "private" or "confidential" from congressional review.[10]

Jefferson's presidency was rarely pressed by Congress for information. The judicial branch, however, held a different view of the executive branch's information privileges. Chief Justice John Marshall subpoenaed documents in the trial of Aaron Burr, and the president complied, although Jefferson insisted that his presence could not be required by the court.[11] Marshall did allow for deference to presidential withholding of confidential information as long as there was no proof that an injustice would result by the nondisclosure.[12]

Subsequent presidents followed Jefferson's model, volunteering much of the information requested, but withholding letters that they considered private or confidential.[13] This practice of claiming executive privilege has been used to varying degrees by all presidents.[14] For example, President Dwight Eisenhower espoused his rights to executive privilege at least forty times, more frequently than any other president. His claim was that if those who spoke candidly with the executive branch knew that their remarks were then subject to public scrutiny, the advice-givers would be less likely to speak frankly. And that, Eisenhower is reported to have said, would mean that "any man who testifies as to the advice he gave me won't be working for me that night."[15]

Presidents John F. Kennedy and Lyndon B. Johnson said that they believed executive privilege was meant only for the president.[16] President Nixon claimed that executive privilege should be narrowly construed, though his subsequent actions during congressional investigations said otherwise.[17] Privilege was not litigated as a primary issue until the Nixon administration. At that time the U.S. Supreme Court heard several cases that hinged on the executive branch, at the specific direction of the president, withholding information deemed public and crucial to congressional review.[18] Soon after came the Nixon impeachment proceedings, which identified, in the first article of the charges, that Nixon withheld information about the Watergate cover-up.[19]

Presidents Gerald Ford and Jimmy Carter issued no executive privilege memoranda to agency administrators, but President Ronald Reagan not only asserted a right to executive privilege but detailed under what circumstances and procedures these should be used. Privilege, the memo directed, would be invoked when the president, the attorney general, and the affected department head agreed that the requested information should not be released.[20]

President George W. Bush issued a variance from the Reagan directive, but President Bill Clinton provided in 1994 a memorandum stating that "[t]he policy of this administration is to comply with congressional requests for information to the fullest extent consistent with the constitution and statutory obligations of the Executive Branch."[21] In contrast, however, the actions of the Clinton White House presumed privilege on most communication, as did the administration of President George W. Bush.

Executive privilege attached by practice to the statutory language of the Housekeeping Act was not the only means of limiting the flow of information out of the White House, however. Congress explicitly gave the president and cabinet another statutory vehicle midway through the twentieth century.

Administrative Procedures Act

Access to executive branch documents and communications was never, by law or tradition, provided equally to all who might have an interest in reviewing them. Congressional committees were routinely kept abreast of international negotiations as they developed, for example, and the general public expected their legislators to keep such information in confidence. But agency representatives found it easier to reject than to shepherd and produce the information requested by those outside of government. News reporters and the public began to agitate for some accountability of the agencies.

As an organizing tool for the mountains of information that government was stockpiling by the mid-1940s and the myriad of requests being fielded by government agencies, Congress adopted the Administrative Procedures Act (APA).[22] The intention of the law was to formalize and systemize the division between information that should be generally, and always, available to the public and that which should be treated with more caution when requested.[23]

Some legislators as early as the 1950s began calling for repeal or amendment of the APA because of the abuses they saw protected by the language of the law.[24] Though the law states that it is "drawn upon the theory that administrative operations and procedures are public property which the general public, rather than a few specialists or lobbyists, is entitled to know or to have the ready means of knowing with definiteness and assurance,"[25] it was said in congressional committee meetings that "executive agencies ... rely on it very heavily as justification for withholding rather than disclosing information."[26] Repeal was unlikely, however, because, as some scholars suggest, Congress has been as much a beneficiary of the information controls instituted by the APA as was the executive branch.

Classification Systems

President Harry S. Truman was the first to issue an executive order in peace time, in conjunction with the APA, that detailed a specific categorization for the safe keeping of government information that was to remain out of public review.[27] The categories for classifying information included non-security information that was considered confidential, secret, and top secret. The eight-page order also included application guidelines that cautioned against over-classification and delegated the specifics of each agency's standards to the chief of that agency.

Though Truman tried to couch the order as necessary to protect the national security, provide for uniform application of these standards, and facilitate clear identification and marking of these materials, some members of the public found it to be more of an erosion of government transparency. The American Society of Newspaper Editors (ASNE), the APME, and the American Newspapers Publishers Association were outspoken in their opposition to the use of this system outside of wartime, as noted in other chapters.

Some members of the science community were also outspoken against the withholding of "secret" government information that was developed or discovered by research specialists. The necessity of sharing information among a wide range of scientists who worked on similar problems was the principle that spurred concern among this group. "Innovation and development depend essentially upon a widespread flow of communication among scientists working on related problems," according to one researcher. "Insofar as governmental secrecy stifles such communication, it hampers scientific progress. ... Scientific achievement is itself regarded as the firmest basis for national security."[28]

Each president since Truman has issued an executive order detailing the authority and parameters of an information security classification system.[29] Not only do the orders detail when and what shall be classified so as to protect it from public scrutiny, but the orders also outline the schedule for declassification of those materials already withheld. Truman's original system directed that classifying officials shall place a notation indicating when the materials may be declassified. The George W. Bush administration, however, began a campaign of re-classifying information, some of which at that time could be easily found on the World Wide Web (WWW), that had already been released or was scheduled for declassification by previous administrations.[30]

During the Reagan administration, there was an additional category of information that received special attention as the use of computer storage became prevalent in the federal government. That category, "sensitive information," first gained legal legs with the passage of the Computer Security Act of 1987.[31] The term was defined as

> any information the loss, misuse, or unauthorized access to or modification of which could adversely affect the national interest or the conduct of Federal programs, or the privacy to which individuals are entitled under section 552a of the title 5 (Privacy Act), but which has not been specifically authorized under the

criteria established by an Executive order or an Act of Congress to be kept secret in the interest of national defense or foreign policy.[32]

Soon after the September 11, 2001, terrorist attacks on New York and Washington D.C., President Bush and Attorney General John Ashcroft instructed agencies to review the guidelines for all information classification categories and include sensitive information as part of their FOIA exclusions. The memorandum[33] included the following guidelines:

Classified Information ...

- If the information is more than twenty five years old and is still classified, it should remain classified ...
- If the information, regardless of age, never was classified and never was disclosed to the public under proper authority, ... it should be classified in accordance with Executive Order 12958. ...
- If such sensitive information, regardless of age, was classified and subsequently was declassified, but it never was disclosed to the public under proper authority, it should be reclassified in accordance with Executive Order 12958. ...

Sensitive But Unclassified Information

In addition ... departments and agencies maintain and control sensitive information related to America's homeland security that might not meet one or more of the standards for classification set forth in Part 1 of Executive Order 12958. The need to protect such sensitive information from inappropriate disclosure should be carefully considered, on a case-by-case basis, together with the benefits that result from the open and efficient exchange of scientific, technical, and like information.

All departments and agencies should ensure that in taking necessary and appropriate actions to safeguard sensitive but unclassified information related to America's homeland security, they process any FOIA request for records containing such information in accordance with the Attorney General's FOIA Memorandum of October 12, 2001, by giving full and careful consideration to *all applicable FOIA exemptions*. [emphasis added][34]

More recently the Transportation Security Administration (TSA) incorporated a classification category that extends sensitive information designation to "sensitive security information" (SSI). This is a class of information that does not reach the traditional thresholds for security designations but is deemed a threat, if publicly available, to national security. The SSI label is used by other agencies under the umbrella of the Department of Homeland Security as well and some wonder if the category is more about avoiding law suits than protecting national security.[35]

An example of information withholding that frustrated some members of the public was during an October 2003 open meeting to discuss a report that recommended increased attention to airline cargo regulations. The details in the report on which the recommendations were made could not be released because they were considered SSI, making it difficult for reporters and anyone outside the government agencies involved in producing the report to ascertain the rationale for some of the solutions sought by TSA.

Conclusion

Between the traditions of executive privilege, the statutory guidelines of the Housekeeping Act, and the APA coupled with the Executive Orders for classifying information, the avenues for review of government-held information have been scrutinized and reorganized with each change in administration. The use and review of the laws highlight, with each new office holder, the range of interpretation available to administrators. The next chapter reports on the specific period immediately before the Congressional push for the 1966 version of the FOIA. During the push and pull of the McCarthy hearings of the 1950s both Congress and the White House became embroiled in a dispute about information privileges that went beyond the skirmishes so far described. It is the particulars of the McCarthy hearing that will be the focus of the next chapter as a way to clarify why the FOIA appeared and took hold when it did.

5

The Paper Curtain

In 1927 the U.S. Supreme Court rendered an opinion in *McGrain v. Daugherty* that congressional investigatory power may spawn from a heritage in Britain's Parliament, but the court went on to say, "In actual legislative practice, power to secure needed information by such means has long been treated as an attribute of the power to legislate."[1] When the issue of executive privilege continued to be a point of contention between Congress and the White House, a 1959 law review article followed the court's lead and harkened to the Massachusetts' House of Representatives with a 1722 quote, saying that it was "not only their Privilege but Duty to demand of any Officer in the pay and service of this Government an account of his Management while in the Public Imploy [*sic*]."[2]

Clearly, the question of authority for demanding information when investigating a particular issue was a long-standing argument between the legislative and executive branches. Not long after the nation survived the threat of World War II, it found itself in the throes of a cold war with the "red menace" both off shore and perhaps inside the government itself. President Truman's 1951 Executive Order 10290 detailing when government-held information should be kept from the public, even in peace time, alarmed some who were concerned about agency rules that were already in place.[3] As Truman tried to put the best face on his order, he urged government officials to avoid over-classifying information that would only appear to help cover-up their mistakes.[4] Members of the press scoffed at this directive and dubbed the classification system "a curtain of secrecy."[5]

As Eisenhower's Republican party members swept the next round of legislative elections, many freshmen delegates found themselves in a majority position of power, and some Democrats were left struggling. As they sought committee assignments and causes that would impress their constituents back home, the issue of controlling government information in this new age of atomic weapons, computers, and imminent total destruction played out in little-known areas of congressional domain.

In 1953 John E. Moss, a Democrat from California, requested for a review of some documents from the Civil Service Commission for the House of Representative's Post Office and Civil Service Committee. Moss simply wanted to verify that the agency had rightfully fired nearly 3,000 employees for security infractions. His request, however, was denied. Moss then wanted to appeal the denial but found there was no system for such an appeal. In his search for a solution Moss became familiar with members of professional organizations outside of government, who had long been hectoring for more responsive bureaucrats. Among this group were the news media organizations like the American Society of Newspaper Editors (ASNE), the Associated Press Managing Editors, and Sigma Delta Chi.

News Media and FOI

As early as 1950 James Russell Wiggins, managing editor of the *Washington Post,* began a systematic collection of directives and standards used by executive branch offices protecting unclassified public information.[6] The results were compiled into a report the next year for the ASNE public records access. About the same time, James S. Pope, managing editor of the *Louisville Courier-Journal,* asked Harold L. Cross, the New York lawyer for several news media organizations, to put together a report on state standards for open records. Right away Wiggins and Cross struck up a correspondence about public records laws that would continue for decades because of common interests and a shared enjoyment of respites in Maine.[7]

Wiggins was well enough known in "access to government records" circles to be asked to serve on many such committees. Many of those requests he accepted, but there were some he declined. When Erwin "Spike" D. Canham, editor of the *Christian Science Monitor,* asked Wiggins to serve on the newly formed U.S. Advisory Commission on Information, Wiggins replied that he thought it "unwise for me to have any formal or official connection with any government agency of any kind." He wrote that he was afraid that "any such connection only exposes us to the charge of partiality to the administration by some of amiable Washington contemporaries."[8]

He did, however, accept committee work for the APME in 1951. During the September 1951 APME meetings held in San Francisco, the convention adopted a resolution "Censorship at the Source" decrying Truman's September 25th executive order. The resolution claimed, in part, "Free people have the right to the fullest information about conduct of their own government. They can safely consent to its abridgment only on the plainest demonstration of national peril." The declaration goes on to a detailed list of six deficiencies "instantly apparent" in the order, and to empower APME president to deliver the resolution to President Truman. Wiggins came home from the meeting and quickly assembled a file of reporters' notes on each federal agency's classification standards. The results were impressive and prepared for distribution by December 1951.[9] The seven-page list included the Bureau of Budget through the Veterans Administration. In all, eighty-six agencies, bureaus, boards, commissions, offices, systems, and authorities had been visited and were part of the report prepared for APME.

When APME met in February 1952, the Freedom of Information Committee reported continued concerns about the "trend" toward government nondisclosure. Edwin Young, chairman of the committee, said:

> Certainly Washington is one source of this trend where the range is all the way from President Truman's order extending military censorship to civilian agencies, to the refusal of witnesses to testify before Congressional committee lest they incriminate themselves. [From] where it stems and regardless of the standing of the individuals promoting this withholding of information, the trend is here. It is a trend that must be fought.[10]

The report included examples of the kinds of nondisclosure that newspapers were experiencing in the hands of government agencies across the nation, taken from the committee's "comprehensive files that has built up in a very short time."[11]

There were instances that continued to flow to Wiggins' office after the committee report and throughout the year. An example came from Spokane, Washington, on April 18, 1952. In a letter to Wiggins from the managing editor of the *Daily Chronicle*, Howard C. Cleavinger reported that a B-36 bomber had crashed near Spokane leaving fifteen killed and two survivors. "Our men who covered the crash encountered considerable difficulties" when they tried to take pictures and get information about the accident. Cleavinger went on to say that he remembers difficulty in other parts of the country when B-36 planes crash. "We feel the difficulty undoubtedly resulted from what might have been overzealous enforcement of the tight security program under which the Strategic Air Command must operate," he said. Cleavinger went on to suggest the issuance of special credentials to news reporters who qualify with government agency guidelines as a way of avoiding this kind of interference.[12]

By 1953, when John Moss was about to experience his request denial, the news organizations were in full throttle over government non-disclosure, and Harold L. Cross' book *The People's Right to Know* was published that year. The title phrase, "the right to know," was credited in the book's foreword to Kent Cooper, citing a January 23, 1945, *New York Times* editorial. Cross' preface to the book opens with these words:

> Public business is the public's business. The people have the right to know. Freedom of information is their just heritage. Without that the citizens of a democracy have but changed their kings.

Cross, a faculty member at Columbia University and a lawyer for the *New York Herald Tribune*, was asked by the ASNE to provide a report on the legal parameters for the public right to know about government's business. That report, eventually published by Columbia University Press in 1953, included a section on the history and rules for public records, the legal sources for access to records at the federal level, as well as relevant state and municipal laws. He also detailed those records traditionally not available for public inspection, as well as the range of judicial records that may be withheld from public review. For good measure, the appendices include an annotated list of state statutes that define public records and that create or define a right of inspection. Much of the text is a legal roadmap to case law and statutes that guided the discourse on public records and "a right to know" about government activities. Supplements to the book were published throughout the 1950s as the laws changed across the nation.

At the April 18 APME meeting, members were told by James "Jimmie" S. Pope, chairman of the Committee on Freedom of Information, that there seemed to be some hope the new Eisenhower administration would see the error of the Truman's executive order. The committee reported on the changes in government bureau department heads. Some were said to "display a lively interest in removing all the news-blocks," and Wiggins was reported as having negotiated with some of the congressional committee chairs for more open hearings. On June 17 President Eisenhower announced he was reviewing and would modify Truman's executive order.

Wiggins, serving as chair of the Freedom of Information Committee for the ASNE and also as a member of the APME committee, spent countless hours with the new attorney general in hopes of significantly changing the use of the classification system. In a memo to members of the ASNE committee dated June 8, 1953, Wiggins wrote, "Not since the President's Executive Order [of 1951] have I been as encouraged and hopeful about its withdrawal and/or modification." His hopes were somewhat dashed when on November 6, President Eisenhower issued a new executive order, No. 10501, "Safeguarding Official Information In the Interests of the Defense of the United States." Twenty-eight agencies were eliminated as having "classification authority," but seventeen nonmilitary and non-State Department agencies continued to have at least some classification authority.

Letters began to fly anew from all corners of the news profession. State committees were actively reporting on problems with government agencies at all levels of bureaucracy. And, the federal legislature was no less immune. For example, on January 19, 1954, Senator John Butler received a letter of complaint from Sigma Delta Chi, the national professional journalists' organization which at the time boasted about 22,000 members. The letter protested the secrecy of committee hearings on "alleged Communist infiltration of some labor unions" and detailed the reasons Sigma Delta Chi thought the hearings should be open. The letter went on to say:

> Because of the importance of this matter, the American people are entitled to a full and factual report of these hearings at the time and not after the fact. Much of the hysteria and confusion in American political life today can be directly attributed to secret hearings and meetings of Congress. In many of these secret Congressional hearings and meetings, the facts and records are never publicly disclosed and the people are given only carefully tailored reports, sometimes slanted for political reasons, by individual Congressmen.[13]

Meanwhile, the second Hoover Commission, called by the president and established by congressional funding from 1953 to 1955,[14] prepared a report that criticized the growing secrecy among federal agencies and suggested some amendments to the Administrative Practices Act as a solution. In the Senate, Joseph McCarthy, a Republican from Wisconsin, was fighting his own battles over the executive branch's withholding of U.S. Army reports. Front-page newspaper stories across the nation reprinted transcripts of senate hearings. Editorials carried headlines that were unambiguous about the debate. For example, a May 9, 1954, story "Special to the *New York Times*" and datelined Washington, declared across the top, "M'Carthy's [*sic*] Secret Paper Reopens An Old Dispute: Executive Departments Have Held that They Decide What Is in Public Interest." It explained the background on executive privilege, beginning with President George Washington. The piece went on to report:

> The basic argument of the Executive Branch is that it, not the Congress, has the constitutional right to decide when it would not be in the public interest to disclose to unauthorized persons information contained in investigative reports. It adheres to its right to classify Congress as an "unauthorized person" if it wants to.

McCarthy's subcommittee was investigating claims that there was Communist infiltration in the military and he was deeply frustrated when Eisenhower refused congressional requests for testimony and documents. McCarthy was later censured by the Senate for his grandstanding and pressure tactics, but Congress was nonetheless without the information it needed to allay public fear of the "enemy within."

Congress Takes Up the Task

All of this prompted Moss to request a congressional study on the existing procedures for information access among government agencies. The House decided that year, 1955, to establish a new subcommittee on government information that would report to the larger House Committee on Government Operations, and named Moss as chair. William Dawson, chairman of the House Government Operations Committee and a Democrat from Illinois, said in his statement establishing the new subcommittee, "An informed public makes the difference between mob rule and democratic government. If the pertinent and necessary information on government activities is denied the public, the result is a weakening of the democratic process. ..."[15]

Moss moved quickly to convene hearings on reforming both the Housekeeping Statute and the Administrative Procedures Act. Harold Cross and Wiggins were immediately in correspondence with each other about the committee's work. Cross was in Ontario, Canada, at the time but offered his services to Wiggins. "Is there anything I can do usefully in this connection?"[16] Wiggins responded three days later that the committee was just in the phase of gathering a library of facts. He added, "They have been interested in obtaining your services as a consultant and I think they will be in touch with you." Wiggins closed the letter with an assessment of Moss as a "very serious and quite careful and conservative fellow ... I think [he] is anxious to do something that will have long time and constructive effects and not just to make a splurge."[17] James Pope, too, wrote to Moss offering ideas, and copied Wiggins on the correspondence. Pope included with his letter a copy of Cross' on the history of information access laws and added, "I think you'll find this bit of history interesting."[18] By September 16, 1955, Moss and Cross were corresponding about the subcommittee's work and hard at work drafting a memo for the Congressional Record about how that work would proceed. In a letter to Wiggins, Cross wrote, "The work of this subcommittee may well become the most important thing that has happened in ASNE's campaign."[19]

Between 1955 and 1959 the House Committee on Government Operations held scores of hearings and issued more than a dozen reports on government information practices and secrecy. Despite complaints and general opposition from federal agency directors, Congress did amend the Housekeeping Statute in 1958 with bills sponsored in the House by Moss and in the Senate by Thomas Hennings. The central reform of the statute was a clarification that agency records are to be stored and used by those offices, but may not be withheld from public review unless so designated by statute or direct executive order.[20]

Celebrations were short lived. Moss and Hennings, as well as their respective committees, soon found that the withholding of information by federal agencies continued unabated. The examples reported within the next congressional session were discouraging. In the first nine months of 1959 Moss' subcommittee found dozens of instances when executive privilege was specifically cited as the barrier against providing agency information.[21] An annotated list provided to the committee included, in part, the following:

- Comptroller General Joseph Campbell [Government Administration Oversight, GAO] formally protests Navy refusal of access to report on procurement activities of the Military Sea Transportation Service. (January 22)
- Complaint from Congressman Richard E. Lankford of Maryland … about the Navy refusal of his request for a report on the Naval Gun Factory, Washington, D.C. (February 17)
- Congressman Porter Hardy, Jr., of Virginia, Chairman of the House Foreign Operations Subcommittee, requests documents relating to the Office of Evaluation in the International Cooperation Administration (ICA) as part of his subcommittee's investigation of the Foreign Aid Program. (February 26)
- Refusal by Acting ICA Director Leonard J. Saccio of Hardy request for documents. (April 2)
- Hearings by the House Government Information Subcommittee on the Navy refusals to Congressman Lankford and to the GAO. GAO lists refusals by the Department of Defense and the ICA including reports on aid to Formosa, Laos, Brazil, India, Guatemala, Pakistan, and Bolivia. (April 20. 21, and 23)
- Senate Subcommittee on Government Organization for Space Activities headed by Senator Stuart Symington of Missouri complained in a report that the imposition of "executive privilege" by the head of the National Aeronautics and Space Administration had hindered Congress "from obtaining basic policy information" about U.S. space plans and program. (Senate Report No. 806, 86th Congress, 1st Session, July 14, 1959)

- Claim of "executive privilege" discussed with Pentagon officials at hearing of the House Armed Services Investigating Subcommittee. (July 17)
- The President signs the Mutual Security Act of 1959 (H.R. 7500) and issues the following statement on the Hardy amendments included in that bill: "I have signed the bill on the express premise that the three amendments relating to disclosure are not intended to alter and cannot alter the recognized Constitutional duty and power of the Executive with respect to the disclosure of information, documents and other materials. Indeed, any other construction of these amendments would raise grave Constitutional questions under the historic Separation of Powers Doctrine." (July 24)
- Congressman Hardy, pointing out the newly enacted Hardy amendments, requests James W. Riddleberger, Director of ICA, to make available ICA evaluation reports on foreign aid operations in Laos and Vietnam. The request was refused informally the same day, and formally by letter on August 5. (July 24)

Things were not going well for Congress. Out on the speakers circuit, Samuel Archibald, staff administrator for the House Government Information subcommittee, summed up the situation at public gatherings. During a forum held on October 17, 1959, in Boulder at the University of Colorado, Archibald localized for his listeners the congressional worries about government secrecy. He told three stories of government information withholding that affected those he spoke to on that Saturday.

One example that Archibald shared was about a request to the Pike National Forest Supervisor's office for a list of ranchers with grazing permits for the forest. The request was denied because, as Archibald quoted, "We have to protect the permittees. We consider their dealings with the Forest Service and their use of Forest Service lands strictly a private affair between them and the Forest Service."[22]

A second story involved the Titan missile site near Littleton, "one of the most widely known 'secrets' of America's top secret weapons program." Chamber of Commerce members were reported to have toured the plant and seen the missile, and the outside shape of the missile had been declassified by the Defense Department since 1958. But the Pentagon's chief press agent, Murray Snyder, would not release an official picture of the missile when asked by news media, so the press went and took their own pictures.[23]

The third story was about evidence of contaminated drinking-water wells around the Rocky Mountain Arsenal chemical plant near Derby, Colorado. When university researchers were hired by the Army Chemical Corps to find out whether the chemical plant might be the cause, the Army refused to make the report public. The report did in fact discover the cause and extent of the water contamination, but the Army said it was only a preliminary, interim report and its release would only cause controversy for the farmers and residents nearby.[24]

Clearly, examples were everywhere. For the entire decade of the 1950s, Congress had not been alone in its frustration with federal agencies. The news media were actively reporting instances of information withholding at every level of government. James S. Pope, managing editor of the *Louisville Courier-Journal* and chairman of the American Society of Newspaper Editors (ASNE) FOI committee during the early 1950s, reported that during his chairmanship he had exchanged hundreds of letters with news organizations across the country who claimed to be operating under government secrecy regimes. His response to all of them was to organize. "Please form a committee, make a careful study of Harold Cross' report … and keep me informed as to your activities. We can help each other."[25] A year later he reported that there were committees in forty-six states.[26]

Harold Cross also reported to the ASNE that for the first ten years of his law practice he had never had a serious refusal of access to information when he was representing newspapers. But in 1951, he said, "Now scarcely a week goes by without a new refusal. The last five years brought more newspaper lawsuits to open records than in the previous twenty-five." His inference from this evidence was that "there is a frightening trend toward suppression of official public records."[27]

Moss was reported to have said, "For ten years the American Society of Newspaper Editors and other newspaper groups have been fighting against restrictions on the flow of information from the federal government. It was largely due to the ASNE that the House Government Information Subcommittee was created."[28] But the workings of statutory change were moving slowly into action.

The American Bar Association continued to urge statutory changes and legal scholars argued long and hard in support. A seminal article in 1959 scrupulously walked through the historical and modern legal issues of invoking executive privilege when Congress requested information from federal agency officials.[29] The set piece for the author was Attorney General Herbert Brownell, Jr.'s 1954 assertion that the president and his cabinet have discretion to keep information secret in the public interest, and that "the President and the heads of departments have an uncontrolled discretion to withhold the information and papers in the public interest."[30]

The claim was expanded, according to Professor Schwartz of New York University Law School, with an additional provision outlined in 1958 during a

Senate subcommittee hearing. "In response to congressional requests for documents, the Executive should exercise discretion as to whether the production would serve a public good or would be contrary to public interest. ... Only the President can make the determination as to disclosure."[31]

Schwartz summarized, "The problem itself—that of ensuring the adequate diffusion of executive information, particularly to the legislative branch—is one of the most significant confronting the country and the Congress at the present time." He concludes, after lengthy review of the relevant legal resources, that "the problem is one which is within the legal power of the Congress to deal with, by statute or otherwise. ... 'We may say that the power ... belongs in the hands of Congress, but only Congress itself can prevent power from slipping through its fingers.'"[32] He continues his conclusion with the following:

> In the absence of effective assertions of the congressional authority to require the disclosure of information, it is hardly surprising if departments and agencies persist in assertions of unfettered discretion in themselves in the matter. To be sure, departments and agencies have a natural desire to be wholly free of investigatory demands. But the possibilities of administrative inconvenience here are surely outweighed by the overriding public interest in having the affairs of the Government carried on free of the "paper curtain" of official secrecy.[33]

Schwartz ends his article with a quote from Patrick Henry that Harold Cross also used in the preface to his 1953 book: "To cover with the veil of secrecy the common routine of business, is an abomination in the eyes of every intelligent man and every friend to his country."[34]

The tendency of administrative bureaucrats just to say no when information was requested after World War II became variously known as a "velvet curtain" or a "paper curtain" or the "curtain of secrecy."[35] In all cases the reference was meant to elicit imagery that came near to the reviled "iron curtain" of Communist eastern block countries in Europe and a lack of transparency that blocked "the light of public scrutiny" often cited in American news columns at that time.

Harold Cross, right up to his death in 1959, was consistent in saying, "The Congress, to which alone the law-making power is entrusted by the Constitution, can legislate, if it will, far-reaching freedom for itself, the people and the press without encroaching on actual powers of the President." Congress did not definitively act until the mid-1960s when it successfully navigated the executive branch roadblocks and public concerns about national security if government information were more readily available. The next chapter will describe the particulars of congressional activity that led to the signing of the 1966 Freedom of Information Act.

6
The Freedom
of Information Act

During the forty years since the passage of the FOIA by the 89th Congress,[1] continuing debate and frustration clouds the value of the act. When President Lyndon B. Johnson signed the law in 1966,[2] he said, "This legislation springs from one of our most essential principles: a democracy works best when the people have all the information that the security of the nation permits." He went on to say, "There are some who have expressed concern that the language of this bill will be construed in such a way as to impair government operations. I do not share this concern."

Even when the protesters against the war in Vietnam and for civil rights gained much of their strength from revealing government documents, President Johnson held firm to his statement that "I have always believed that freedom of information is so vital that only the national security, not the desire of public officials or private citizens, should determine when it must be restricted."[3]

The following chapter outlines the history of the FOIA in order to provide background and context for the subsequent chapters that focus attention on particular aspects and uses of the act. While the history provided here is not intended to be exhaustive, it is intended to report and review the primary documents that were fundamental to the initial passage and many revisions of the act. It is hoped that this work satisfies the scrutiny of those who are experts in legal research as well as those who are not scholars but serious readers.

Beginnings as a Quick Review

The first session of the first congress of the United States worried about the public's need to know what government was doing. During that session there was some debate about how best to provide the necessary reports, but there was little delay in congressional action. On September 15, 1789, Congress required the secretary of state to publish, in at least three of the public newspapers printed within the United States, every bill, order, resolution, vote of the houses of Congress, as well as presidential objection to these actions.[4]

Though this early resolve in American history might suggest a continuing and empowering atmosphere of government disclosure, this was not the case. A constant power play between each of the branches of government led to a yoyo effect for access and denial of what the executive branch deemed necessary to keep secret, and what it would divulge to public scrutiny. In times of open conflict there was little discussion about the need for secrecy, and the courts denied any attempts to force an easing of secrecy.[5]

Often, however, during times of relative calm the president and his cabinet were forthcoming about their activities, with Congress pressing the case, and the courts responding with some support.[6] But peace was rare enough that Congress often found it necessary to push hard where the path was not already well trodden for any disclosure about executive branch decision-making and follow-through.[7]

By the mid-twentieth century, Congress passed the APA,[8] bolstered by a Senate Judiciary Committee Report particularly favoring the language of Section 3:

> The section has been drawn upon the theory that administrative operations and procedures are public property which the general public, rather than a few specialists or lobbyists, is entitled to know or have ready means of knowing with definiteness.[9]

The evident problem with Section 3 was that government agencies were given discretion to withhold documents that the agency thought, in the public interest, should be kept secret. The law also allowed the agency to decide which documents were public records subject to disclosure.[10] Frustration with the shortcomings of the APA led to more hearings and further efforts to force the executive branch to open up. President Harry Truman's expansion of the military's information classification system to include documents from all executive branch agencies did not make things easier with the legislature.[11] Nor did his expansion of executive privilege endear him to Congress.[12]

The struggle for more public review of executive agencies during the 1950s and the cold war was a continuing priority among legislative members. Continued evidence that the executive branch was not only refusing requests from the public, but increasingly rejecting requests from Congress, forced members to launch an investigation and publish a damming report.[13] For example, the findings included the revelation that during the ten years before 1940 there had only been three occasions when an agency refused a congressional request for information. During the next twelve years, there were fifteen refusals. During the period between 1955 and 1960, there were as many as seventy-five instances when congressional requests for information were rejected.

Congress was not the only entity concerned with or investigating executive branch secrecy. The ASNE established a committee to compile a report on freedom of information problems. That report, *The People's Right to Know: Legal Access to Public Records and Proceedings*, was published in 1953, and its author, Dr. Harold L. Cross, served as a resource to congressional subcommittees that later wrote the FOIA legislation. More broadly the American Bar Association recommended that the entire Administrative Procedure Act be revised,[14] as had the Hoover Commission in 1955.[15]

There were several early attempts at what would become the FOIA. Senator Thomas C. Hennings, Jr., a democrat from Missouri, said these efforts were being made in order to "make it clear beyond any doubt that the basic purpose ... is to insure the dissemination of the maximum amount of information reasonably possible."[16] The statement was reiterated in the final Senate report that accompanied the 1966 bill:

> It is the purpose of the present bill ... to establish a general philosophy of full agency disclosure unless information is exempt under clearly delineated statutory language and to provide a court procedure by which citizens and the press may obtain information wrongfully withheld.[17]

In 1957 there were, initially, extensive amendments to Section 3 of the APA, and to the Housekeeping Statute,[18] offered in both the House and the Senate to override the discretionary language used to withhold information. The amendment to the Housekeeping Act was simple, and said that the statute "does not authorize the withholding of information from the public or limiting the availability of records to the public."[19] The bill was passed unanimously by the House and Senate in 1958[20] and was signed into law on August 15 of that year by President Dwight D. Eisenhower.[21]

The victory, however, was short lived. In 1959 a House subcommittee investigated the effectiveness of the Housekeeping Statute amendment and found that no changes in the executive branch agencies' procedures had resulted.[22] Instead of revising the amendment to the Housekeeping Statute, more effort was put into the Section 3 revisions of the APA.

Senator Hennings had offered the original Section 3 amendment bill which had languished while the Housekeeping Act revisions sailed through Congress. When the Senate came back to Hennings' bill it was favorably reported to the Subcommittee on Constitutional Rights.

The proposed amendments included public disclosure of all "records, files, papers, and documents submitted to and received by the agency,"[23] with three exceptions. Those were materials exempt by statute, or requiring secrecy for national security, or unwarranted invasion of privacy. There was vigorous lobbying, but before the bill reached the Senate floor Hennings died and with him went the attention to the Section 3 amendment.

The Struggle Toward Passage

When Congress convened in 1963, there was new interest in freedom of information legislation. Cold war rhetoric was stepping up, and Congress was concerned about how the executive branch was managing the enforcement and defense agencies. Senator Edward V. Long, a democrat from Missouri, took up leadership of the Judiciary Committee's Subcommittee on Administrative Practice and Procedure. The Section 3 revisions were contained in S. 1666, and the witnesses to committee hearings strongly favored the bill.[24] And additions to this version of the bill included a right to seek a court order that would compel an agency to produce any record improperly withheld. Though it passed the Senate, the House adjourned without action on the bill, and it was reintroduced in the 89th congressional session as S.1160.

Senator Long again sought witnesses and suggestions for any improvements on the bill's language before sending it to the floor for a vote. Witnesses included media group representatives, American Civil Liberties Union, the Chamber of Commerce for the United States, and American Bar Association members, as well as a few representatives from government agencies. Senator Long said, as part of the record for new hearings, that he was disappointed in the executive branch response to his questions. He said agencies were "remiss and derelict in offering any constructive suggestions as to how Congress can strike a balance of the right to know and the necessity to withhold certain information."[25]

The bill was passed by the Senate in October 1965 and referred to the House. Again, the House members were uninterested in the bill, but Representative John E. Moss, a democrat from California, was determined to move the issue forward. He had, earlier in the year, submitted an identical bill in the House but identified it as an amendment to the Housekeeping Statute in order to have it reported to a somewhat more enthusiastic subcommittee. Moss' bill, H.R. 5012, was introduced in February, 1965 with hearings held in March and April.[26] When the executive branch would not budge on redrafts of the bill to meet their objections of it, the work got bogged down, and as a result no bill was reported out of the committee.

In October, however, when the Senate bill was sent to the House it was referred to Moss' subcommittee and they decided to hold no hearings, thereby squelching administrative efforts to slow progress, or make any changes to it. Knowing what the objections were to the bill from previous hearings, however, the House report that accompanied it recommended passage without amendment, but included passages that seemed to contradict the bill itself. It was passed by the House in June, 1966,[27] and was signed on July 4.[28]

The two-page bill not only included the nine exemptions to information availability, but also said that agencies must provide notice of public information availability in the Federal Register. The required information in the Federal Register must also contain descriptions of central and field offices, officers, and methods for securing information made available. It also required that agency opinions and orders be published, as well as agency records, proceedings, and the limitations on exemptions. The codification of the amendment to the APA, known as the FOIA, went into effect July 4, 1967.

Early History

The June 1967 memorandum containing guidelines for agencies compliance with FOIA came from the attorney general's office less than a month before the new law came into effect.[29] The House and Senate reports that accompanied the bill were used for specific language in the memorandum, and where there were differences between the reports, the language that excluded the most information from review was adopted. Though the policy statement at the beginning of the guidelines said the general rule was one of openness, there was little in the guidelines to suggest radical changes from custom.

Many government agencies were slow to take the FOIA seriously,[30] but when law suits were filed against them for noncompliance the bureaucrats snapped to attention.[31] The court's initial reading of the law favored the Senate report's intentions for full disclosure, much to the consternation of those agencies who favored the House report's language favoring exemptions.[32] Hundreds of suits were filed and the Department of Justice (DOJ) was obligated to defend these suits,[33] so that by 1970 there was serious review in Congress and by activists about the effectiveness of the law.[34]

When Congress wanted reports of FOIA usage, the House Subcommittee on Foreign Operations and Government Information requested a survey to be conducted among the executive branch agencies.[35] Unfortunately the law did not require that statistics of requests and responses be kept and so ad hoc results were the best that could be collected. For example, some of the larger agencies reported that more than 250,000 formal requests were received between the years 1967 and 1971. But since the Department of the Air Force treated all requests for information as FOIA requests, the totals were probably skewed.

Among the figures that were somewhat easier to collect were the refusals to supply information. Among the major agencies, there were about 1,500 denials for access, and about 650 were requests made by corporations and their law firms. Though most of the witnesses during initiation hearings were media members, only about ninety media requests were denied, and public interest groups came in at about the same number. Congressional members received about thirty-five denials of information, and the rest were nonfederal government agencies, or other kinds of requesters.

The survey also reported that the FOIA exemption most often cited for denials was for trade secrets, Exemption 4. This exemption accounted for more than four hundred denials. Exemption 5, agency memorandums accounted for about 375 request denials, and personnel files, Exemption 6, was used 344 times to deny requested information. Exemption 1 for national security only accounted for thirty denials, while one hundred denials were based on Exemption 2, internal rules. Exemption 3 for those provided by other statutes contributed to 206 denials, and investigatory records, Exemption 7 accounted for 244 denials.

FOIA 1974 Revisions

With the results of the survey in hand, and a litany of complaints by users and agency providers, Congress set about to remedy the problems as quickly as it could.[36] The House and the Senate each passed amendment bills that went to a conference committee late in 1974. Both House and Senate agreed to the conference report, which was then sent to the president on October 1, 1974.[37]

Among the significant changes to the original law that the separate bills addressed was a more careful delineation of more than a dozen aspects of the original legislation. These included quarterly publication of indexed reports on departments' FOIA activities and annual reports that included a list of officials responsible for FOIA, along with an annual report by the Attorney General's office detailing FOIA litigation; provisions of de novo judicial review for appeals as a response to the Supreme Court's 1973 decision in *EPA v. Mink*;[38] shortening the agency response time from sixty days, to ten days for the initial response from the agency, and twenty days response time when an administrative appeal was requested; broadening of the definition of agency to include all executive departments like the executive office of the president, military, and government controlled corporations, and independent agencies; and relaxing the definition of identifiable records in a request to that of more simply, reasonably described.

The Exemption 7 definition of investigatory records was also modified to allow the withholding of records only when the disclosure would interfere with enforcement proceedings, deprive a person of a right to a fair trial, or constitute an unwarranted invasion of privacy, or disclose the identity of a confidential source, expose investigative techniques, or endanger the life of law enforcement officers. Other modifications included the awarding of attorney fees and court costs to the requester if the litigation ended in strong support of the requested information. There was also a provision that the courts impose sanctions where agency employees wrongfully withheld information.

President Gerald Ford received the bill with many political concerns. Though Watergate investigations two years earlier and the resignation of the President that Richard Nixon formally accepted on August 7, 1974, had eroded public esteem of the White House, Ford was said to have concerns about the long-term effects of too much disclosure by the executive branch.

President Ford had supported the original FOIA legislation when he was a member of Congress, but his shift to the executive branch also shifted his view of the problems detailed in the amendments. His primary advisors during his administration were Chief of Staff Donald Rumsfeld and Deputy Chief of Staff Richard Cheney, both of whom later served as senior advisors under Republican presidents through George W. Bush. They were joined in their opposition of the amendments bill by Central Intelligence Agency (CIA) Director W.E. Colby and the Justice Department's lead counsel Antonin Scalia, who would later become a U.S. Supreme Court Justice.[39]

In a memo to the president dated October 16, 1974, from the OMB, the agencies recommending a veto included the OMB; the CIA; the DOJ, Treasury, Commerce, Defense, State; and the Civil Service Commission. The GSA offered no objection, and the Department of Health, Education, and Welfare deferred.[40] Ten days after receiving the bill, President Ford issued a veto, based on concerns about the heavy burden placed on the executive branch to justify nondisclosure and the shorter turn-around time for agency response to the high volume of requests.[41]

Though Congress was scheduled for a recess, the next day—October 18—members shot back at the veto. Senator Edward Kennedy said that he did not believe the president wanted to perpetuate the kind of secrecy that characterized the Watergate years, but the president's veto would have that result.[42] President Ford issued some specific suggestions to amend the language of the bill, but Congress set about to override his veto. On November 20 the House voted 371 to 31, with 32 abstentions, in favor of the override[43] and the Senate followed on November 21 with 65 in favor and 27 against.[44] The FOIA amendments, then, became effective on February 19, 1975.

Congressional Oversight of FOIA since 1975

The DOJ took the leadership role within the executive branch for interpreting and implementing the FOIA regulations. In early December 1974, an eighteen-page memorandum was sent to all agency heads suggesting interpretation of the amendments that would go into effect in February 2005.[45] A longer, more detailed guide was issued in February.[46] There was much attention paid to the Exemption 7 amendment on investigatory records, and specific interpretation about the revision, allowing courts more latitude in reviewing classified documents, was also provided in the memorandum.

The DOJ was also interested in avoiding FOIA litigation at all the agencies because it was responsible for representing those agencies when requests were denied and appealed. At that time there were about 600 cases pending at one stage or another.[47] To aid the reduction of the number of suits, the attorney general's office wrote a letter to every agency that said the DOJ would "defend FOIA suits only when disclosure is demonstrably harmful, even if the documents technically fall within the exemptions of the Act."[48] In addition, the DOJ established the Office of Information Law and Policy, dedicated to coordinating FOIA's implementation across all agencies, to providing consistent advice and training to agency officers responsible for responding to FOIA requests.[49]

The Office of Information Law and Privacy changed to the Office of Information and Privacy and reported to the DOJ's Office of Legal Policy during the Reagan administration. Not only did the office coordinate efforts across agencies, it also provided regular publication of updates on the most recent interpretations of FOIA's regulations, and made these guides available to the public upon request.[50]

Despite attempts to improve the communication, lawful interpretations of FOIA court cases continued to work very slowly through the system.[51] Two cases lasted nearly a decade and received much notoriety. Unfortunately, they were not the only cases of this sort. One case involved a dispute about the availability of computer tapes used by the Internal Revenue Service (IRS) for reviewing tax payer compliance. An economist, Susan Long, requested an edited version of the tapes to use in her research on the effectiveness of audits in taxpayer compliance.

A 1976 District Court in Seattle held that the computer tapes were not records as defined by FOIA and therefore were not required to be available. The 9th Circuit Court of Appeals in San Francisco disagreed with the lower court, but further litigation to halt compliance kept Long from getting the tapes from either the IRS or the Department of Commerce, who also had a copy of the tapes. Congress responded by passing a law to allow IRS withholding of selected returns for examination in determining standards.[52]

The 1986 Freedom of Information Reform Act

In nearly every session there were some amendments to FOIA offered in Congress. Senator Orrin Hatch, a republican from Utah, initiated changes in 1981, supported by the Reagan administration.[53] Eventually the Senate passed an amendment bill by February 1984, but the house let the legislation die.[54] Reform provisions were again introduced in both the House and Senate during the next congressional session, with most of the attention given to Exemption 7 amendments. These revisions included a broadening of the description of information, and records for law enforcement materials, and a narrowing of what constituted investigatory records to be protected from disclosure. The expression of the probability of harm from disclosed records that the agency expected was lowered to what could reasonably be expected.

There were also concerns about the fee structure and waiver provisions, and so statutory instructions were included that called for the OMB to create guidelines and fee schedules. New guidelines for fee waivers, minimum fees, and the advanced payment of fees were to be established so that requesters could calculate before a request was made of what costs might be involved. There was also an additional distinction to be made between the kind of requesters and the requisite fees attached to providing information. Public interest requests were to be changed only for document duplication, while commercial requests were to be charged for search, review, and duplication fees. A third category was designated and required to pay for search and duplication only.

With much haste and a minimum of explanation, both the House and Senate agreed on a single version of the FOIA amendments and passed the reforms[55] attached to a more popular bill, the Anti-Drug Abuse Act of 1986.[56] President Reagan signed the bill on October 27, and the law went into effect immediately.

FOIA in the 1980s

Though revisions and burgeoning numbers of requests dogged the Act, most agencies had regularized their responses to the extent that reports on FOIA compliance were issued and assessments of its value began to appear routinely. For example, the GAO prepared a tally of agencies' costs in responding to the FOIA requests and presented the results to the Senate Committee on the Judiciary. The 1983 report covered the 1981 budget year and carried a disclaimer, "A precise determination of direct and indirect costs of implementing the FOIA is not possible because agencies generally lack detailed supporting records."[57]

The twenty-four-page report detailed what sorts of costs were considered. They included personnel, personnel benefits, facility rent and utilities, copying, printing, supplies and materials, mailing, filing, and travel. Though the GAO acknowledged that the figures were incomplete, they totaled the expenses reported by forty-two of the seventy-three agencies filed in 1981. These initial figures came to $54.7 million.[58] Housing and Urban Development reported no FOIA costs except for the cost of preparing a three-page response to a DOJ study on FOIA.

At the other extreme was the DOJ with $17.1 million, the Department of Defense with $7.6 million, the Department of Treasury with $5.6 million, and the Department of Health and Human Services with $5.1 in costs. When further investigation added in the overlooked or misstated figures, the GAO reported a total of $61 million spent in FOIA compliance by federal agencies in 1981. The GAO also recommended uniform cost reports be instituted as part of FOIA compliance, and the OMB was given the task.

The GAO was also asked to gather information from the cabinet-level departments, the Veterans Administration (VA), and the General Services Administration on the more specific costs of collecting and processing fees charged to those who requested documents under FOIA.[59] The report estimated that the Department of Agriculture and the Department of State were the most expensive, at the cost of $25, for collecting and processing FOIA fees per request. VA and Housing and Urban Development were the least expensive at less than $2 per request.[60]

In 1989, the GAO prepared a report on the Department of State's FOIA requests response procedures for the House of Representatives' Subcommittee on Government Information, Justice and Agriculture, and Committee on Government Operations. The report detailed the processing of 7,567 FOIA requests received by the State Department from the beginning of 1985 to the end of 1987.[61] The investigation found that it took longer than six months for three-quarters of the requests to be completed, and that at the beginning of 1988, there was a backlog of about 3,700 requests.

In a smaller sample, of the 1,329 requests received during the initial six months of 1986 about half of those requests took longer than 360 days to complete.[62] The delays, according to the GAO report, were caused by initial processing complications so that the assignment of requests to a particular agent took several weeks where it should have taken no more than a single week. Once searches were complete there was found to be significant delays of as much as five weeks in processing the completed search for agency review before it was sent to the requestor.[63] The GAO investigation also found that the department had simply closed, without notice to the requesters, 220 cases because they had been in process for several years.[64]

The cost of FOIA compliance felt by the agencies was not the only issue visited by Congress during the 1980s. Part of the 1986 amendments included a fee schedule with lower fees charged to requests from news media, scientific, and educational institutions, and higher fees for commercial users, and the OMB was asked to establish guidelines for determining into which category a particular requester fit.[65]

The definition of a commercial user was broadened to include "a use or purpose that furthers the commercial, trade, or profit interests of the requester."[66] The final guidelines also defined "representative of the news media" as a "person actively gathering news for an entity that is organized and operated to publish or broadcast news to the public."[67] Scientific and educational institution requesters were to be considered noncommercial if the purpose of the research and scholarship conducted at the institution was not intended to promote a particular product or industry.

In addition, the new guidelines required that agencies reduce or waive fees "if the disclosure of the information is in the public interest because it is likely to contribute significantly to public understanding of the operation or activities of the government and is not primarily in the commercial interest of the requester."[68]

Costs to both the requester and the agencies continued to be calculated throughout the 1980s, but an additional concern related to cost was finding its way into the discussions. Recoverable costs of record searching and preparation has long been part of the fees imposed on requesters. But a new kind of record format was creating special costs and special headaches for everyone using FOIA. Documents were increasingly stored as digital files in order to save the space of mountains of paper generated by government agencies. The digital records not only saved space but could save time for those well-trained in information storage and retrieval.

In 1987 Congress passed the Computer Security Act (CSA),[69] which was to protect unclassified computer information that was deemed to have "sensitive" standing among government documents. The CSA specifically provided that it was not to be used to avoid FOIA requests,[70] but the use of a new category of documents, "sensitive" sent red flags up for FOIA advocates. Soon, there were requests for clarification and litigation to determine when agencies must provide information contained in digital format that was, by the very nature of the request for that information, required to create a new document or record in order to deliver the information.[71]

President Reagan also issued an executive order dated June 23, 1987, that required agencies to inform commercial information suppliers with a written notice that their records were being requested by a third party. The notice was intended to give those who submit commercial information the opportunity to protest the information disclosure.[72] Agencies were instructed to consider carefully the objections raised when a commercial information supplier objected to disclosure, but the order also instructed that there were six situations in which the agency did not need to notify the original commercial information submitter.

These included when the agency decided on its own that there would be no disclosure if the information had already been published, if the information was already officially available, if the disclosure was already required by law or by agency rules, and if the objections by the information submitter would pose a frivolous desire for confidentiality. In this case the executive order was accomplishing something that some members of congress had tried but failed to do with legislation.[73]

Privacy issues in conflict with FOIA were also coming more frequently to the courts during the 1980s. In a case heard at the end of the decade, the Supreme Court favored privacy over access in the *Department of Justice v. Reporters Committee for Freedom of the Press*.[74] The particular kind of record at question was the rap sheet—the record of individuals picked up or suspected in a crime that police use to keep track of that person's interactions with the police. The Justice Department claimed rap sheets were exemption from disclosure under Exemption 7, and the court agreed, even in the face of strong public interest in favor of the disclosure.[75]

In another Exemption 7 case, *John Doe Agency v. John Doe Corp*, the Supreme Court also held that documents "compiled" by an agency simply meant that the any records provided by any source that were put into an investigatory file by that agency, rather than personally collected by that agency, met the exemption standard.[76] As a result, the DOJ issued new guidelines instructing agencies to apply privacy interests to personal items other than rap sheets and deny public access to all information in any investigatory file no matter its original, non-law enforcement source.[77]

At the end of the decade, and nearly twenty-five years after the passage of the FOIA, Congress asked the DOJ to provide a comprehensive report on the FOIA and the agencies' increasing electronic records issues as they related to privacy.[78] The sixty-page report included a survey of all agencies to learn whether these offices had, in place, a regulation or policy statement about how to handle electronic records requests—meaning either that the records only existed in electronic form, or the requester wanted the records in electronic form. The survey also asked respondents to suggest appropriate policies, and to report the extent to which individual agencies' records were generated and stored electronically.[79]

Though the Justice Department had already clearly instructed agencies that records in computer databases were records under FOIA,[80] the department hoped to gather enough responses from the survey to answer four continuing questions. These included whether FOIA (1) was requiring agencies to create new or modify computer programs in order to search and retrieve records tailored to a particular requesters questions, (2) was requiring agencies to create new or modify computer programs in order to segregate disclosable from non-disclosable electronic records, (3) was requiring agencies to provide requested information in the database formats specified by requesters, and (4) was FOIA including computer software as an agency record.[81]

There were eighty-three departments or agencies that responded to the survey, but thirteen of them said they had little or no experience with electronic records and therefore had nothing to contribute to the results. Of the seventy that did respond substantively, fifty-three said that FOIA requests had prompted them to create new or modify existing computer programs in order to provide search capability, but only thirty-three said that they had been required to create or modify computer software for segregating record portions. Forty-one respondents said they thought FOIA required them to provide records in the particular format specified by the requester, but there was a nearly even split on whether computer software itself was deemed an agency record under FOIA.[82]

Clearly some modification to the FOIA was required to meet both the needs of the agencies in record construction and requesters in record requests in an ever-enlarging electronic environment. But those were not the only kinds of problems experienced by requesters in the 1980s. In a survey done by the Society of Professional Journalists in 1989, the results pointed to a general laxness in adhering to FOIA guidelines for response time, politically selective application of exemptions, and wide variations in policies among agencies on FOIA request policies.[83]

The report included not only a general survey to journalists but also in-depth interviews with those who used FOIA often to investigate a story. The survey respondents were a small number because most reporters who had any experience with FOIA requests readily admitted they avoided further experience because of delays, poor response from agencies, and better sources elsewhere.

The biggest complaints among those reporters who continued to try to use FOIA were the length of response time most of the journalists experienced. A majority of the respondents claimed it took more than thirty days to get information, and it was usually because of a personal contact within the agency about the request itself that freed up the requested material.[84]

By 1990, the frustration felt by many constituencies of FOIA requesters was gaining enough attention that a conference was held in Washington, D.C., and coordinated by Jerry J. Berman. Its findings were forwarded to Congress as part of an effort to step up progress toward a legislative solution.[85] The seventy-page report included a section that specifically identified nine issues for computerized information storage and retrieval in the context of FOIA.

These issues included when to apply the definition of "agency record" under the FOIA for new forms of electronic records, whether or not software was a record under FOIA, what constituted a reasonable search of electronic information, whether programming created a new record in itself, whether agencies should be allowed to redact electronic information, who should be allowed to choose access formats, whether legislation was the solution to the FOIA electronic records problem, what costs should be allocated to FOIA requesters for electronic information, and what oversight strategies should there be for educating agencies about FOIA obligations in an electronic environment.[86]

With the change of White House administrations in 1992, there was some hope of change in attitude among agencies about FOIA. On October 4, 1993, President Bill Clinton issued a one-page FOIA memorandum to heads of departments and agencies. He asked agencies to renew their commitment to FOIA and "its underlying principles of government openness." He also reminded agencies that "our commitment to openness requires more than merely responding to requests from the public. Each agency has a responsibility to distribute information on its own initiative and to enhance public access through the use of electronic information systems."[87]

Congress continued to review bills of reform for FOIA,[88] and agencies continued to provide specific agency reports. In 1996, J. Kevin O'Brien, chief of the FOIA section at the FBI, provided a report to the House Subcommittee on Government Management, Information and Technology of the Committee on Government Reform and Oversight.[89] The report detailed the cost of administering FOIA compliance and the kinds of requests and requesters that came to the FBI. The report said that in 1995, for example, the FBI budget required $21 million and 263 full-time staffers to meet the FOIA requirements. He estimated there were 15,259 requests in the bureau with an estimated 5.4 million pages to review.

O'Brien estimated that an average of 13,100 new requests came to the agency each year, and that some big projects among these requests took several years to complete. He also reported that the vast majority of requesters were private individuals (74.6 percent), with prisoners the next largest group of requesters (14.7 percent). Scholars, news media, authors, business organizations, and others made up the remaining 11 percent.[90]

As executive, legislative, and judiciary branches continued to make sporadic attempts to meet the demands of public access to government-held information, the U.S. government-sponsored Internet began playing a larger role in the universe of information distribution. Before the 1990s, most of the Internet network was devoted to linking universities. Case Western Reserve University established the first "Freenet" for the Society for Public Access Computing in 1986.

In 1990 there were about 300,000 computers connected to the Internet. By 1996 there were about 10 million, and by January 2000 there were estimates of more than 70 million Internet computer servers, or hosts, connected to the Internet.[91] The news business community quickly began capitalizing on the shift in communication formats. Soon, every major newspaper developed Web sites for breaking stories as well as the entire newsprint versions of their products. Broadcasters experimented with pod casts that let viewers receive bulletins as well as entire news segments on hand-held devices.

Into this mix of technology experiments, President Clinton championed and signed into law the Electronic Freedom of Information Act (EFOIA).[92] This expanded version of the original FOIA required agencies to provide Internet access to routine documents, forms, and contact information. Initially it seemed like a boon for activist citizens, but soon it was clear that the implementation of the law was going to be slow and uneven.

Several studies at the end of the twentieth century evaluated the range and depth of government information available on the World Wide Web (Web).[93] The work by West and by the federal OMB attempted to catalogue not only what materials were available, but also to report how well these materials were said, by the state-level civil servants making the reports, to serve their government offices' distribution demands.

Soon after the federal passage of EFOIA, every state in the nation developed or maintained a Web site for some level of public information distribution. Studies on the qualities and content of state-mandated information distribution through the Web or other online formats found that although there was much available, the content varied greatly from state to state. One report evaluated the homepage for each state's legislative branch, for example, and found most sites provide legislators' contact information, but most did not provide legislative session reports.[94]

Another study of state governments' electronic initiatives found that most state-level chief information officers thought their e-government Web sites improved service delivery and that this form of communication had also reduced government costs.[95] When this report is coupled with research describing many kinds of content found on state-supported Web sites, it was clear that web delivery of state government information had grown dramatically in the ten years after the Web was launched in 1993.[96]

FOIA in the Twenty-first Century

During the history of FOIA's many legislative modifications, including DOJ reinterpretation and court review, there continued to be questions about the value of the bill's intentions. As the information collection, storage, and retrieval technology changed there were fresh attempts in nearly every congressional session to update or restrict fundamental access to government-held information. Although some issues were resolved, others continued to be problems. Timeliness in response to requests, even in the age of Internet communication, continued to be a problem across all agencies.

For example, the GAO report on FOIA processing statistics said there were 1.9 million requests across twenty-five agencies during 2000, and 82 percent of the requests processed during the year resulted in full records returned to the requester.[97] But about 140,000 requests could not be processed within the twenty days that was the median amount of time for most of the agencies.[98] Not only did timeliness continue to plague FOIA administration, but costs and fees seemed uncontainable.[99]

The question that lingered over every request, however, was exactly what should be released and what should be withheld. Even after forty years of review, the answer had to be rediscovered every time a new query came to an agency's FOIA officers.

Homeland Security and FOIA

When the World Trade Towers in New York City were struck and then burned for days and when the Pentagon was hit almost simultaneously on September 11, 2001, the fate of information seekers changed in a flash. Among the first things that the Bush cabinet did in response to these attacks was to shut down Web access to government information that had been publicly available. The nonprofit research organization OMB Watch in Washington, D.C., began keeping a list of materials that were withdrawn from government Web sites:

> OMB Watch submitted FOIA requests to a number of federal agencies asking for a list of any information removed from agency web sites in response to the Sept. 11 terrorist attacks, and any criteria used in making decisions to remove such information.[100]

That list of agencies included Department of Defense, the National Imagery and Mapping Agency, Department of Energy, Department of Health and Human Services, Department of Interior, Department of the Treasury, Environmental Protection Agency, and the Federal Energy Regulatory Commission.[101] Slowly some agencies began selectively disallowing specific and previously available information that some groups had come to rely on for daily updates.

On March 14, 2002, the EPA announced that it would no longer allow direct access to its Envirofacts databases, which had previously been available on demand. Instead, it would be available only to certain government employees and contractors. Although some of the Envirofacts information could be gathered in person from the EPA main library, the library was closed in October 2006.[102] The Federal Register statement accompanying the closure announcement said, ironically, in part,

> With more material available online and electronically, EPA has found that its employees and the public are finding the materials they need from EPA's web site and they are requesting more information electronically. In addition, with tighter security at Federal facilities, the public's physical visits to the EPA Headquarters Library have been declining. These trends, in addition to reductions in the library's FY07 budget, suggested to EPA that it needed to use information technology to improve its delivery of library services to EPA and public patrons.

Separate from the problems of finding and reviewing documents has been the question of classification – those restrictions that FOIA allows based on the necessity of secrecy. The federal office of Information Security Oversight reported in 2005 that 15.6 million documents were classified in 2004, about double the number in 2001.

The rate of declassification, however, did not keep pace, according to the same report. In 1997, 204 million pages were declassified, but in 2004 only 28 million pages of previously classified documents were released. The tendency toward secrecy increased with an expansion of the classification system used by many government agencies.

For example, with the establishment of the Homeland Security Office, new employees of the department were required to sign a nondisclosure agreement that prohibited them from giving anyone "sensitive but unclassified" information. Determining what might be sensitive but unclassified was a major problem for those afraid of being caught afoul of the provision since the traditional classification system for government documents had been confidential, secret, and top secret.

About 35,000 employees were affected by the requirement and were subject to adherence inspections at any time or place.[103] Adherence to the nondisclosure agreement, then, might mean denying a FOIA request that normally would have met the traditional classification exemptions for release because the document was not classified confidential, secret, or top secret.

So, at the time of writing this chapter, the boundaries of information access remain unclear. The executive branch continues to push back on what it will release, and Congress argues the merits of government transparency with no certainty of success. The next several chapters will continue our discussion of specific examples in U.S. history where government transparency plagued the democratic model, and the news media found itself in the forefront of struggle for balance between too many stories and not enough news about government activities.

Part Two

Freedom of Information Act in Practice: Introduction

Nearly five decades of litigation and continued congressional attention since the passage of the Freedom of Information Act (FOIA) attest to the importance of the legislation. With each report of FOIA activity produced by the administering Justice Department, there are increases in the number of requests and the subsequent expansion of dedicated work hours required by each executive branch agency office. The American Society of Access Professionals (ASAP) assists government employees who are responsible for responding to FOIA requests so that the learning curve is not quite so daunting to them. The organization's membership is not limited to public sector employees but is concerned with responsive administration of the law. To that end ASAP says it intends to "promote and facilitate citizen observation of and participation in government decision-making through open official meetings or hearings. ... And the availability of records or information."[1]

Avid user groups and watchdog organizations have generated volumes of examples when FOIA not only gave entry to government documents but aided in the collection of evidence that agencies were doing good work as well as a bad job. Largest among the public service groups that focus on FOIA administration are the Center for National Security Studies (CNSS), founded in 1974, and the National Security Archive, founded in 1985. The CNSS was established to protect civil liberties that might be infringed by the work of the Federal Bureau of Investigation

(FBI) and the Central Intelligence Agency (CIA). The National Security Archive includes an extensive database of declassified documents as well as released materials that were specifically requested by researchers and staff members.

Also, to a slightly lesser extent, the Public Citizen Foundation founded by Ralph Nader in 1971, and the American Civil Liberties Union which pre-dated the enactment of FOIA have also joined in many of the lawsuits that established the working guidelines for access to government information. There are news professionals' organizations that give special attention and continuing support to FOIA use and litigation. These include the Reporters Committee for Freedom of the Press and the Society of Professional Journalists.

Few would dispute the usefulness of the law in discovering malfeasance among some of the government bureaucrats, but there are critics who claim that the groups who championed the law have laid little claim to its use. One report on FOIA queries to four government agencies found that corporations, not law makers or news organizations, were the highest number of requesters. The agencies sampled included General Services Administration (GSA), Environmental Protection Agency (EPA), Transportation and Education during the January to June period of 2001. Corporations accounted for 910 requests, while media accounted for only 119 requests. Individuals made 373 queries; lawyers, 567; and nonprofits, 181, according to the report available on the Web.[2] While this may surprise some advocates of the Act, it should not cloud the fact that the law is being used by a range of constituencies across the nation.

As noted in the previous chapters, the founding framers clearly understood the necessity of public dissemination of reports about government activity. The first session of the first congress included an act directing the publication of congressional bills offered and votes taken, as well as the enactment or veto of these laws by the executive branch. Subsequently, President George Washington instituted the original Housekeeping Act to protect some of the executive branch documents from public inspection. These early actions on the part of the legislature and the executive set the stage for scores of public efforts at open government and the counterbalancing periods with severe censorship. Each of the world wars brought new efforts to control what was known about both war effort and life at home. There are some low points throughout U.S. history, but also explicit gains in the right of access to government-held information and the resulting exposure of government misuse of the public trust.

At no point in the history of news media support for open access to government records did the publishers and reporters claim that they would be the sole or greatest beneficiary of the availability of executive branch information. The claim that was made, instead, was that access to government information should be and was a public right necessary for good governance. The next group of chapters reviews in greater detail some of the uses made of the FOIA once the rights of access to government-held information had been gained in 1966.

The next chapters will review cases-in-point that helped develop the criteria on which specific kinds of information might be provided to those requesters or interest groups that might seek clearer understanding of government activities, or who simply like to check up on what those in powerful agency positions are doing. These chapters are devoted to examples and groups who have been the subject of government data collection and subsequent FOIA requests. The stories were gathered from news reports and books written during the past forty years of FOIA experience. The examples included here are just that—examples. The inclusions are not an exhaustive list but rather a survey of the kinds queries and ways that FOIA has been used by private citizens, journalists, and special interest groups throughout the more than forty years since passage of the FOIA.

As early as 1975 the news reports of FOIA frustrations for both government and the public were common. In May 5, 1975, *U.S. News & World Report* article summarized the ten-year history of the act's use by quoting John E. Moss, "It immediately freed many areas of information for the public. But it also tended to create more artful ways of withholding—many delays, many devices developed." At that time it was reported that most agencies responded to requests in an average of thirty-three days, and an additional fifty were required for appeals if the initial request was denied. The State Department, FBI, and CIA received the bulk of requests at that time, the article notes.

A partial explanation provided in the *U.S. News & World Report* story was that some agencies had simply destroyed their records in order to avoid review, and others had simply opened the records so widely that requests were not necessary. Mark Lynch, an attorney for the Center for the Study of Responsive Law, said, "There is a real question whether a government can operate effectively in the open. No government in history ever has."[3]

As the edges of access developed, the courts were asked for specific guidelines. In two 1980 Supreme Court cases, the justices ruled that federal officials no longer in office need not make their records available for review, nor must private groups that receive federal grants make their reports available for public inspections. The particular instances involved Henry Kissinger's telephone diaries and a government-funded drug study.[4]

When President Ronald Reagan signed into law some major revisions of FOIA that allowed greater withholding of investigative materials, some reporters cried foul. Concern had been expressed since FOIA's initial enactment that criminals could piece together sensitive investigation materials that could be requested under the act. *New York Times* reporter Linda Greenhouse wrote:

> Proposals for addressing the problem have been the subject of numerous hearings and several bills over the years, none of which passed both houses of Congress. But this year a bipartisan compromise resurrected the revisions in the last weeks of the Congressional session, adding them to the $1.7 billion anti-drug bill. In signing the anti-drug bill on Monday, Mr. Reagan singled out the information act provisions for special praise, saying they would "considerably enhance the ability of Federal law-enforcement agencies" in their fight against drugs.[5]

Also included in the revisions was explicit language about fees for the agencies' time spent finding materials and document duplication in response to requests. Elaine English, then director of the FOIA Service Center of the Reporters Committee for the Freedom of the Press, was quoted as saying that the fee structure was a good change in the law. But she went on to say, "agencies tend to interpret whatever discretion they're given as broadly as possible."

When the age of computing was firmly part of the federal government's information storage framework, FOIA advocates began to agitate for more explicit guidelines about that particular format's challenges. In another *New York Times* story, Alan Westin, a Columbia University computer technology researcher, summed up the problem: "It's as if you've created a great no man's land of information. Traditionally, thinking has been in terms of paper environments and without any sophistication about electronic information."[6]

The issue raised at that time, and most frequently among requesters and agencies' FOIA officers, was whether computer records were records contemplated by the FOIA regulations, and if they were, then how much time and effort should be expected of agency personnel already overworked by traditional requests. Jerry Berman, director of the information technology project of the American Civil Liberties Union, said of the problem, "We have to make the Government focus on this ... and we need to view technology in general as a means for making Government more accessible to citizens."[7]

At the turn of the century the computing problem had not been solved, but continued attention to the effectiveness of FOIA was ever-present. In another *U.S. News & World Report* article, March 18, 2002, the concern about executive branch secrecy was put to the George W. Bush staffers. The rationale sounded remarkably like the George Washington years.

George Bush's attorney general, for example, issued a memo explicitly concerning FOIA requests instructing officers to release documents only if there was a sound legal basis for doing so. Vice President Dick Cheney was said to have fought the General Accounting Office requests for the list of those who attended his energy policy committee meetings simply as a matter of principle. "In fact, some close to Cheney say they were looking for this fight to reassert eroded executive branch privilege."[8]

The next three chapters describe in more detail some of the circumstances that troubled both requesters and agency personnel as the contours of the law were developed through experience and practical concerns. The first of the three chapters focuses on the federal agencies' general responsiveness and management of FOIA issues. The next chapter pulls together those examples that concern the business of government and the concerns of government intertwined with commerce. The third chapter focuses on the individuals or identifiable groups of persons, some famous and some not-so-famous, who have been the subject of FOIA requests. These case reviews will provide not only a context but also a hopscotch history of FOIA during the past forty years of practical use.

Federal Agencies through the Lens of FOIA

Some federal agencies regularly make announcements about the documents they are releasing for public review, and a few agencies even provide the documents in "electronic reading rooms" where document search windows are part of the Web-interface homepage.[1] Though all federal agencies were required to replace paper documents with digital copies whenever practical, not all offices have gone so far as to put all public information on the World Wide Web.[2] Despite the best of intentions there are cases where government agencies have provided misinformation to the public and purposefully misled Congress in order to circumvent the FOIA program.

An example predating electronic reading rooms reported in 1991 *Common Cause Magazine* was that the Reagan administration and the National Aeronautics and Space Administration (NASA) urged Congress in 1987 to close access to all NASA information because Japanese scientists were leaching space shuttle technology from the United States by using FOIA to get at information used in the program. Some time later it was learned that the "Samurai Shuttle" episode, as it was called, was a foil to keep reporters and others from learning more about the program's 1986 Challenger explosion.[3]

Compliance and Classification Standards

Presidents issue executive orders as they take office that indicate how agencies should handle, and classify, documents and routine information collected by staffers. Each president has his own concerns about what kinds of information should receive special treatment, but some observers have claimed that President

George W. Bush set a new standard for government secrecy as soon as he took office. A measure of this mindset is the comparative number of documents designated for some kind of restrictive classification. During the Bush administration's initial two years more than 44 million records were designated to be classified, which was twice the rate of the Clinton administration during its final four years. In addition, the Bush administration began a program to reclassify records that were about to become or already were public documents upon expiration of a previous classification order.

These broad statistics do not provide an accurate comparison, however. For example, more than eighty federal agencies reported to the National Archives in 2004 that 15.6 million decisions to classify information had been made, but this total excluded the vice president's office. When asked why Vice President Dick Cheney withheld even a tally of his office's decisions, a spokeswoman said that Cheney's view was that his office was "not under any duty" to provide such statistics.[4]

Whereas the summary statistics tell one part of the story about public access to federal records, it is the individual's efforts and frustrations that reveal the oddities of FOIA's history. For example, when Terry Anderson, a U.S. citizen taken hostage and held for nearly seven years in the Middle East, began working on a book about his experience he requested from thirteen federal agencies any relevant information about his captors. Some documents were released to him under FOIA guidelines, but Anderson told a *Washington Post* reporter, they were "so heavily censored as to be nearly useless." Most astounding to him, however, was the response he got from both the State Department and the Drug Enforcement Administration (DEA). DEA wrote to him that before it would begin processing the request Anderson would need to provide either proof of death or an original notarized authorization from the men who were his captors. DEA said that without these waivers of privacy rights the agency could neither confirm that there were such records nor provide information about their contents.[5]

Another example, in 2001 Joseph McCormick, a former U.S. Army Ranger and resident of Floyd County, Virginia, wanted to understand the impact that a thirty-inch natural gas pipeline was going to have on his community. When he sought from federal regulators a project map that had been made public earlier in the planning process, he was denied access. The Federal Energy Regulatory Commission reportedly said the route of the pipeline might be used by terrorists and was therefore no longer public information. "I understand about security," McCormick said, but he also observed that once construction began, the pipelines route was going to be pretty obvious.[6]

In contrast, in 1980 an antinuclear activist group was successful in getting some of the routes for transporting interstate shipments of radioactive atomic wastes that had been set up by the Nuclear Regulator Commission (NRC). The map information was released to the Potomac Alliance through FOIA requests made to Virginia state officials rather than going to the NRC, though the information originated in the federal agency.[7]

McCormick's experience, however, wasn't an isolated incident. After the newly empowered TSA was up and running, there were many stories about passengers denied boarding passes or removed from flights. It was not until 2004, however, that passengers got some idea of how the system was reviewing them. FOIA released records from the NASA showed that at least one airline, Northwest, provided information on millions of passengers for a then-secret government air-security project initiated soon after the September 11, 2001, attacks.[8]

Mohammed Ali Ahmed, a naturalized U.S. citizen and a Muslim, is an example that actually predated the establishment of this secret security project. After he and his three children were removed from an American Airlines flight, Ahmed sued on civil rights grounds. When he requested information about the incident as part of his case preparation, Ahmed's lawyer was told by the government that supplying the records would compromise airline security and so would not be forthcoming.[9]

Appeals Strategies

Efforts to loosen federal agencies' hold on the declassification cycle have met varying success. When a request for documents fails, the usual route of appeal is to file a petition in the federal court system. An interagency appeals panel was also established by executive order of President Bill Clinton in 1995 to review classified documents within the system of standards set by various agencies. However **CIA**, for one, challenged the authority of that avenue to access, however. The director of the CIA, George Tenet, in 1999 claimed that his statutory obligation was to act as the ultimate determiner of document classification status for his agency, and he was unwilling to cede that responsibility to the Interagency Security Classification Appeals Panel.[10] While presidents may set the parameters for records access during their administration, some federal agencies have histories of dubious activities across many administrations that have been belatedly discovered through patient generations of FOIA requests.

Central Intelligence Agency

A 1978 release of CIA documents revealed a handful of studies, one of them code named "Artichoke," beginning in 1949 that experimented with mind control. Among the released documents was a January 1954 memo that posed a "hypothetical problem." Excluded from the public version were the identifying details. The proposal began:

> As a "trigger mechanism" for a bigger project, … an individual of [deleted] descent, approximately 35 years old, well educated, proficient in English and well established socially and politically in the [deleted] government be induced under Artichoke to perform an act, involuntarily, against a prominent [deleted] politician or if necessary, against an American official.

The batch of memoranda included conclusions about this particular effort. "After the act of attempted assassination was performed, it was assumed that the subject would be taken into custody by the [deleted] government and thereby 'disposed of.'" Though there was no evidence in the documents that "Artichoke" had been tested, there was a follow-up note that said, "Considering the speed with which we had to operate, I believe [Artichoke] went extremely well. We were ready when called upon for support, even though the operation did not materialize."[11]

John Marks, author of *The Search for the "Manchurian Candidate": The CIA and Mind Control*, opened his 1979, two-hundred-page volume with the note that sixteen thousand pages of CIA documents were released to him because of FOIA requests, and that "without these documents, the best investigative reporting in the world could not have produced a book." He went on to give a special thanks to the congressional sponsors of FOIA, "when they passed into law the idea that information about government belongs to the people, not the bureaucrats."[12] In his endnotes for chapter after chapter of the book, Marks meticulously reports which CIA documents were used in his work. For example, in Chapter 2, he wrote:

> The origins of the CIA's ARTICHOKE program and accounts of the early testing came from the following Agency Documents #192, 15 January 1953; #3, 17 May 1949; A/B, I, 8/1, 24 February 1949. … Documents giving background on terminal experiments include #A/B, II, 10/57; #A/B, II, 10/58, 31 August, 1954; #A/B, II, 10/17, 27 September 1954; and #A/B, I, 76/4, 21 March 1955.

The ellipse here indicates that a long list of document identification was left out simply for ease of reading. But all twelve chapters in Marks' book contain similarly extensive notes on the documents reviewed and cited. Clearly, the author relied heavily on a paper trail made available by FOIA and successfully told a story that, most likely, would have otherwise gone unreported. He was not the first, however, to have reported on the CIA's MKULTRA behavior experiments of the 1950s and 1960s that were tested at about eighty private and public universities. In 1977, as thousands of pages of records began to trickle out of the CIA to the affected universities, the documents showed that the university administrators were unaware of the projects.[13]

The CIA was again linked to experiments with mind control drugs used in 1963 on prison inmates. Documents released in 1980 reported that at least eight prisoners at a Lexington, Kentucky, facility who were twenty to forty years old and former morphine addicts were given hallucinogens. The study reported that one of the subjects had a psychotic reaction lasting three days, and that another subject tried to kill nonexistent mice. The drug tested was said to be different than Lysergic Acid Diethylamide (LSD) because it caused "a great deal of obvious confusion and sedation."[14]

Other forms of misinformation provided by the CIA came to light in a *U.S. News & World Report* series titled "Mysteries of History" that reported the $200 million 1974 deep-sea sailing mission of the *Glomar Explorer*.[15] At the time of sailing, the ship was said to be gathering information about minerals. The truth was a long time in coming. What the ship was really doing was salvaging a Soviet nuclear submarine about three miles below the surface and about 750 miles off the coast of Hawaii. Reporters learned something about the *Glomar's* mission in 1975, but when a *Rolling Stone* reporter, Harriet Ann Phillippi, filed a FOIA request to get details, the CIA would neither confirm nor deny that there were any documents of such a mission or vessel. This kind of FOIA-compliance evasion became known as a "*Glomar* response."

Pieces of the story came to light in 1977 when Phillippi had moved to another job, this time in broadcast television, and some of her FOIA request was filled. She decided to alert some of the Washington reporters about the documents' contents because she thought they might still be interested. The *Los Angeles Times*, *New York Times*, *Washington Post*, and *Parade* magazine had, in fact, learned what the mission, called Projects Jennifer, of the *Glomar Explorer* was, but were asked by the CIA to not report it.[16]

The rest of the story, unlike the Soviet sub, finally emerged more than a decade later. The mission was not a complete success. The Soviet sub broke into pieces while being raised and several of the nuclear warheads were lost, apparently. In a 2005 lengthy story by *U.S. News & World Report* that referenced the misinformation technique of "*Glomar* response," a sidebar story highlighted the public use of the CIA's "reading room" Web site www.foia.cia.gov, where documents released during the past fifty years could be "virtually" viewed.[17] Among the most popular search terms at the site, as reported in the story, were No. 1, UFO; No. 3, Area 51 and No. 5, mind control. Others among the top ten were Vietnam, China, Iraq, Bay of Pigs, Afghanistan, Guatemala, and Iran.

Some researchers have used FOIA requests to one agency as a way to get the CIA to respond. An example is the way Stephen Schlesinger, coauthor with Stephen Kinzer of *Bitter Fruit: The Story of the American Coup in Guatemala*, found the CIA unresponsive to original queries. Rather than quit the project, Schlesinger requested transcripts of cable traffic kept by the State Department concerning the embassy in Guatemala.

What he received, he said, was "about a thousand pages of communication" between Ambassador John Peurifoy and the State Department in Washington.[18] At that point, Schlesinger said he went to the CIA and filed FOIA requests for very specific documents and files. Though the CIA eventually admitted there were about 180,000 documents about the 1954 coup, the agency resolutely would not release them on the grounds of national security. By 1997 the CIA had released about fourteen hundred pages,[19] but Schlesinger said he didn't expect to ever see many more pages.

More recently some agencies have worked with the CIA to ensure larger bodies of classified documents. The Associated Press learned that a 2002 agreement between the CIA and the National Archives allowed the reclassification of documents, already made public through the Archives, to be sealed from further review. Though some of the documents were more than fifty years old, the National Archives staff was directed to not even mention that the reclassification had occurred and which documents were affected by the new order to seal. The story reported that the agreement stated: "It is in the interest of both [unnamed agency] and the National Archives and Records Administration (NARA) to avoid the attention and researcher complaints that may arise from removing material that has already been available publicly from the open shelves for extended periods of time." The agreement was originally stamped "Secret." NARA provided a redacted copy of the agreement to AP under the information act this week and then posted the document on its Web site.[20]

It was estimated in 2006, however, that 55,000 pages of 10,000 documents had been withdrawn from previously public papers. Some of these pages included materials as old as information about riots in 1948 that occurred in Colombia and 1962 translations of news stories about China.

Federal Bureau of Investigation

The CIA is not the only agency with a history of frustrating FOIA requesters. The FBI was long known to circumvent public reporting mechanisms, to the irritation of congressional members and the general public alike. In Athan Theoharis' 1978 book, *Spying on Americans: Political Surveillance from Hoover to the Huston Plan*, the author candidly notes in the preface that

> Federal intelligence agencies devised separate filing systems, the intent of which was to safeguard even "national security" classified documents from public discovery. ... The reports of the Senate Select Committee on Intelligence Activities recounts numerous instances either where the recognized "sensitivity" of certain projects resulted in decisions to devise secretive procedures, where intelligence officials were unable to produce documents involving activities or proposals the committee learned about through testimony, where incomplete records were created in part to ensure "plausible deniability" or to confine knowledge to those "who need to know," or wherein contemporary orders were issued to destroy documents pertaining to proposed questionable or abhorrent activities.[21]

Theoharis spent many years working with presidential libraries, and it became increasingly evident that special practices in communication between the FBI and the White House made a paper trail almost impossible to follow. Theoharis went so far as to suggest to researchers that the Select Committee's hearings and reports were the best preparation available for investigating domestic security policies. "[T]hey provide the necessary background about key policy decisions, make it possible for the researcher to file intelligent Freedom of Information Act and mandatory declassification requests, and outline the areas where our knowledge is presently incomplete or deficient."[22]

Another, more recent review of government surveillance on individuals and domestic organizations is Angus Mackenzie's 1999 *Secrets: The CIA's War at Home*. While much of the book focuses on CIA activities, Mackenzie also relied heavily on FBI documents released after FOIA requests were made. An appendix to the book, "Targets of Domestic Spying: Annotated List of Some FBI Surveillance Targets during the 1980s," reports that he requested files on 127 political groups. The agency's response took five years, and "the vast majority of the files were denied," Mackenzie wrote.[23]

Mackenzie's inclusions in the appendix do note, however, what could be learned in the request rejections. For example, the American Committee on Africa/ Africa Fund opposed apartheid in South Africa. Mackenzie reported that the FBI's response to his request for any documents on the organization was to withhold

425 of the 615 pages "in the interest of national defense or foreign policy." Another group, the Black Student Communications Organizing Network, was intended to bring black student groups together. The FBI's response to Mackenzie's request was to withhold the files entirely to protect "national defense or foreign policy." In the FBI's file on the Union of Concerned Scientists, 296 pages were withheld as secret to "protect foreign policy, privacy, and confidential informants." What could be learned by Mackenzie was that the group of faculty members and graduate student at Massachusetts Institute of Technology maintained no formal membership rolls and that they were interested in "turning scientific research applications away from military technology and toward the solution of environmental and social problems."[24]

An almost comical counterpoint is the experience of Diane Solway, author of a 1998 biography about Rudolf Nureyev, the famed Russian dancer who immigrated to the United States in 1961 and was subsequently denounced by the Soviet government. Solway requested any files that either government held on Nureyev. She told a *Washington Post* reporter in 1999 that she received the Soviet file within a year of her request and that it was "completely" uncensored, but, she also said, the FBI took six years to produce anything for her and "much" of that was heavily censored.[25]

In a similarly surprising turn of events, the Soviets told the State Department in 1991 that it condoned the declassification of correspondence during 1962 between Nikita Khrushchev and John F. Kennedy. The letters were sought by an American University professor, Philip Brenner, as part of a FOIA request that had already yielded more than a thousand pages, but had denied access to about seven hundred more pages. The letters were part of that cache yet withheld. An official with the State Department told a reporter that the twenty-five letters Brenner sought "haven't been released in part because they contain information still relevant to current policy questions."[26] State Department officials had also noted in 1990 that about eighteen thousand pages on the Cuban missile crisis in October of 1962 had already been released under FOIA.[27]

The FBI's surveillance of U.S. citizens is not news, but several authors have written long books about specific programs or individual subjects of agency snooping. Herbert N. Foerstel's 1991 book, *Surveillance in the Stacks: The FBI's Library Awareness Program*, relies on agency documents as well as interviews and congressional committee reports about the program that grew out of the 1950s Red Scare. Librarians thought to have ties to the Soviet Intelligence Service were originally the targets of investigation. But the Library Awareness Program continued for decades and ultimately required a court order to force the release of documents that provided evidence of the agency's activities. FOIA requests from individuals and the American Library Association, as well as the National Security Archive, eventually prompted Judge Louis Oberdorfer to issue an initial order that thousands of pages of FBI internal documents on the program, as well as more than one hundred internal records searches on individuals affiliated with libraries, be processed in response to the FOIA requests.[28]

The FBI was similarly interested in the Supreme Court from the early 1930s until at least the mid-1980s, according to documents released to Alexander Charns and reported in a 1988 *New York Times* story.[29] More than two-thousand pages were contained in the general file about the court. Conversations were monitored that included Justices Earl Warren, Abe Fortas, Potter Stewart, and William O. Douglas, who was characterized in a note that said, "Douglas, of course, is crazy and is not in too good health," according to the *New York Times* story. Charns also wrote that

> [i]n the late 1950s, the FBI became increasingly concerned about what it believed were pro-Communist decisions by the Court. FBI records ... show that Justice Douglas' loyalty was questions by Mr. Hoover and his top aides in that era because of his views involving the Constitutional rights of Communists.

During the Rosenberg atomic spy case in the early 1950s, court employees acted as informants about what was heard in the halls and who was in the Supreme Court offices. After the Rosenbergs were executed in 1953, two court employees were singled out for special appreciation of their cooperation with the FBI informants program, according to documents Charns said he reviewed.

There was, in contrast, a special relationship between J. Edgar Hoover, long-time director of the FBI, and Justice Earl Warren.[30] Throughout the file of about thirteen hundred pages released in 1985, there was clearly a trust between the two men that began when Warren was a district attorney in California. From 1948 to 1953, Hoover authorized confidential information to be provided to then Governor Warren. "He should be advised that the information is furnished in strictest confidence and none of the information can be attributed to the FBI," Hoover wrote, according to documents released under FOIA. The documents also report that the FBI provided favors to Warren, including a personal car and driver on several occasions. "Whatever the governor requests I want prompt attention accorded it," Hoover wrote in 1951. Though Hoover felt stung by the Warren Commission Report on the assassination of President John F. Kennedy, he seemed to have forgiven the slight. When Warren announced his resignation from the Supreme Court in 1968, Hoover wrote to the chief justice, "You have contributed untiringly and unselfishly to furthering the best interests of the nation and your record of achievements will long stand as a monument to you."

Of course, there were instances of lengthy investigations of groups opposed to the U.S. policies toward foreign governments. One such group, the Committee in Solidarity with the People of El Salvador (Cispes) evidently received some attention. The evidence was a stack more than a foot tall of about seventeen hundred documents collected during a decade of observation in the 1970s and 1980s. According to a 1998 *New York Times* article, "the Cispes inquiry took the equivalent of five agents' full-time attention annually for its entire duration, whereas the bureau's investigation of the right-wing Aryan Nation group received 52 agent-years of attention in 1985 alone and, by comparison, the FBI spent 1,600 agent-years on organized-crime cases that same year."[31]

Over the decades since the passage of FOIA, the number of requests directed to the FBI has steadily increased. It was reported that during the decade of the 1980s, the number of requests grew from about eleven thousand annually to more than fifteen thousand, while the number of staff members to handle those requests fell from 224 to 193. As a result the average response time went from 180 days to 340 days.[32] Like the CIA, the FBI now puts some of its public files on a "reading room" Web site, http://foia.fbi.gov/room.htm, for speedier response to the most common requests. But some requests simply take many years to process. David Garrow, a historian and author of several books about Martin Luther King, told an interviewer in 1998 that he had waited seventeen years for some documents.[33]

David T. Hardy, a Tucson lawyer, did not have to wait so long for copies of infrared videotape and conversation transcript to be released by the FBI, but it did take a court order. The documents requested were about the enforcement agency's standoff with the Branch Davidian at Waco, Texas, that ended in a deadly fire at the compound April 19, 1993. Hardy filed suit in 1996 for any videotapes that might have been made prior to 10:42 a.m. that day and was told there were none. Three years later, in 1999, not only was an early morning tape from April 19 handed over to Hardy, but $32,000 in attorneys' fees was also paid to him.[34] Hardy along with co-author Rex Kimball wrote a book, *This Is Not An Assault,* about the Waco incident that relied on some of these documents and was published in 2001.

In at least one instance, however, an FBI agent said he thought authors stole the thunder of the agency's work. When the *Washington Post* published a 1992 story marking the twentieth anniversary of the Watergate break-in, Special Agent Angelo J. Lano said that he thought he and his partner, Daniel C. Mahan, discovered much of the break-in's details before reporters Carl Bernstein and Bob

Woodward appeared to crack the case on the front pages of the newspaper. Lano agreed to talk on the record in 1992 because much of the FBI's files, about sixteen thousand pages, on the break-in had been recently released under FOIA. "I resent that they have been perceived as the individuals who responded and solved the investigation," Lano told a reporter. "I feel the bureau … solved it, even though the public doesn't know that."[35]

Other Agencies and FOIA

NASA was peppered with a spate of FOIA requests about the space shuttle *Challenger* that exploded soon after lift off in 1986. At issue in particular was the tape recorded conversation between the shuttle astronauts and ground control crews. According to the official transcript originally made public by NASA, the *Challenger's* seven crew members seemed to be unaware of the impending disaster until the final moments of the lift off on January 28. The taped transmission stopped seventy-three seconds after the *Challenger's* launch and immediately before the shuttle exploded in mid-air.

The FOIA request, and then the court papers filed by the *New York Times,* said that there were questions about the completeness of the official transcript and that independent experts should be allowed to examine the original tape. NASA denied the requested tape to the *New York Times*, and others, on the basis of Exemption 6 of FOIA that allowed exclusion of private medical and personnel files.[36] Initially the courts found in favor of the FOIA request, but after several years of appeals working through the system, a 1991 opinion held that the tape recording was exempt from disclosure.[37]

The Bureau of Engraving and Printing provided FOIA requested documents when one of their own employees, Robert Patrick Schmitt, Jr., was arrested in 1994 after depositing thousands of brand new $100 bills in nearby banks where he had personal accounts that he shared with his mother. Documents also revealed when his car was searched and as much as $650,000 in $100 bills was found in the trunk. The bureau officials said that, at that time, it was the largest theft in the agency's 132 years.[38]

The Commerce Department found itself in 1995 forced by a District Court judge to release, sooner than it wanted, 30,000 documents about Secretary Ronald H. Brown's trade missions. Judicial Watch, a nonprofit advocacy group, had requested the documents in September of the previous year, and the department had asked the court to give it time until September 1995. The judge ordered the documents to be available in June, and also told the Commerce Department it had twenty-four hours to decide whether to waive a $13,000 photocopying charge.[39]

In 2004 the effectiveness of the Environmental Protection Agency's (EPA) enforcement of drinking water testing and standards was called into question when a *Washington Post* story reported that hundreds of records, released under FOIA, from just a few, recent years showed cities and states ignored the federal standards with impunity. EPA's then Acting Assistant Administrator, Benjamin H. Grumbles, said," We have not identified a systemic problem," when queried by congressional members about water quality. The agency at that time did not seek an overhaul to its regulations, according to the *Washington Post* story.[40]

When reporters were frustrated by the limited response from the Washington D.C.'s Metro Subway management office to their request for a 1980s construction evaluation report, they turned instead to the federal National Transportation Safety Board. The single page of the report provided by Metro "generally praised the transit authority's current construction management," the story reported. A complete copy was supplied by the federal transportation agency in response to the FOIA request submitted by the *Washington Post* in 1990. From that complete report, the Metro's practices were highly criticized, the story said.[41]

The National Institutes of Health (NIH) found itself barraged during two years when John Crewdson, a reporter for the *Chicago Tribune*, filed nearly one hundred FOIA requests asking for information about scientist Robert C. Gallo. The NIH provided about five thousand pages between 1988 and 1990, the agency noted. The NIH records were evident, too, in the series of stories published during those years that Crewdson wrote about acquired immune deficiency syndrome (AIDS) virus research. Crewdson, however, became the subject of a FOIA request when a *Washington Post* reporter queried NIH in 1990 about Crewdson's FOIA activities and received a report from the agency on what had been asked for and what had been provided to the *Tribune* reporter.[42]

In a case of the left and right hands working without knowing about the other, the Department of Defense (DOD) was reported to have ignored its own data-release standards when it provided 1.4 million servicemen's names and addresses on twenty computer tapes in response to a FOIA request by the Reagan-Bush Campaign Committee in 1984. The usual handling of FOIA requests to any DOD unit was to start at the central clearinghouse which then forwarded the request to each division. In this case it would have been each branch of the armed services. Instead, this particular time, the request went straight to the Defense Manpower Data Center. Concern about fulfilling the request surfaced only after an Air Force liaison at the data center "voiced concern" to the Air Force FOIA coordinator. That concern grew to "a strong objection" which was apparently dismissed. The fallout for subsequent requests was that the court ruled in 1985 that the Navy could not withhold service members contact information when an insurance company requested it because, in part, the Pentagon had "provided similar information to the Reagan-Bush Campaign Committee."[43]

The long-running and always nagging question of "what did you know and when did you know" plagued the Army intelligence community half a century after World War II. When fifteen thousand pages of Russian documents on the slaughter of Jewish residents of Belarus at the hands of German soldiers in 1941 were provided to the U.S. Holocaust Museum in 1996, the FOIA requests for National Security Agency's (NSA) release of parallel reports arrived immediately. Richard Breitman, an American University history professor, told a *Washington Post* reporter that he had requested about a million pages of German transcripts intercepted by the British government and that was subsequently provided to the NSA. "The extraordinary thing about these documents is that they contain new information about ... what the West knew about the Holocaust" during the war, Breitman said.[44]

Similarly, when fifty-three boxes of National Archives materials were released in 1996, they seemed to document the government's practice during the Vietnam conflict of declaring Vietnamese commandos who were in the service of the CIA to be dead when they were in fact being held in enemy prison camps. The 200,000 pages released in response to a FOIA request provided evidence that there were at least sixty commandos who had been declared dead but who were in fact living in the United States, according to John Mattes, a lawyer for some of these refugees. Hundred of commandos were enlisted by the CIA to increase local resistance to the communists during the 1960s. A reporter for the *Los Angeles Times*, however, said that more than two hundred of them were living in the United States in the mid-1990s.[45]

Even the Department of Housing and Urban Development (HUD) found itself scrutinized in the news media when FOIA-requested documents revealed that loans insured under the federal mortgage insurance program during the 1970s and 1980s had cost the tax payers about $90 million. HUD Secretary Jack F. Kemp announced a closing of the program in 1989 when the possible abuse was made public. But according to news reports, Kemp's office was quick to say, "the decision to cancel the mortgage insurance program did not represent any shift in the Secretary's thinking. ... Mr. Kemp had not acted because of the FOIA requests for documents about his handling of the program."[46]

There was evidence of serious problems long before the FOIA documents were made public. In a 1986 audit by HUD's inspector general, the loan program was deemed "risky to the government and [it] had failed to accomplish its statutory goals of encouraging moderate- and low-income housing," according to a news report in 1989. The story went on to report on the largest default, and obviously a counter to the goals of the program, found among the released documents. The Desert Falls Country Club, in Palm Desert, near Palm Springs, California, included a $7 million golf course, an $8 million clubhouse, two swimming pools, a spa, and seventeen tennis courts. The audit was said to have found that sixteen of seventeen projects were for housing that was not affordable to families in economic brackets described by the program, and that half the active projects supported by the loan program were in default.[47]

This experience at HUD, however, did not sour Kemp on FOIA. Instead, the agency made access easier than was often the case at other agencies. A few months after the loan program story, reporters were given quick, frequent and direct access to HUD repositories. According to an August 28, 1989 *New York Times* story,

> [R]eporters covering the department's influence-peddling scandals have been allowed in to rummage through another portion of what has become a journalistic El Dorado: the office files of former Secretary Samuel R. Pierce Jr. and his senior aides. For Mr. Pierce alone, that has meant 48 boxes of personal correspondence, speeches and memorandums. ... Mr. Kemp, eager to prove to the press corps and Congress that he is not covering up malfeasance by officials in the Reagan Administration, has ordered that the housing department documents be turned over to reporters quickly, often within days after receiving a request.[48]

Clearly, not all agencies embrace the use of FOIA by the public, but many public interest groups have benefited from the insistence that government documents should be available and provided on request. The next two chapters describe a number of instances where consumer groups have been able to learn from government reports about the dangers in products that were widely sold and embraced by the unwary. So, too, did individuals learn that the errors of fact about the lives of the famous and the not-so-famous members of American society were dutifully collected and preserved by the government until exposed for correction. The stories noted here are examples, available through news reports, interviews and book projects developed during the course of more than forty years of FOIA history, but there are hundreds more that are told every year, beyond these few among the pages of this book.

8

The Famous, the Not-So-Famous, and FOIA

It is sometimes said in jest that "some people are more special than others." It is apparently no joke, however, when agencies decide on the kinds of records kept by the government about individuals in the United States. When John Wiener, in 1983, began seeking files that were amassed on the activities of John Lennon, a popular member of the music group "The Beatles," Weiner said he was just curious about what kind of information was collected and stored. Lennon had been a peace activist who opposed the Vietnam war, President Richard M. Nixon's administration, and was shot dead on the street in front of his home in New York City in 1980.

At the end of 1988, Weiner was still waiting for the CIA and the FBI to release their records on Lennon. "How can fourteen-year-old documents on the peaceful activities of a dead rock star jeopardize national security?" Weiner said to a reporter for a *New York Times* article. The FBI's response was reported to be "that even the explanation of how the materials might jeopardize national security would itself threaten national security."[1] Then in 1997 he received a batch of 248 pages, and in 2004 a U.S. district judge ordered the FBI to hand over another ten pages. Though Weiner has written two books about John Lennon that relied on some of the released files, he said that decades-long pursuit of these records is more about principle than the facts found in the documents. "It's not really a case about Lennon anymore; it's a case about government secrecy and freedom of information. ... [F]reedom of information is the cornerstone of democracy," he told a reporter.[2]

As has been revealed in dozens of instances, some of the information about individuals that was gathered by agents was no more than a whispering campaign, but remained, unverified, in the files. J. Edgar Hoover, director of the FBI for nearly five decades, was said to have kept large, gossip-filled files on anyone he thought might eventually be important. A 1983 *U.S. News & World Report* story noted that more than seven thousand pages of these files, marked "official and confidential," had just then been released because of a FOIA request made by Athan Theoharis, a historian. Though more than ten thousand pages remained classified, the story said that Hoover had kept even top bureau officials from reviewing any of these files, sometimes referred to as "O & C," during his directorship.[3] The story reported a number of items about well-known political figures including presidents and politicians:

> The record does show that when Hoover picked up a report of sexual misconduct by an important politician, he often found occasion to pass the word on. "I know there's no truth to this. I'll never speak of it to anyone," Hoover would promise. "It was one of his favorite speeches, one he gave often to politicians," recalled the late William Sullivan, a longtime aide who had a bitter falling-out with him in 1971. ... Agents vied with each other in providing tidbits on political figures that ranged from corroborated intelligence to outright gossip. A 1940 memo told how Supreme Court Justice Felix Frankfurter was pulling strings with his "stooges in the administration" to influence the appointment of the Secretary of War. Decades were to pass before historians caught up with the bureau's inside knowledge of how politically active Frankfurter was while holding a position supposedly above politics.[4]

The pages available for review also showed that every president took some advantage of Hoover's attention and special interests. Sometimes, however, the result was not what the president expected. For example:

> In June, 1965, Johnson, by then President, complained to Hoover about a number of adverse articles and cartoons in the *Washington Evening Star*. A Hoover aide reported to the director that he had "discussed this matter on a very discreet basis with at least five officials of the *Evening Star*, including the editor, Newbold Noyes," and received an accounting that showed the paper had published more favorable than unfavorable articles about the President.

Presidential hopefuls were also tracked in Hoover's special "O & C" files. The director was reported to have declined a request to investigate whether Wendell Wilkie had changed his name from Wulkje. But on other occasions he was more inclined to create very hefty files, as was true for Adlai Stevenson and George McGovern. Stevenson was rumored to have had Communist associations, and the documents released showed that agents had a very difficult time spelling his name correctly. McGovern had made the mistake of publicly maligning the bureau, and though Hoover very much wanted to bring special pain to McGovern's life, Hoover eventually was persuaded that such activity might help McGovern's political career.[5]

Mere association was enough sometimes to generate Hoover's interest. For example, Edward Prichard, Jr., became a subject of wiretaps when in 1945 he served as a young lawyer for Fred Vinson. Vinson was head of the Office of War Mobilization and Reconversion during a period of transition between the Roosevelt and Truman administrations and later became Secretary of the Treasury. Prichard admitted that he had had a "dim view" of the Truman appointees and that he may have even called them "numbskulls" while working for Vinson, but when he learned in 1983 of the wiretap records from 1945 he said, "[t]he whole thing is a damned outrage … it was illegal as hell."[6]

Hoover was not the only executive-branch employee to have kept extensive notes that eventually found their way into FOIA requests. Oliver North, the storied military operative during the Reagan administration, also kept diaries of all his meetings. Among 1,200 pages of notes released in 1990 were excerpts from 1986 meetings that appeared to corroborate Manuel Noriega's claims that U.S. officials knew about his smuggling and Nicaraguan government plots. The diary pages suggested that Noriega, a Panamanian, volunteered to sabotage Nicaraguan targets and to provide intelligence to the United States on what he found there.[7]

In something of a reverse tack, however, The National Security Agency (NSA) disclosed in 1998 that more than a thousand pages had been gathered about Princess Diana, first wife of Prince Charles of Great Britain, but that none of the documents were the result of a targeted surveillance of her, and that none of it would be released.[8] Needless to say, British tabloids made much of this revelation at the time. The NSA reiterated its earlier statement again in 2006 when Scotland Yard was preparing a final investigation report of the Princess Diana's 1997 death in a car accident on Paris streets.[9]

The Famous

Kitty Kelley, a biographer of the rich and famous, made First Lady Nancy Reagan the subject of a book. Though Kelley relied on interviews and popular media reports for some of her work, she said she also used FOIA. "The information [about Nancy Reagan's adoptive parents] should have been released to me … all the people involved are now dead … but the FBI refused," Kelley told a reporter in 1991.[10]

David J. Garrow, with much greater success using FOIA, has written several books about Martin Luther King, Jr., and much of that work relied heavily on federal agency files. In his 1986 biography, *Bearing the Cross: Martin Luther King, Jr., and the Southern Christian Leadership Conference*, Garrow listed in the bibliography six federal divisions that released documents to him because of his FOIA requests. These included the CIA, the Civil Rights Division and the Community Relations Service of the Justice Department, the FBI, the Army, and the U.S. Information Agency of the Department of State. He also noted in his acknowledgments that he owed special thanks "to the many individuals who have labored long and hard in retrieving and processing the tens of thousands of pages of federal documents released to me pursuant to Freedom of Information Act requests."[11] This work was not the first time that agencies had been asked to help Garrow with his research on King.

In an earlier book, *The FBI and Martin Luther King, Jr.: From "Solo" to Memphis*, Garrow specifically examined the course of the agency's surveillance of King. Garrow wrote that the intention of the book was to explain why "the FBI developed such a viciously negative attitude toward King ... why would the United States' major police agency devote so much energy and resources to an intense pursuit of one man. ..." Several pages of the book's preface describe Garrow's FOIA requests to obtain as much as he could from the FBI, and how his queries were limited at first by his understanding of the bureau's investigation system and then by the sheer number of work hours required to review all the documents. What he found, however, led him to conclude that the bureau's reasons for investigating King changed over time. He also suggested that what he found about the King surveillance "was indicative of more than just [FBI] attitude toward one man ... [but also] why the FBI acted as it did toward a whole range of individuals and organizations."[12]

Some of those other individuals included a New York lawyer and friend of King's, Stanley Levison. He was characterized in FBI files as "a secret member of the Communist Party" and the subject of wiretapping in the 1960s.[13] By 1987, the bureau had released more than ten thousand pages of bugging and wiretap transcripts gathered from Levison's office between 1962 and 1972. But Taylor Branch, an author who was very frustrated by FOIA requests and bureau rejections, said that there were still 863 pages of crucial material protected by bogus exemptions. "If the government can win in a case of this import—involving documents more than 30 years old, protecting sources already identified and dead ... then it seems to me the FOIA law is far gone toward dead-letter status."[14]

James Baldwin, author of *Go Tell It on the Mountain,* and essays "Nobody Knows My Name" and "The Fire Next Time," during this period was also the subject of FBI surveillance. His biographer, James Campbell, requested files from the FBI and received some documents in time for publication of *Talking at the Gates: A Life of James Baldwin* in 1991. Other pages were denied release on the grounds of national security and legitimate law enforcement purposes. Campbell's court petition for the additional pages spent ten years in the system. When the appeals court ordered the agency to review the requested documents again for release, it was about seven years after publication, and more than ten years after the death of Baldwin. To reinforce the court's displeasure with the delayed response, it also told the FBI it could not deny a fee waiver to Campbell for the copying costs.[15]

Karl Evanzz, author of *The Judas Factor: The Plot to Kill Malcolm X* and *The Messenger: The Rise and Fall of Elijah Muhammad*, also waited patiently for FBI documents that would help his research on the two black leaders. When 15,000 pages on Malcolm X and 3,000 pages on Elijah Muhammad began arriving in the 1980s, there were pages from reports as early as the 1940s.[16]

The FBI and more specifically J. Edgar Hoover seemed to have a special dislike for Frank Sinatra, evident when Sinatra was reported to have volunteered the names of Hollywood Communists. Hoover responded by saying that he wanted, "nothing to do with him," according to a 1998 report on the release of 1,275 pages of FBI documents under the FOIA.[17] Sinatra's file began at least as early 1946 when Hoover attached a note to a news article about screaming girls at a Sinatra concert that said, "Sinatra is as much to blame as are the moronic bobby-soxers." Though Sinatra was investigated frequently until he died in 1998, he was never charged with any crimes, and some of the reports about him were just plain wrong. A 1971 memo said that Sinatra had cancer and would live no more than two months.

Julian Bond, a Georgia state senator in 1975 shared the fact that a seventy-eight-page FBI file about him also included a letter from Director Clarence M. Kelley. Mr. Bond, then thirty-five years old, had been the subject of threats, and the letter from Kelley advised him that the "investigation of this matter resulted in an individual being arrested, tried, and found guilty of violating the Federal Extortion Statute."[18] The file obtained by Bond's FOIA request also included monitoring of his nationwide speeches and notes that reported Bond had called J. Edgar Hoover "a little tyrant" and "a sissy."

Even local government politicians with seemingly out-sized personalities and well-known social leanings were the subject of Hoover's special attention. Richard J. Daley, mayor of Chicago and friend to several presidents, filled about three hundred pages of Hoover's files. One document noted, "After Daley was elected [mayor] in April, 1955, the CP [Communist Party] felt that its concentrated effort ... contributed greatly toward the victory of the Democratic Party and Daley."[19]

FOIA requests are sometimes in aid of exonerating those who were or believe they were under suspicion, but sometimes FOIA documents reveal a possibility of guilt. Such was the case when Athan Theoharis asked to see the FBI files on Supreme Court Justice Abe Fortas. Some of the documents, Theoharis said, suggested that Fortas supplied both the White House and the FBI with notes on the court's deliberations because there was some information contained that could be used to discredit then-Senator Robert F. Kennedy.[20]

And sometimes the documents released upon FOIA request cast a shadow on the character of individuals who were favored by the U.S. government. Securities and Exchange Commission documents released in 1977 brought to light the fact that a South Korean intelligence agent was under investigation for conspiracy and bribery. Tongsun Park had acted as a purchasing agent and confidant of a Saudi Arabian prince and other well-known celebrities in New York as part of a bank defrauding scheme.[21]

Another example was Raymond Bonner's book, *Waltzing With a Dictator: The Marcoses and the Making of American Policy,* about Filipino strongman Ferdinand Marcos and his wife Imelda. Making dozens of FOIA requests, Bonner gathered almost twelve thousand pages from State Department files for his five-hundred-page book detailing how the Marcoses worked the foreign policy system to their advantage for more than twenty years.

Samuel R. Pierce, Jr., was Secretary of Housing and Urban Development (HUD) for eight years, but in 1989 FOIA-released documents revealed that he provided personal assistance to well-known Republicans including Lionel Hampton, a famous jazz musician. In a story reporting the substance of the files, the following statement provided context: "More than 10,000 pages of documents reviewed by the *Times* do not offer direct evidence of wrongdoing, but they give a detailed view of the degree to which politics and friendship permeated the top levels at H.U.D."[22]

A follow-up story suggested even more strongly that hundreds of thousands of pages released under FOIA "provide the strongest evidence so far to contradict [Pierce's] assertions that he had only a limited role in the selection of projects that received billions of dollars in Federal aid."[23]

At about the same time, Oliver L. North, a Marine lieutenant colonel and staff member of the National Security Council, was testifying before Congress about the U.S. government involvement in Nicaragua. He was also, apparently, keeping voluminous notes about the lies he told in those hearings. The National Security

Archive requested North's notebooks under FOIA, and eventually received about 2,600 pages covering the period between 1984 and 1986. "They raise a lot more questions than they provide answers," Tom Blanton, the deputy director of the archive told a reporter.[24]

Another insider to the surveillance world, Robert Hanssen, who worked for the FBI but was also a spy for the Soviet Union's KGB, left his initials on nearly three thousand pages of files obtained under FOIA while he was supervising a program in the 1980s that probed the loyalty of U.S. citizens. "It's astonishing that the very guy who was going after dissenters was in fact working for the Soviets," Michael Ratner, of the Center for Constitutional Rights, and the subject of FBI monitoring, told a reporter.[25]

At other times a FOIA request resulted in documents that made individuals seem more silly than scary. Jack Abramoff, a regular lobbyist at the White House during the first term of the George W. Bush administration and who was involved with scamming his Indian tribe clients, used email as fluidly as the telephone. Dozens of exchanges with David H. Safavian, a White House budget aide, showed a casualness that borders on the banal. The two men met regularly for a variety of reasons at Abramoff's restaurant, Signatures, in Washington, D.C. FOIA-released documents reported that one sequence of email exchanges initiated by Safavian began, "When you spurned my invite, I called one of the industry sycophants and offered him an opportunity to suck up." Abramoff replied, "Damn, I want to be the one to suck up!!!"[26]

Similarly, Grover Norquist, an associate of Abramoff, was a frequent visitor at the White House, FOIA-released documents showed. Norquist and eight others suspected in a corruption scandal between 2001 and 2006 were identified in the White House visitor logs as being cleared by security at least 236 times during that period. But at least one of those clearance actions did not result in a trip through the security gate. A meeting scheduled for September 11, 2001, never took place. The records, blemished as they might be, were handed over to the Democratic National Committee in 2006.[27]

Luis Pasada Carriles was once a scary person. He admitted to bombing hotels, plotting Fidel Castro's assassination, and was accused of participating in an airline explosion. But in 2006, at seventy-nine years of age, Posada was more of a CIA and FBI embarrassment than a feared criminal. Documents released to Peter Kormbluh at the National Security Archive suggest that Posada worked with the intelligence community and then found himself in a perpetual state of limbo. Attempts to simply deport him out of U.S. legal jurisdiction, so that he would not be testifying in court, proved impossible.

Apparently Canada, Mexico, Guatemala, Panama, Costa Rica, and El Salvador would not take him.[28]

The Supreme Court had also been the target of investigations as was noted in the previous chapter. Occasionally, though, the wiretapping of justices was a byproduct of some other target's investigation. In documents released in 1989, there were at least twelve justices whose conversations[29] were recorded between 1945 and 1975. Those who were caught on tape included Chief Justices Warren and Vinson, and Justices William Douglas, Felix Frankfurter, Hugo Black, Stanley Reed, Robert Jackson, Frank Murphy, John Harlan, Potter Stewart, Harold Burton, and Abe Fortas.

The most extensively taped justice was Douglas, though the real target for the wiretaps was Thomas G. Corcoran who had served in President Franklin Roosevelt's administration. President Truman had asked for the wiretaps and Hoover apparently had them installed without waiting for the attorney general's approval.[30] The wiretap summaries may have contributed to Truman's sour attitude toward Justice Douglas. Truman was said to have referred to Douglas as a "professional liberal" and that he belonged to a crowd of "crackpots whose word is worth less than Jimmy Roosevelt's."[31]

The Not-So-Famous

FOIA requests can also reveal records about groups of people, as was the case when a 1990 report said that more than 350,000 people were listed by the government as foreigners who had not been or would not be admitted to the United States because of political or security reasons. The Lawyers Committee for Human Rights had initiated the FOIA request in 1986. The Immigration and Naturalization Service argued that certain information be exempt because disclosure would jeopardize those who had sought entry and also might reveal too much about U.S. intelligence activities. The documents produced four years later revealed that those barred from entry came from 146 countries, and that China had the highest number of denials at that time. The information did not contain specific names, but instead relied on a heavily censored list of the dates that visits had been denied and the grounds for denying the visitor's entry to the United States.[32]

In a related case, a Florida lawyer sought the names of Haitians who were involuntarily returned from the United States to Haiti. Michael Ray was trying to build a case about the treatment of Haitians seeking asylum and wanted to talk with those who had been denied refuge. He filed a FOIA request with the State Department which was denied on the grounds of privacy rights for those who had not won asylum. In a 1991 unanimous opinion, the U.S. Supreme Court found in favor of the State Department's rejection of the FOIA request and agreed that privacy rights should be accorded to the deported Haitians.[33]

Though thousands of names were not released in these two cases, the lists of immigration services investigations are not faceless. Choichiro Yatani, a Japanese student studying at the Stony Brook campus of the State University of New York, spent more than five years searching for the records that would explain why he was stopped at Kennedy Airport as he returned from an academic conference in the Netherlands in 1986. He was asked at the airport if he had ever been a Communist, and though he adamantly denied the accusation, he was jailed for forty-four days while deportation was initiated. His wife, and two children who were both born in the United States, waited and worried while his case worked its way through the legal process. He admitted that as student body president of Kyoto's Doshisha University, he was arrested once in 1968 during an antiwar demonstration. But he insisted that occurred a long time ago and was not a Communist party activity. By 1991, five years after the airport detention, the government still refused to allow Yatani to see the documents that drew attention to him, and would not remove his name from the "lookout list" of suspect aliens.[34]

Members of organizations have also been found among classified documents. For example, a 1979 *New York Times* story reported that 50,000 members of the California Peace and Freedom Party (PFP) were indexed in CIA records. "The actual indexing ... of registered members of the California P.F.P. was undoubtedly deemed justified and was based on policy emanating from the Director of Security's Office," it was noted among the documents.[35] Though the documents were released in 1978 under a FOIA request, the purpose of the index was not revealed.

An index kept by the FBI of more than one hundred members of the Socialist Workers Party was developed to identify "individuals deemed dangerous to the internal security and who would be afforded priority investigative coverage in the event of a national emergency," said Clarence M. Kelley, the Bureau's director, according to a *New York Times* story December 18, 1975. The index was revealed as part of a $27-million lawsuit against the FBI brought by the Socialist Workers Party. Kelley told a congressional House committee that same year that the list was updated monthly and included "only those individuals who pose a realistic, direct and current danger to the national security."[36]

More recently the American Civil Liberties Union pressed the FBI to release files under the FOIA that were kept on the J. Roderick MacArthur Foundation.

The organization was established in the early 1980s and was reported to have spent about $2 million a year in support of human rights and civil liberties organizations. The FBI was willing to release only eighteen heavily censored pages in 1990 in response to a request made in 1988. Arlie W. Schardt, then-vice president of communication of the Council on Foundations, said, "It is an intimidating discovery and will give pause to grant-makers who support groups that have been critical or challenged government policy."[37]

College campuses were also easy surveillance targets during the 1960s, according to documents released by the CIA in 1977. One memo said that field agents "developed files on the universities and colleges, came to know all the campus security people, special units in the local and state police," so that they could identify potential college trouble spots.[38] The released pages also included a warning memo from Richard Helms, director of the CIA at the time, and sent to Secretary of State Henry A. Kissinger. The documents said that surveying student dissidents could be embarrassing to the government because "this is an area not within the charge of this agency," and that the agency "should not be reporting at all on domestic matters of this sort."[39]

As laughable as some of these reports might seem, there are many examples that leave no one smiling. When a secret mission to release American hostages held in Iran failed in April 1980 it was hard for the soldiers and the administration to understand what had gone wrong. Nearly a decade later the questions and errors still seemed to haunt the participants and the public. After thousands of pages that carried some of the mission's details were released by FOIA request, and evaluated during a year of study by staffers at *U.S. News & World Report,* the answers were few and far between:

> The results are a mixed bag of great success, good intentions and bad results, well-meaning initiatives and those that ran fatally afoul of law and procedure. For the most part it is the story of a group of men, some of whom recognized the limitations of power and tried to halt excesses and others who decided that they alone knew what was best for the country.[40]

On a less dramatic scale, the family of Staff Sgt. Edward A. Carter, Jr., used FOIA to learn why he was banned from further service in the military–a banishment that had broken his health. He died at the age of forty-seven in 1963. In 1999 he was posthumously honored for heroism in combat, without apology for the delay or Carter's heartbreak. What the fifty-seven pages of U.S. Army files showed was that Carter had been watched and reported on by his unit members since the day he joined in 1942. During the five years of his career, records showed that he had subscribed to *Popular Science* and *Popular Mechanics*. He had joined the Masons. His neighbors and landlord were interviewed. His service record was exemplary. Ultimately, however, there was a note, a single line, that hinted he might be a Communist because his parents had been missionaries to China where Carter spent some of his youth.[41]

Elias P. Demetracopoulos, living in Washington, D.C., after he fled the 1967 military junta in his home country of Greece, spent six years peppering the CIA, FBI, the State Department, and Immigration and Naturalization Services to find out why he had been identified for surveillance. He even came to the attention of the *New York Times,* and in 1977 a profile by David Binder was published about Demetracopoulos that cast doubts about his Greek wartime resistance activities and suggested his association with foreign trouble-makers. The report was based on information supplied in part by the CIA, and Demetracopoulos told a *Washington Post* reporter that the story was a "hatchet job." Demetracopoulos eventually was successful in getting CIA documents about himself that appeared to refute the earlier statements in the newspaper story attributed to CIA officials. "That was vindication," Demetracopoulos told a reporter. "The important thing was for the CIA to admit in writing and for the *New York Times* to publish [it]."[42]

Frank Varelli, an El Salvador evangelist, had tried to keep a low profile, but a car burglary that exposed FBI files also blew Varelli's cover as an informant. Subsequent investigation into Varelli's role with the FBI revealed even more than either he or the agency wanted known. Varelli, it seemed, had fabricated most of the information he provided to the FBI about groups thought to oppose the U.S. policies in Central America. Varelli told congressional members that the FBI knew his reports were tall tales, but that those reports were what provided the agency an excuse to harass political opponents of U.S. foreign policy. The FOIA-released files verified the statements Varelli made during congressional hearings.[43]

Varelli wasn't the only foreign agent taken a bit for granted. Nicholas M. Nagy-Talavera said that in 1957 he provided the CIA with military information about resistance in Hungary, where he was a native, and that he helped trap Soviet agents. But his relationship with the CIA changed when he went to Cuba in 1959, as a student from the University of California at Berkeley. Upon his return he wrote an article for the student newspaper that suggested the United States was forcing Castro into the arms of the Soviet Union. After requesting the release of any information that the CIA, the FBI, and the State Department had about him, Nagy-Talavera said he was convinced that his trip to Cuba marred his record. Though he became a U.S. citizen in 1962, he was denied a Fulbright-Hays grant in 1965. By 1967 he was accused by the agency of being a Soviet spy despite having earned a Ph.D. from Berkeley and joining the faculty at University of California at Chico.[44]

The career problems of Morris Starsky were even more of a surprise than Nagy-Talavera's troubles. In 1975 the FBI admitted to filing an anonymous, derogatory letter about Starsky in 1970 so that a review committee at the Arizona State University might be encouraged to dismiss him from the faculty. Starsky's file began in 1968 when he was an associate professor and had helped to organize an antiwar teach-in. FOIA-released documents disclosed that Starsky was just one example of what was thought to be dozens of similar cases across the country and evidence of an FBI initiative called the Counterintelligence Program, or Cointelpro.[45]

Not Always a Happy Ending

Sometimes the queries that spur FOIA requests are the result of life-long curiosity, and the discovery that government files are the only place to find the answers to some questions. Robert J. McDonnell spent most of his lifetime studying accounts of the 1934 *Morro Castle* passenger ship disaster. The *Morro Castle*, owned by Ward Line out of New York, burned and sank off the New Jersey coast, killing 134, and appeared to be the work of arson. McDonnell became acutely interested in the story when in 1959 he read *Fire at Sea*, by Thomas Gallagher, retelling what was known about the tragedy at that time.

McDonnell's curiosity grew when evidence of murder became part of the story as he pursued further accounts of the disaster. After decades of investigation on his own, McDonnell decided that the federal agencies might have details that had eluded him. In 1984 his nearly life-long interest turned to anger when initial FOIA requests received little attention and few intelligible documents. Eventually McDonnell received more than a thousand pages of memoranda, reports, and testimony from survivors and Ward Line employees. Those documents suggested a culpable arsonist, but rather than pursue the suspect, the Justice Department and the Department of Commerce held him "blameless and protected." An FBI special agent told McDonnell that a notation in the margins of several documents indicated that the suspect might have had "informant privilege" protection. McDonnell acknowledged his obsession with the case. "Why ... obsessed? Because ... we have been lied to."[46]

Lewis H. Diuguid, writing for the *Washington Post Magazine* in 1999, wanted to find out what happened to a German-extraction family in Baltimore, Maryland, during World War II. Through FOIA requests to the Justice Department, Diuguid learned that his American-born but German speaking neighbor, Otto Franke, had been part of the federally instituted Exclusion Program that forced residents living and working near either the east or west coasts to move to interior locations, in this case, Ohio. Though Franke had an excellent work record, with letters of recommendation following him throughout his repeated firings at the behest of the federal agencies, he was scarcely able to make a living for himself, his wife, and two children. After the war, Diuguid reported, the Franke family returned to Baltimore and led productive lives. The children, Robert and Lehn, told Diuguid that they remembered their mother saying she'd sue the government over its treatment of her family if she had the money, but that the children had "no memory of their father expressing any bitterness. He waited until they were grown to explain, sketchily, but without rancor, what had happened."[47]

Jennifer Harbury was very angry in 1995 when she finally received copies of five pages from the Defense Department about her husband, Efrain Bamaca Velasquez. Harbury had asked the State Department and the U.S. Embassy in Guatemala City for information about Bamaca when he disappeared there in 1992. She thought there was some hope that he was alive because a comrade of Bamaca's, Santiago Cabrera, had testified in 1993 that he saw Bamaca tortured but alive inside a military base during the summer of 1992. Harbury told a reporter for the Associated Press that she could get no confirmation about Cabrera's report or locate her husband's body. "The official story from the Guatemalan army is that Bamaca was either killed during a firefight with government troops or, in lieu of being captured, killed himself," the redacted pages said. In another portion of the file Efrain Bamaca was said to have been "held incommunicado, interrogated a number of times and then killed." Harbury said she felt American officials had betrayed her by waiting so long to release even the few pages that they had.[48]

Sister Dianna Ortiz, a nun who claimed that she was kidnapped, tortured, and raped in Guatemala during 1989, told reporters that FOIA-released documents about her showed how the U.S. Embassy had been biased against her. "[They were] paying lip service to the need to find the truth in my case, and secretly undercutting me, slandering me, and trying to prevent the truth from emerging," Ortiz said at a news conference held in 1996 when she first reviewed the pages of her file.[49]

Lisa Leff, a reporter for the *Washington Post* in 1989, wrote a story about Frank Perdue, the poultry magnate, that reported on his driving license history. What she found, based on extensive records checks that in some cases required FOIA requests, was that Perdue had thirty-four speeding convictions in a twenty-year period, at least once caused the death of another driver in a head-on collision, but had never lost his license. The collision report, and subsequent involuntary manslaughter charges, had been expunged from Perdue's record because the case had expired. In 1974, the time of the fatal accident in Pennsylvania, the state law required criminal trials to begin within 180 days of arrest, which did not happen in Perdue's case, prompting the cleared record about a decade later.[50]

General Barry McCaffrey used the release of documents in 2000 as proof that he was cleared of charges he had engaged the enemy in the Persian Gulf after a cease fire had been declared in 1991. Hundreds of pages of records were provided under FOIA just before the publication of a *New Yorker* magazine article by Seymour Hersh that McCaffrey claimed was going to dredge up the old allegations without adequate rebuttal. "All of these issues were fully investigated 10 years ago, and there was a full exoneration," Bob Weiner, a spokesman for McCaffrey, told an Associated Press reporter.[51]

Sheldon Himelfarb, a writer, found humor in his long-delayed FOIA responses that began with his requests in 1982. He sought documents pertaining to the negotiations between the United States and Czechoslovakia for claims of settlement and restitution resulting from World War II activities. After more than a year of waiting for anything to be released to him, Himelfarb called on a friend who worked in the State Department, and he began to appeal some of the deletions in the few pages he had received. Documents began appearing in his mail soon after that, and by 1987 he was receiving a steady stream. "Not all of the sensitive information came to me on appeal," Himelfarb said in an editorial published in the *New York Times.* "Sometimes one of my reviewers would mistakenly send me a duplicate of a document that the other had already censored and released to me. Usually, the second would have entirely different passages blocked out."[52]

John R. Burke, deputy assistant secretary of state, however, was not so amused by Himelfarb's prose. In a letter of response dated September 22, 1987, and carried in the *New York Times,* Burke reported what Himelfarb had left out. About 10,000 documents had to be located initially in response to Himelfarb's request. "Since the negotiations were public knowledge and the subject of debate in press and Congress, secrecy was less a hindrance than sheer volume," Burke wrote. About 3,500 documents were found to be relevant to Himelfarb's specific questions, and Burke said that about 90 percent of those documents were released to Himelfarb in their entirety. Burke reminded readers, "The only cost to Mr. Himelfarb was postage and reproduction; the expense of retrieving, screening and reviewing material was borne entirely by the taxpayer."

Jesse Trentadue may have appreciated Himelfarb's protracted FOIA experience. Trendadue wanted to find out all he could about his brother's 1995 death during Kenneth's incarceration on a parole violation. Though Trentadue, a Salt Lake City lawyer, was told his brother Kenneth had hanged himself while in an Oklahoma City federal prison, there were also severe cuts and bruises on the body.

Trentadue told a reporter for the *Chicago Tribune* that he believed his brother was mistaken for a suspect in the Oklahoma City Murrah Building attack of four months earlier and that his brother was accidentally killed during interrogation. But in his search for clues about Kenneth's death, Trentadue found himself petitioning the FBI, the Bureau of Alcohol, Tobacco, Firearms and Explosives, as well as the Justice Department with FOIA requests and follow-up lawsuits in order to get even a few more pages of documents about events surrounding his brother's prison stay. Many of the hundreds of pages of documents he received were about the investigation around the bombing suspects as well. "I didn't start out trying to solve the Oklahoma City bombing," he said of his decade-long search for missing evidence in his brother's death. "I started out to find out why my brother was killed, and it led me to the bombing." [53]

Relatives of victims in the World Trade Center attacks on September 11, 2001, were the beneficiaries of a *New York Times* request for emergency radio and telephone transcripts that day. The Port Authority agreed to release the transcripts in 2002 but then changed its response when concerns for the victims' families were raised. The two thousand pages of transcripts included more than two hundred hours of recorded calls that occurred during just a few hours that morning. At least thirty-six victims were identified on the tapes, and an additional thirty who were thought to have been recorded that day were also included on the list of participants. Families of all sixty-six were given personal invitations to read or listen to the materials first-hand. The transcripts were released in 2003, but some families chose not to review the materials. [54]

The Business of Government, Consumers, and FOIA

The previous chapters focused on the ways in which FOIA is used to understand how federal agencies work and how individuals may find themselves the subject of public records. This chapter will look, instead, at the uses of FOIA for those who want to be better consumers both of government products and products made for the government. Critics of FOIA who were from the business community were particularly outspoken during the 1980s. Their anger arose because of a number of embarrassments and costly exposures that resulted from the mishandling of proprietary and confidential information required from companies by government agencies like the Food and Drug Administration (FDA), the Environmental Protection Agency (EPA), and the Patent office.

For example, in 1982 it was reported that the EPA had disclosed Monsanto's secret formula for its most profitable herbicide, Roundup, when the EPA responded to a FOIA request by an attorney for Monsanto's competitors. "What we are concerned about is that a competitor could pick up this data legally and register it in Japan or France without spending a dime except for copying costs," Jack Early, a spokesman at the time for the National Agricultural Chemical Association, told a reporter.[1] The FDA came under attack again that same year when one drug company received a confidential list of ingredients and the molecular structure diagram for a competitor's new product because of an inadvertent inclusion of materials provided to a FOIA requester. "They always apologize but that doesn't help," James T. O'Reilly, a lawyer for Procter & Gamble, said.[2]

Sometimes the route to discovery about the business of government is confused by assumptions about who the government favors and who is an enemy of the state. For example, during the years that Henry Kissinger served the White

House in various capacities, he met with Chinese leaders, then thought to be political enemies of the United States, and offered them a "hotline" to a U.S. early warning satellite system so that the Chinese could detect possible Soviet attacks on China. The discovery of this political entrepreneurship was made in 1999 by the National Security Archive Research Center, more than twenty-five years after the conversations were recorded and translated in top secret memos delivered to President Richard Nixon.[3]

A 1990 story about the Bureau of Alcohol, Tobacco, and Firearms (BATF) created some controversy for the George H. W. Bush administration. Based on BATF documents released under FOIA, it was reported that the government's initial ban on the importing of assault weapons had not stopped the practice altogether. New versions of Uzi, AK-47, Galil, and HK-91 had been altered to remove grenade launchers and other military-style attachments, but the gun still accepted large magazines of up to thirty rounds of ammunition and sported pistol-grip stocks that allowed quick reloading. Although the ban on the older versions of these weapons had been scoffed at by both detractors and supporters of gun possession, the effectiveness of the law in the face of these modified weapons was clearly not impressive to either side. Evan H. Whilden, a Philadelphia importer of guns, told a reporter that he thought the import ban was meaningless. "It's all baloney," he said.[4]

Consumer Guides

Many books have focused on the particular hazards or improvements that specific industries provide to the American public. For example, soon after FOIA enactment, several consumer groups began to comb government reports about product safety. *Small—On Safety: The Designed-in Dangers of the Volkswagen*, published in 1972, relied primarily on in-depth studies done by the independent Center for Auto Safety but also included some government sponsored crash tests, recall notifications, and safety violation reports. Another book by the same Center for Auto Safety provided a consumer manual on what to do if the purchased automobile seemed to have more repair problems than might be expected. *The Lemon Book*, published in 1980, again was based on the experience of consumers and explained the procedures for successful complaining and consumer rights. One chapter was devoted to appropriate federal government addresses and telephone numbers to facilitate easy consumer action.

Some important consumer-based investigations on automobiles and transportation do not result in book-length projects. A report released in 1997, built on

FOIA-released documents generated during the 1990s by the Federal Highway Administration, estimated that Washington, D.C. drivers spent more than $100 million a year on car repairs that were required after traversing District potholes. The report, "Potholes and Politics," was prepared by two groups, The Surface Transportation Policy Project and the Environmental Working Group, and minced no words on the quality of road conditions in the capital.[5]

Though automobiles have been expensive purchases for many Americans, even small purchases got special, book-length attention once FOIA made government reports even more accessible. *Over the Counter Pills That Don't Work*, published in 1983, was the work of another independent consumer organization, Public Citizen Health Research Group. Many of the assertions about which products were a waste of money originated in government-supported studies that were made available when completed.

The drug industry was confronted a little more forcefully in 2005 by several states' suits that alleged Medicare patients and state governments had been overcharged for prescriptions. One example was Illinois Attorney General Lisa Madigan's investigation that relied on FOIA requests for contracts with as many as forty-eight drug companies who supply pharmaceuticals to state-served patients. Investigators on the federal level had claimed that the prices charged by drug manufacturers has cost the government insurance, like Medicaid, about $800 million annually, and that patients, who must also provide a co-payment for the prescriptions, are adding $200 million a year to this over-charge.[6]

A book that was based on the absence of government information was James Bamford's 1982 *The Puzzle Palace: A Report on American's Most Secret Agency*. Bamford was able to tease out much detail from government documents that provided only silhouettes around the National Security Agency (NSA) whose budget is even a top secret classified mystery. Soon after publication, devotees of Lyndon LaRouche claimed that the Agency had been investigating him and his Schiller Institute. Group members of LaRouche, who had a political following after several campaigns for the presidency, told an Associated Press reporter in 1987 that their FOIA request about records relating to the group revealed that there was a file but that the agency would not release its findings. They said they suspected that LaRouche was being watched because his wife was a German citizen.[7]

Another author, Evan Hendricks, also wrote books that relied on government documents, but his work is concerned with consumer services rather than working widgets. *Credit Scores and Credit Reports: How the System Really Works, What You Can Do* by Hendricks is just one of several of his works that not only relied on FOIA-released information but that also warns consumers about how to use FOIA and how to avoid being caught up in FOIA-generated databases. Public records database sales are huge, Joseph W. Duncan, an economist at Dunn & Bradstreet, told a reporter in 1991. "[Computer records] evolved to the point now that its so inexpensive to redistribute data that public data has in effect become a commodity with very low overhead," Duncan added.[8]

That ease is what troubled Hendricks and prompted his book. "This information was created for one purpose—government. But now technology has made it possible to get this stuff online and beam it around and match it to other data." And the larger concern is that inaccurate information from one agency may end up in hundreds of files which will be almost impossible to track and correct.

The Business of Governing Government

Much of the day-to-day government business can be tracked through federal agency contracts with specialists. When an oil pipeline across Virginia burst and spilled hundreds of thousands of gallons of diesel oil near Reston in 1993, the National Transportation Safety Board (NTSB) released all the paperwork covering not only the pipeline installation but also all the permits and site reports for nearby construction. In that case the FOIA-released information did not provide an explanation but did exonerate some of the early suspects at the spill site.[9] Similarly, when a lawsuit was filed in a Kansas federal court during 2006 against Boeing and its suppliers for manufacture of its 737 passenger airliner, FOIA requests netted an instructive, though not conclusive document. An investigative report by the Defense Criminal Investigative Service noted that the military inspectors assumed that Federal Aviation Administration was providing inspection services as the aircrafts were being built and that, despite complaints and queries by finishing assembly workers and whistle-blowers, no further examination for defective parts was necessary.[10]

A couple of 1978 stories about a federal "goodwill" agency, established in 1971, relied on FOIA-released information to report on the program's spending priorities with its $100 million budget. The American Schools and Hospitals Abroad program, under the direction of the Agency for Internal Development, was set up to advance American ideas and practices in the education and medical fields. But what the story suggested was that hundreds of thousands of dollars were spent on projects that program evaluators thought were nothing more than international pork barreling.[11]

In 2006, as another example, grant contracts that became public under a FOIA request showed that 132 recipients were paid to provide human rights seminars, as well as training and advising leadership in newly developing political parties working toward establishing democracy, in Venezuela.[12] The U.S. Agency for International Development censored the names of the recipients for fear of reprisals in that country, but the 1,600 pages of contracts still provided the gist of the work to be done. Among the projects supported by the grants contracts were $47,459 for a "democratic leadership campaign," and $56,124 for analysis of the country's new 1999 constitution.

Special payments to employees at federal agencies have gotten attention through FOIA requests and the resulting released documents. A 1979 story based on information about that the Pennsylvania Avenue Development Corporation, for example, disclosed that fourteen of its thirty-eight employees had received tens of thousands of dollars in bonuses under a federal incentives program directed by the Office of Personnel Management. The program distributed about $25 million in awards that year to about 125,000 federal contract employees to encourage superior performance, so judged by supervisors within the entity under federal contract.[13]

Similarly, a 1984 story based on FOIA-released information about federal pension payments described a former senator who left Congress in 1978 with a pension at that time of $38,000 a year. Six years later, the story reported, that same retired senator was collecting $62,880 because he had not only served six years in the Senate, but also six years in the House and twenty-six years as a federal attorney. William L. Scott of Virginia, the lead example in the story, said simply, "I think a person who has worked for the government for more than 38 years is entitled to a large annuity."[14]

Audits and Self-Studies

Domestic spending is easier to audit, as the National Aeronautics and Space Administration (NASA) learned in the mid-1980s. In 1988 the settlement provided to families of the *Challenger* explosion astronauts was released as part of a FOIA request. The builder of the shuttle's solid rocket booster agreed to pay more than $4 million, and the federal government agreed to pay about $3 million to survivors of four of the seven astronauts, according to Department of Justice (DOJ) documents.[15]

An unflattering report based on FOIA-released audits of NASA also suggested that billions of tax dollars were wasted by the agency's contractors and bad management practices.[16] The audits were done by NASA's Inspector General's office, the Pentagon's Defense Contract Audit Agency and Congress' General Accounting

Office. The audits came to light after the *Challenger* launch explosion, but had been prepared and delivered to NASA in years preceding the accident. C. Robert Nysmith, a management administrator with NASA told a reporter in 1986 that "Getting the agency to identify weaknesses is not a natural culture [but] the system is improving every year."

Near the top of the list of problems at NASA, according to auditors, was the heavy reliance on private-contracts employees in critical areas of the agency's work. Nearly half of all NASA employees were hired by and paid by contractors, auditors found in the early 1980s. Though NASA officials were not happy to talk about it, the Senate Governmental Affairs Committee chairman John Glenn made the topic part of committee hearings in September 1989.[17] "The more contracting there is the more difficult it is to monitor," Senator Glenn, a former astronaut, told a reporter.

The same sort of problem was found to be at the root of the military's problems with Black Hawk helicopters from United Technologies, a private company contracted to furnish the Black Hawks, F-15 Eagle, and F-16 Falcon fighter jets. In 2004 FOIA requests for contract documents were delayed and rejected on the rationale that private contractors were not subject to FOIA because of the "state secret privilege." When the Department of Defense (DOD) seemed to be on the verge of releasing the requested information, United Technologies filed suit against the defense department in order to prevent the documents from exposure.[18]

Though the work of a particular contractor might well be just fine, the way that contractor receives further federal dollars may be questionable. FOIA-released documents in the paper trail of Mitchell J. Wade led to a review of his contributions in the bribing scandal of Randy "Duke" Cunningham initiated in late 2001. A blanket agreement and hundreds of millions of dollars in Defense Department funds that were paid to Wade's MZM consulting firm led him to eventually plead guilty and testify against Cunningham, who until then was a Congressman that funneled funds for MZM through earmarked budget approvals to the Pentagon.[19]

Less costly to taxpayers, but equally embarrassing, the Pentagon had hoped to "wait out" a request for information, made by Congresswoman Patricia Schroeder, a twenty-four-year member of the House National Security Committee, in June 1996, about military officers working on Capitol Hill for legislative members. Her query came after she learned that the then-Speaker of the House Newt Gingrich had several officers working for him as "fellows." Initially the Pentagon's legislative affairs office did not respond to Shroeder's several letters of inquiry. When she formally filed FOIA requests for the information, she was told that she could be charged up to $45 an hour for searching of documents, and $0.15 per page for copies. "There were people in legislative affairs who thought they could just wait it out," an unnamed Pentagon official told a *Washington Post* reporter in October 1996. Shroeder, a Democrat from Colorado, was to retire from Congress within a few months of her query. What happened, instead, was an order to review the Pentagon's "fellows" program.[20]

Audits of the Department of Housing and Urban Development (HUD) plagued Secretary Jack F. Kemp in the late 1980s, too. The problems turned up by the audits were for acts committed during the 1970s, but Kemp found himself saddled with righting the wrongs done by his predecessors. By June 1989 Kemp announced that he would end the federal mortgage insurance program because it was "riddled with abuse" and was costing the government about $90 million in defaults.[21]

Tens of thousands of documents were released in response to FOIA requests in the late 1980s that precipitated substantial housecleaning at HUD. For example, Deborah Gore Dean, executive assistant to former HUD Secretary Samuel Pierce, contributed more than twenty thousand pages of files released in October of 1989. Though Dean was apparently an uncooperative witness during congressional hearings, her voluminous filing system was much appreciated by the investigating panel.[22]

FOIA-released documents that included delinquent loan records, board meeting minutes, and investment strategy notes added fuel to a political fire that burned during most of the first term of President Bill Clinton's administration. The Whitewater Development Corporation was part of a savings and loan collapse that led to James McDougal, a partner of the Clintons, facing bank fraud charges in 1990. Though he was found not guilty, many were interested in the details that the Resolution Trust Corporation, entrusted with sorting out the bankruptcy paperwork, found when reviewing all the banking documents. In 1994 about 8,000 pages were released to news media, under FOIA, on loan activities throughout the 1980s.[23]

Agency self-studies can be even more embarrassing when the document released upon FOIA request is compared to the original report that was leaked and clean of redaction. When the National Highway Traffic Safety Administration's (NHTSA) report on how it handles nonpublic information was initially made public, there was no mention of internal concerns over the lax access to offices and paperwork. In contrast, the unexpurgated version reported that "Some offices … have expressed frustration because they perceive that industry sources sometimes seem to know what NHTSA is doing before they do."

The audit was initiated after Ralph Hoar, a safety advocate, saw an agency videotape that showed test dummies being ejected from a Chrysler vehicle when a faulty latch blew open. Hoar claimed that the agency withheld the evidence in aid of Chrysler sales. Sam Dubbin, NHTSA's counsel at the time of the self-study report, told a reporter for the *Washington Post* that the redactions contained information about the agency's relationships with the safety community that required protection.[24]

In a review of the Federal Aviation Administration's (FAA) handling of safety test reports, the National Transportation Safety Board (NTSB) found errors from start to finish in responding to FOIA requests. The review was initiated after a *Los Angeles Times* request for Boeing 757 turbulence tests was initially too narrow and limited. An appeal prompted the FAA to produce about two hundred more pages. After an internal review of the FAA's response to FOIA requests and the agency's FOIA practices, about five thousand pages were released.[25]

Though agency self-studies may not be easily available through FOIA requests, there are times when separate reports can be compiled to generate a portrait across time about a particular group of federal employees. When President George W. Bush announced his intention to increase the number of troops serving in Iraq and Afghanistan without reinstituting the draft, the *Los Angeles Times* submitted FOIA petitions to the DOD asking for statistics about the quality of those already recruited and serving in the military. Between 2004 and 2006 the number of new soldiers with high school diplomas had fallen, compared with previous recruitment campaigns, but the number of recruits with general equivalency diplomas had increased. The statistics also showed that the Army had issued more "moral character" waivers than in previous recruitment years. Waivers are issued to recruits when their records indicate "serious misconduct" such as substance abuse, weapons misconduct, or crimes. In addition, the Army increased the bonuses offered to new recruits who would commit to extended tours of duty. "They are having a difficult time signing up recruits into the armed forces, and that does seem to be tied to the unpopularity of the Iraq war," Anita Dancs, research director at the National Priorities Project who conducted the study for the military that was later made available in response to the FOIA request of the *Times*.[26]

The intricacies of daily work life among the upper echelon of Justice Department appointees were exposed when in 1991 FOIA-released documents reported that the director of the U.S. Marshal's Service had upgraded his leased car and added a dining room to his office suite. Though details of this sort don't usually make news, this case was intended as an example of particular attitudes among new executive branch appointees. Federal law at that time allowed presidential appointees about

$5,000 to decorate or upgrade their offices. In 1989 K. Michael Moore replaced his predecessor's 1988 Mercury Grand Marquis, leased for $3,075 a year, with a 1990 Lincoln Town car, leased for $5,100 a year, according to the released documents. He also ordered the installation of a dining room near his office, at a cost of $15,707. In 1991 it was reported that the dining room had been used seventeen times in sixteen months. When asked to defend the expenses, a spokesman for the Justice Management Division said that the limit did not apply in Moore's case. A spokesman for the Senate Appropriations Committee, which approves requests for more than the limits, told an Associated Press reporter that he disagreed.[27]

The Department of Agriculture was similarly shamed when Justice Department documents revealed, after a FOIA request, that the Payment-in-kind (PIK) program may have been abused by an Agriculture official. About eight hundred pages reported an investigation that ended with a scolding letter to Everett G. Rank, Jr., an administrator for the Agricultural Stabilization and Conservation Service, when his farm received more than $1 million from the PIK subsidy program. The program was designed to encourage farmers to reduce production and surpluses of certain crops.[28]

In another instance with the Agriculture Department, Secretary Mike Espy was momentarily embarrassed by the revelation that he had been charging the government for travel costs when he went to his home in Mississippi. The travel records were part of a FOIA request, and once made public Espy admitted he may have been inattentive to how the expenses would look. "I regret that deeply and have taken full responsibility to correct those perceptions," he told reporters.[29] Espy was not the only agency secretary to get a close review. In 2004 it was disclosed that HUD Secretary Mel Martinez had made many trips to his home state of Florida just before he left the Bush administration to run for the Senate.[30]

Work Papers

Policy directives and work-in-progress papers are harder to get and to describe when FOIA requests are made. During the George W. Bush administration, there were several instances of internal memos that were not disclosed on the grounds that what was asked for by the FOIA requester was merely executive branch information gathering and not appropriate for disclosure. In 2002, for example, a federal judge ordered several agencies to release work papers that were provided to an energy task force led by Vice President Dick Cheney.

Congressional members had sought access to the pre–decision-making information, and after threatening to subpoena the desired documents, the White

House agreed in 2001 to give a Senate committee access.[31] But environmental groups had to petition the federal court for similar access after they failed with FOIA requests to these agencies. They sought the documents for the same reason that Congress had—because they were concerned about policy directives that might be based on skewed task force reports.[32] When the documents were released there were about 11,000 pages, and some complained about heavy-handed redaction. Ari Fleischer, then White House spokesman, said, "The government … has to protect the rights of government to have deliberative meetings."[33]

Concerns about influence peddling were not based on phantoms and imagination. FOIA-released letters from the treasury secretary's office during both the Clinton and Bush administrations provided hard evidence that Enron Corporation's chief executive had worked hard at establishing and relying on his personal relationship with that office. Kenneth Lay offered Robert E. Rubin a seat on Enron's board of directors in 1999, when Rubin announced he was stepping down as secretary of the Treasury Department. This offer was made while Enron was lobbying Washington, D.C. against efforts to regulate its energy trading business. Rubin turned down the invitation, but the Clinton administration did decide against federal oversight of the energy trading businesses. Congress, the following year, adopted that recommendation under the Bush administration. Even as Enron was closing in on collapse, Lay pressed forward with the company's lobbying efforts against oversight.[34]

Incoming Secretary Lawrence H. Summers received a congratulatory note from Lay expressing his confidence. "I can't imagine anybody better prepared," Lay wrote. Subsequent letters petitioned Summers much as Lay had written to Rubin, but the effect, Summers told a reporter, was clear in his response to Lay's messages. "My formulaic response to Lay's letter speaks for itself," he was reported as saying.[35] Rubin and Summers, of course, were not the only object of Lay's attentions. The Bush family also had many letters and gift exchanges with Lay while George W. Bush was governor of Texas, according to documents released under that state's freedom of access laws.[36]

Several examples of the executive branch working hard to protect internal memoranda came to light in 2005 during several appointment confirmation proceedings. Two U.S. Supreme Court nominees had previous working associations with the federal government, generating paper trails that court watchers wanted to review. John Roberts, Jr., had served as a legal advisor in the Ronald Reagan and George H.W. Bush administrations. As many as fifty thousand pages were sought under FOIA by congressional members as well as reporters. The White

House claimed attorney-client privilege in denying the release of many of those pages.[37] Samuel Alito, Jr., had also worked during the Reagan administration in the Justice Department where he advised the director with opinions on policy stance. Some of these documents, too, were denied from release, based on attorney-client privilege.[38]

When John D. Negroponte was nominated as the first director of the newly formed national intelligence agency, the State Department was petitioned for his work papers that had accumulated during his long career as a diplomat. Much of what was requested had already been released to Negroponte when he retired from the diplomatic service in 1998. Hundreds of pages were thus easily provided at the time of his nomination hearings in early 2005, though some were said to be delayed for processing.[39] But during the nomination of John Bolton to the position of United Nations ambassador, the White House was more adamant about FOIA rejections. To avoid congressional review of the nominee's work papers, President George W. Bush proceeded with Bolton as a recess appointment that could be given formal attention by Congress only during the next session's cycle seventeen months later.[40]

A more recent example of federal agency protectionism came out in 2006 when the CIA acknowledged that two classified documents did exist about the detention and torture policies of prisoners held at Guantanamo Bay prison, but that the memos were too sensitive for release. The American Civil Liberties Union (ACLU) had petitioned a federal court in 2004 asking for documents that detailed the interrogation and prison policies there and had received more than 100,000 pages. But two important documents were missing from the cache, lawyers for the ACLU complained. One was described as a directive signed by the president, and the other was a 2002 memo from the legal counsel of the Justice Department to the corresponding counsel at the CIA on the legal definition of torture. "The documents are withheld in their entirety because there is no meaningful non-exempt information that can be reasonably segregated from the exempt information," a CIA lawyer reported.[41]

Details about life at the Guantanamo Bay prison were difficult to learn and required inventive use of FOIA requests by those reporters willing to stay with the story over many years. In a 2006 story by the *Washington Post*, for example, reporters compared testimony transcripts where the prisoners' names had been blacked out with that of detainees who had been named and released in Pentagon reports. The reporters claimed that in this way they were able to determine which prisoners remained in detention but had achieved "no longer enemy combatants" status.[42]

Quality of Life and Government Agencies

Among the federal agencies charged with protecting the basic qualities of human well-being, the Food and Drug Administration (FDA) has long been near the top of the list. However, in a story from the mid 1990s, the FDA logged about one thousand blood bank errors and accidents in 1989, and by 1992 the annual error rate had increased to about ten thousand. FOIA requests by *U.S. News & World Report* resulted in a cover story about blood banks and the risk of disease through transfusions. When, for example, it is discovered that contaminated blood is part of a bank, the units involved are recalled, according to the June 27, 1994, story. FOIA-released documents from the FDA indicated that more than 370,000 units of blood or blood products were recalled between October 1989 and the date of the story's publication. Tainted blood products, however, is not the only concern for the FDA and those receiving transfusions. About a million test kits and blood screening components also were recalled because of malfunctions and defective use between 1990 and 1994, the date of the story's publication. Here is the research statement that accompanied the story:

> *U.S. News* reporters used the Freedom of Information Act to obtain nine government databases related to blood safety. *U.S. News* also created four databases. One merged 1,007 Food and Drug Administration records on recalls with data hand extracted from 2,978 pages of FDA reports. Two databases drew on more than 10,500 visually scanned microfiche documents describing FDA enforcement actions. A fourth database was based on a survey of 15 blood banks.

Though somewhat smaller in scale, the FDA also released a critical report in 1988 on the manufacturing procedures of a drug company that prepared medication for the critically ill. The report was released after FOIA requests were made to review it, and the specific allegations were a list of forty-four violations of "good manufacturing practices" found during a three-month inspection tour of the LyphoMed facility in Illinois.[43]

When violations are documented or accidents result in headlines and emotional testimony, federal agencies sometimes exact fines as punishment that may reach millions of dollars. Collection of these fines, however, is another matter. In a 2006 Associated Press story, reporters petitioned dozens of agencies for documents about the outcomes of large fines assessed by them across the country. What they found, for example, was that the Labor Department's Employment Benefits Security Administration reported that among a dozen penalties issued, that ranged from more than $80,000 to $180,000, no more than $2,000 was actually paid.

The Occupational Safety and Health Administration actually had a policy statement about how to reduce, by as much as 95 percent, those penalty payments proscribed by the agency.[44]

Waste and manufacturing practices at nuclear munitions plants received almost constant attention once the facilities began to close in the late 1970s. For example, a 1983 story reported that the Department of Energy (DOE) knew but did not release information about the loss of 2.4 million pounds of mercury during a thirteen-year period at the Oak Ridge, Tennessee, site. Union Carbide who managed the facility for DOE had reported that mercury levels in local fish was higher than Food and Drug Administration (FDA) guidelines and that stream beds were contaminated, but that information was apparently not shared with local health officials. The reports did not come to public attention until they were released by FOIA requests made by Tennessee residents.[45]

Also close to home was a 1986 report based almost entirely on DOE FOIA-released documents about radioactive waste stored on a three-hundred-acre site in South Carolina. The Savannah River Plant, where millions of gallons of waste have been stored for about thirty years, was owned and operated by the DOE and E.I. DuPont de Nemours & Company. Among the documents released was a 1976 internal study reporting that more than a dozen workers had developed leukemia, more than double the expected rate per capita.[46]

In a follow-up 1988 story, E.I. DuPont de Nemours & Company officials acknowledged that accidents had occurred at the plant between 1957 and 1985 and that all reports of the accidents had been turned over to the government as required by law. The accidents, however, were news to Troy E. Wade, acting assistant secretary for Defense Programs at the DOE at the time of the October 3 story. One environmental group said it had received copies of the technical reports that should have contained the accident details, but "These did not describe the accidents considered the most significant by DuPont. The monthly technical reports, in which DuPont says it described the accidents, were denied to the group by the Energy Department on the ground that they were classified."[47] Similar waste sites near Boulder, Colorado, and Fernald, Ohio, were the subject of FOIA requests at about the same time.[48] It was estimated that about 600,000 former employees of the nuclear defense industry may have been affected.

A request for documents about radioactive emissions that may have affected the health of those living and working around Washington's Hanford Reservation produced about nineteen thousand pages of information. That 570-square-mile processing complex owned by Westinghouse Electric Corporation, supplied the first atomic test explosion July 16, 1945, in the New Mexico desert.[49]

By 1990 so much of the FOIA-released information pointed to culpability, the Energy Department admitted that the radiation levels around the Hanford plant were high enough to have caused serious health risks for as long as two decades during the 1940s and 1950s.[50] The effects of radiation contamination during the test launches of the 1950s were still being debated in 2006. A nuclear accident near Simi Valley in 1959 may have contributed to cancer illness and deaths, according to a study by independent health and science experts. Much of the foundational information used in the study was gathered through FOIA requests to the DOE.[51]

In July 1990 the Energy Department acknowledged that the Richland, Washington, atomic weapons plant emissions were high enough to cause illness, and that about twenty thousand babies born in the region may have been affected by the high levels of radiation discharged between 1944 and 1960. These estimates were made public when a government report by a panel of scientists was issued after a two-year study that was initially spurred by the 1986 FOIA-released Energy Department documents.[52]

And in a 1999 news story about the Union Carbide Corporation uranium-handling plant in Paducah, Kentucky, Energy Department Secretary Bill Richardson promised to compensate sick workers during the 1950s through the 1970s at that plant. The health of employees at that particular work site had long been the subject of investigation by both Union Carbide and the DOE and so FOIA-released documents were available quickly enough for news reports about findings to be written within months of requests. In December 1999, the Energy Department also announced that its 2000 budget would increase spending on health studies and medical monitoring of affected employees.[53]

The stories continued in 2000 with reports that the Paducah plant had also leaked plutonium into ground water around the facility. Maps of soil and water testing, done by the facility's managers, beyond the plant's parameter during at least ten years belied earlier officials' statements that no more than trace amounts had ever been found. The minute levels acknowledged in those earlier statements had been dismissed from concern because, it was claimed, traces were found everywhere after weapons testing. The newly released maps were posted on the DOE's Web site in 2000 in response to a FOIA request. Levels noted on the maps that were dated 1989 and 1999 extended to the Ohio River and included a state wildlife park. The concentration levels recorded from the tests were as high as hundreds of times the normal background levels and exceeded the maximum safe limits set by the government.[54]

Americans in the Pacific Ocean were also vulnerable to the government's testing of biological warfare during the 1960s. The DOD decided to test 112 possible weapons programs and one of these, the Pacific Project, experimented with flyby spraying of barges with various bacteria and germs. When Mark J. Rauzon, a wildlife biologist, sought more information from DOD,

> A trove of information arrived, including heavily redacted documents with intriguing names: Operation Fearless Johnny, Magic Sword, Shady Grove, Green Mist. In all, ... 50 or so operations had been conducted during the '60s by about 20 ships transporting more than 6,400 sailors.[55]

U.S. soldiers captured during the Korean War who were subjected to harsh interrogation at the hands of Soviets provided, in some cases, a wealth of information about U.S. military tactics and routines. Though the intelligence reports were gathered during the early 1950s, the documents were not made available to the Pentagon until a 1990s effort by the United States and Russia to account for American POWs. The forty-year-old files were initially denied to Associated Press when it made a FOIA request in 1993 for them. Subsequently the Pentagon decided to respond with the documents in 1997.[56]

Closer to home, the contaminants in children's school lunches were the subject of a 5,000 word story in the *Chicago Tribune* during 2001. The sources for the report included FOIA-released documents from Department of Agriculture, the FDA, dozen's of states' health and food safety agencies, and publicly available documents from the Center for Disease Control and Prevention. The statistics and thousands of cases of illness spanned the country, coast to coast, and the decade of the 1990s.[57]

In late October of 2001 no one was particularly surprised to learn from FOIA-released EPA reports that daily monitoring of the World Trade Center site showed that chemicals and metals were leaking into the ground and poisoning the air around the demolished buildings. Low levels of contaminants were found in the Hudson River, and the ground and air near the trade center also carried concentrations, at higher than federal standards, of dioxins, PCBs, lead, and chromium. Hundreds of pages of test results were posted on the EPA's Web site, though an EPA spokeswoman said the agency was still examining the data for ongoing investigations.[58]

Another demographic group unable to represent itself, the mentally and physically ill living in Washington, D.C., group homes, were the subject of a series of stories in the *Washington Post* during 1999. Using documents released by FOIA requests at the Department of Human Services, the story reported on the skimming of federal funds and poor oversight that led to untimely deaths just blocks from the nation's capital.[59]

Documents from the EPA in Illinois that were supplied after a FOIA request by Citizens Alliance for Responsible Development in 1997 contributed to suits filed against the St. Charles water treatment facility to force it into pollution guidelines. A previous suit filed against the water treatment plant by the same citizens' group was dropped by them when the Illinois attorney's office filed a similar lawsuit against the facility.[60]

The Department of Health and Human Services (HHS) during the 1980s was deeply involved in the study of the little-known AIDS virus. Documents describing experiments that intended to identify the various strains and characteristics of the virus were still in development stages and sometimes were closely guarded secrets. An extensive report on the sharing of research information was published in 1989 and relied heavily on FOIA-released documents from HHS, acquired after suits were filed to force the agency's compliance.[61]

The National Institutes of Health (NIH) is usually the subject of FOIA requests for reports on research. For example, the 1991 release of a study on an AIDS vaccine that resulted in at least one person's death was provided because the researchers had claimed that the researched had harmed no one.[62] But a year later the NIH also inadvertently released documents about the development of AZT, a drug tested in the treatment of AIDS, that did not support the George W.H. Bush administration's assertion that NIH scientists had been the co-inventors with researchers at Burroughs Wellcome. The FOIA-released files given to Burroughs Wellcome included confidential documents containing legal opinions that argued against the Bush government's position. Burroughs was reported to have earned about $150 million in sales of AZT during 1991 alone.[63]

The Challenges of System Abuse

The Corporation for Public Broadcasting was the subject of targeted presidential disapproval in the early 1970s. Documents released almost a decade later indicated that President Richard Nixon sought ways to cut funding for public broadcasting when he learned that Robert MacNeil and Sander Vanocur would anchor a new program on that network. The revelation was reported in a 1979 story based on about ten thousand pages of documents released under FOIA at the request of the Carnegie Commission. In one memo quoted in the newspaper story, Nixon's aide Charles Colson admonished coworkers to be less direct in their correspondence about the ways to cut funding. "This is a serious mistake for whatever records this piece of paper might ultimately end up in, or perish the thought, should it get out."[64]

Government spending on publicly funded art has also become the subject of disputes and FOIA requests. The Art Censorship Project filed court of appeals papers against the National Endowment for the Arts (NEA) in 1994 when NEA did not produce all the documents requested on behalf of three photographers who were denied grants. The difference of opinion sprang from the NEA's contention that it need not provide anything from the "working groups" meetings held by its advisory arm, the National Council on the Arts, who in this case had overruled the photographers' peer panel recommendation in favor of funding.[65]

Chicago artists wondered why it seemed that most of the public spending for art in public spaces went to artists from out-of-state, and in some cases out of the country. In order to understand how selections were made, the Chicago Public Art Program and Department of Cultural Affairs board meeting records were requested under FOIA. The meeting records showed that committee members voted for Chicago artists, but that the vote was overturned during the planning and construction negotiations. The final decisions were made during closed-door sessions that subsequently were forced by open meetings laws to allow public attendance.[66]

There are, of course, instances of FOIA requesters trying to abuse the system. That was what a judge accused Michael Antonelli of in 1985. Antonelli, a convicted bomber in 1980, spent much of his jail time making FOIA requests about anything and everything. Many of his requests required him to file a lawsuit, and by the mid-1980s he had filed about one hundred of them in Chicago alone. Prison inmates were usually allowed to file lawsuits at no charge, but a judge decided in Antonelli's cases to impose the requisite fees. Antonelli also had to provide the copy costs that his requests garnered. He paid the Drug Enforcement Administration (DEA), for example, nearly $2,000 for photocopying between 1983 and 1985. Though Antonelli would not divulge the source of his funding, he suggested that it came from grateful clients.[67]

Edwin P. Wilson, jailed as an arms smuggler in 1983, discovered through FOIA-released documents that his conviction was in part based on misleading testimony that the CIA provided at his trial.[68] The CIA had claimed in court that Wilson had never been asked by the agency to provide intelligence services after his retirement from service. The newly released pages attested to at least eighty instances when CIA senior offices talked with Wilson between 1971 and 1978 about intelligence matters and his willingness to provide weapons to foreign governments. "I'm not mad at the CIA," Wilson told a *Washington Post* reporter in 1999. "I'm not mad at our government. I love our government."[69]

States and Freedom of Information

Though every state in the nation has government information access laws, the date of adoption and the range of particulars within each state's laws varies dramatically. As noted in an earlier chapter, many of the states' acts were promulgated in the latter half of the twentieth century. There are some notable exceptions. Nebraska, for example, not only had open records laws as early as 1866, but litigated whether some numerical indices kept by the county clerks were public records,[1] and if non-court personnel were entitled to inspect certified copies of the court reporter's records before they were offered in evidence.[2]

The following list provides an overview of those state regulations or guidelines adopted in legislative and court documents, organized here by year:

State	Public Records Act Citation	Year
Alabama	Ala. Code 36-12-40 et seq.	1983
Alaska	Alaska Stat. 09.25.100 to .220	1962
Arizona	Ariz. Rev. Stat.Ann.39-121 to 1-24	2000
Arkansas	Ark. Code Ann. sec. 25-19-106 et seq.	1967
California	Cal.Gov.Code 6250 to 6270	1957/1968
Colorado	C.R.S. 24-72-201 et seq.	1963
Connecticut	Conn. Gen. Stat.sec. 1-200 et seq.	1949
Delaware	29 Del. C. sec. 10001 et seq.	1977
District of Col.	D.C.Code Ann. 25-61-10 & sec. 2-531	1968
Florida	Fla.Stat.Ann. 119.01 to .165	1967
Georgia	Ga.Code Ann. secs. 50-18-70 to 76	1959

State	Public Records Act Citation	Year
Hawaii	Haw. Rev. Stat. sec. 92F-1 et seq.	1988
Idaho	Idaho Code 9-338 to -347	1990
Illinois	5 ILCS 140/1	1983
Indiana	Ind.Code Ann. 5-14-3-1 to 10	1983
Iowa	Iowa Code Ann. 22.1 to .14	1984
Kansas	Kan.Stat.Ann 45-215 to 225	1984
Kentucky	Ky.Rev.Stat.Ann. 61.870 to .884	1976
Louisiana	La.Rev.Stat.Ann. 44:31	1968
Maine	Me.Rev.Stat.Ann. 1-13 sec. 408	1975
Maryland	Md.Code Ann., sec. 10-611-628	1957
Massachusetts	Mass.Gen.Laws Ann. Chs.4, 7; 66,10	1975
Michigan	MCL 15.231	1976
Minnesota	Minn. Stat. Ann. 13.03	1979
Mississippi	Miss. Code Ann. secs. 25-61-1 et seq.	1983
Missouri	Mo.Ann.Stat. 109.180 to .190	1961
Montana	Mont.Code Ann. 2-6-101 to 111	1935
Nebraska	Neb. Rev. Stat. secs. 84-712	1866
Nevada	Nev.Rev.Stat.Ann. 239.005 to .040	1977
New Hampshire	N.H. Rev. Stat. 91-A:1	1967
New Jersey	N.J.S.A. 47:1A-1 et seq.	1963
New Mexico	14-2-1 NMSA 1978 et seq.	1941
New York	NY Pub. Off. Law Sec. 84	1974
North Carolina	N.C. Gen. Stat. sec. 132-1 to 10	1935
North Dakota	N.D. Cent. Code 44-04-18 to -18.8	1957
Ohio	Ohio Rev. Code Ann sec. 149.43	1963
Oklahoma	Okla. Stat. Ann. 51,24A.1 to .18	1959
Oregon	Or. Rev. Stat. Ann. 192.410 to .505	1973
Pennsylvania	Pa. Cons. Stat. Ann. 65, 66.1 to .4	1957
Rhode Island	R.I. Gen. Laws sec. 38-2-1 to -14	1974
South Carolina	S.C. Code Ann. secs. 30-4-10	1978
South Dakota	S.D. Codified Laws Ann. sec. 1-27-1 to -19	1939
Tennessee	Tenn. Code Ann. sec. 10-7-503 et seq.	1957
Texas	Texas Code sec. 552	1973
Utah	Utah.Code Ann. 63-2-101 to -207	1953

State	Public Records Act Citation	Year
Vermont	1 V.S.A. sec. 316	1975
Virginia	Va. Code sec. 2.2-3704	1968
West. Virginia	W.Va. Code sec. 29B-1-1	1977
Washington	Wash. Rev. Code Ann. 42.17.250 -.311	1973
Wisconsin	Wis. Stat. Ann. 19.31 to .39	1981
Wyoming	Wyo.Stat.Ann,9-2-407, 16-4-202	1953/1969

Generalizations Among the State Laws

There are fundamental aspects of access laws that must be dealt with in every state. These characteristics are either defined explicitly by the legislature or through the courts by custom and practice that often relies on common law. Determining what constitutes a public record is often the first point of reckoning, and definitions range from the simple to the highly detailed. Indiana, for example, defines a public record as any writing, paper, report, study, map, photograph, book, card, tape recording, or other material that is created, received, retained, maintained, used, or filed by or with a public agency and which is generated on paper, paper substitutes, photographic media, chemically based media, magnetic or machine readable media, electronically stored data, or any other material, regardless of form or characteristics.[3] New Hampshire, on the other hand, does not define public record in its access statutes.

The reason for inspection of government records may be a point of contention that divides advocates and government agencies. As a result, some states require that a request to examine government-held information also explain why the request is being made. North Carolina law states specifically that no person requesting review of public records, or copies, is required to disclose the purpose or motive for the request.[4] Ohio law, however, allows a public office to limit the number of records it transmits to any one requester. If that requester provides written certification that the records sought will not be used for commercial purposes, the public office may provide more than the ten allowable records.[5]

Another important element that many states detail in the law is who may exercise the right of government information review. When states relied on common law for this determination, the courts often found that inspection of public records was limited to those who were citizens, with appropriate interest or proper purpose.[6] The intention is often to exclude those who have no more than an idle curiosty.[7] Tennessee, for example, requires that if law enforcement records are the subject of inspection, then any requester making an inspection of those records must provide his or her name, address, business telephone number, home telephone number, driver license number, or other appropriate identification prior to inspecting the records.[8] Colorado law, on the other hand, makes no requirements of the requestors' identification.

Once the courts have determined that the information requested is in fact a public record, is not exempt from review, and that the request is being made by a recognized legal entity, then determining the enforcement procedure, if not detailed by statute, may prove the most difficult task of all. In those states that rely on common law, the usual process for compelling record keepers to allow access is the writ of mandamus. But this disclosure by court order is not always satisfactory. Some states have recognized the writs only to require the reasons for nondisclosure be made available to the courts, while other states expect only that the requested records be reviewed by the judge to determine if disclosure is appropriate.[9] In some states the limited legal standing of a petitioner to ask for mandamus has frustrated those who seek access. In a few cases the states have allowed only the attorney general or a designated official to petition on behalf of those who seek public access to records.[10]

With these points of litigation for reference, the rest of this chapter will review some of the experiences that record access advocates have had when using states' government information laws, sometimes called access laws, to provide detail about the ways that local governments conduct public business. All states are not represented in the short stories noted here, but instead the sample is intended to provide a snapshot of local gains and losses in public information agendas.

Agency and Quasi-Agency Reports

Alaska and Exxon Mobil

Near the close of 2003, Exxon Mobil had already paid $900 million for cleanup efforts necessary after the 1989 Valdez tanker spilled 11 million gallons of oil into Prince William Sound. Alaska and the federal government, however, were still evaluating whether to pursue additional damage claims that could amount to $100 million more. The decision rested with the Exxon Valdez Oil Spill Trustee Council's recommendation, and that recommendation was to rely on ecological study reports that only became publicly available after the *Wall Street Journal* requested them through the Freedom of Information Act (FOIA). Among the study results that were reported by an Associated Press story on October 1, 2003, were a rise in the death rate for pink salmon eggs, fewer surviving harlequin ducks, oil in mussels, and large pockets of oil just beneath the sand surface.

Georgia and Soil Safety

In 2001 Alfonso Mallory and Scott Davis were concerned about hazardous contamination in DeKalb's Wade Walker Park but didn't know for sure that there was a problem. After requesting county soil tests, they learned that the land there had a history of landfill problems. The result was that Mallory and Davis wanted the local landfill closed until more safety measures were instituted.

Davis told a reporter that he doubted that he and Mallory would have been able to make a strong enough case to force state action on the landfill if they had not had access to the test results records. Mallory added, according to a March 13, 2005, *Atlanta Journal-Constitution* story, "Without accountability, without people having access, then democracy,—your civil liberties—would cease to exist. This is how we use information to ask the right questions."

Georgia and Corporate Documents

Cobb County Superior Court ordered the Clary Lakes Recreation Association (CLRA) to provide corporate documents in response to a request from Phillip Parker. Parker, a resident and member of the homeowners association, wanted to "inspect all accounting and/or corporate records of CLRA for the purpose of determining the performance of management and the condition of the corporation," according to court documents. The court decided that all of these records were not public, but that board meeting minutes were documents that Parker should have had available to him.

The court's standard of review was that the trial judge must determine "whether the purpose named (in the request for review) is a proper one, whether the request is vexatious or arising from idle curiosity, whether the documents called for are relevant material, and not over burdensome, [and] whether granting the request would violate principles of confidentiality." [11]

Idaho and Research Data

Twin Falls lawmakers were considering legislation that would protect research data from public records disclosures, according to an Associated Press June 19, 2003, story. But a faster solution to the problem of releasing research data that some Idaho residents were also considering was to simply contract the research work out to a nongovernment, private research corporation. Ron Sherffield, a University of Idaho researcher, said he was surprised to learn that Idaho law did not protect research data as he had experienced when working in North Carolina and Virginia.

Sherffield ran into data collection problems in Idaho because dairymen there refused to participate in a study he was conducting unless they were promised confidentiality. That is the point at which third-party contractors were considered to solve the open records problem. "I don't want [us] to lose another season," state Senator Tom Gannon said. "It would be nice to think that by this time next year we would have this [study] in the hands of the Ag Department."

Illinois, Children and Family Services

A letter of program assessment dated 2003 and sent to the Department of Children and Family Services claimed that Maryville Academy leadership had threatened the jobs of staff members there, withheld health information about children assigned to the institution, and had ignored state directives. The children's services office released the letter in response to a state FOIA request soon after a change in the leadership of Maryville Academy was announced.[12]

Illinois and Park District Board

At a June 8, 2000, Butterfield Park District board meeting, resident Lisa Saunderson turned on her tape recorder to audiotape the actions and discussion of the members. She had taped the May 17 and May 30 meetings, but at this meeting she was told by the board president to stop recording. That order was reinforced by others at the meeting, including the board attorney and another commissioner. At one point on her tape she was threatened with the prospect of a 911 call to force her to turn off her machine.

Saunderson and other contended that the park board was holding closed meetings and failed to report in board minutes key decisions. The Illinois open meetings act says that "any person may record the proceedings at meetings required to be open ... by tape, film or other means." Saunderson said she agreed to turn off the recording if she was promised a copy of the board's tape of the meeting. She also told a *Chicago Tribune* reporter that she never received the promised copy. "This is my park board. ... They're elected to represent me, not to coerce me," Saunderson said.[13]

Indiana and Nonprofit Corporations

In a 1991 Supreme Court ruling, the Indianapolis Convention & Visitors Association was deemed a public agency and therefore required to disclose records dating back to the passage of the state's public records act promulgated in 1984. The five-justice court found that, because the association funding was in part from county levied hotel/motel tax, they were indirectly supported by public revenues and subject to state board of accounts audit, and the state's auditing of the association brought it squarely within the definition of a public agency under the public records act.[14]

Kentucky and Summaries of Records

Charles W. Riddell began a series of requests in 2001 for Madison County records on building permits and electrical inspection fees. Riddell received summary information but not the opportunity to see the original records, and so he filed suit with the state's attorney general to find out if he was owed more. Amye L. Bensenhaver, assistant attorney general, wrote in her 2003 opinion, "The requirements of the [open records] statute are not fully discharged until Mr. Riddell is afforded an opportunity to inspect existing documents."

New Hampshire and Electric Company Reports

The Supreme Court ruled in April 2005 that individuals' privacy interests outweighed public interests in the disclosure of residential names and addresses contained in a report on voltage complaints filed with a utility company. Brian D. Lamy, a Bedford resident, asked in 2003 to see a consultant's report investigating the quality of electric service provided by the Public Service Company of New Hamshire. The report had been submitted to the New Hampshire Public Utitlities Commission and included the customer names and addresses of both residential and business subscribers.

Lamy's request was initially met with a copy of the report that had removed the list of customers involved with voltage complaints. Lamy asked for the complete report and a lower court decision ordered the public utitlities commission to comply. But after an appeal, the higher court determined that residential customers had a high stake in privacy issues and so the final court decision ordered only that the business customer names and addresses may be included under New Hampshire's right-to-know laws.[15]

New York and Not-for-Profit Corporation Records

The Supreme Court agreed with Southern Tier Economic Development, Inc. (STED) that it was not required to comply with the state's information access laws when public inquiries were made in 2004 for a copy of financial audits. Walter C. Ervin had asked to see the budget statements of STED, and his request was denied on the grounds that Southern Tier was not a public agency.

The audit in question was to assist the Elmira mayor and other city officials determine if a land transfer had been properly settled and not to determine if STED owed money. "The outcome of the audit does not bear on the rights and obligations between STED and the City ... [STED's] Agreement does not set forth any obligation on the part of STED to furnish any records, including audit reports, to the City," the court wrote. Justice Robert C. Mulvey concluded that "[t]here is no evidence that STED has ever acted as or held itself out as an agent of the City. ... For these reasons the Court finds that STED is not an agency within the definitions set forth. ..."[16]

Oklahoma and Insurance Records

Michael Farrimond asked in 1999 to see insurance records that were part of a receivership order dated 1997. The receivership order designated that all of Mid-Continent Life Insurance Company records be placed in the state's Insurance Commission office, and the court at that time issued a protective order prohibiting disclosure of some insurers' policy information.

Farrimond wanted access to some of Mid-Continent's documents and petitioned the comission office for them on the grounds that it was a public agency and the records he sought were in that office's possession. The Supreme Court decided in 2000, however, that the documents that Farrimond wanted did not constitute commission office records but were still covered in the original proactive order.

In support of their decision, the court referred to a similar Kentucky case and wrote, "The court held that the fact that *possession* [emphasis added] by the Insurance Commissioner of records of the insurer who was in receivership did not convert the insurer's records into public records, subject to disclosure."[17]

Washington and Construction Documents

In 2000, Seattle announced it would hold public hearings about a city council bill to begin construction on a light rail transit system. Rick Hangartner requested all documents relating to the city council bill's proposal. Though the city produced many of the requested documents, some were withheld as exempt from public review under a "controversy" exemption of the state's public disclosure act.

Hangartner petitioned for review of the exclusions, and the trial court ordered the documents to be made available and deemed them not exempt under Washington's disclosure laws. But the state Supreme Court reversed that decision for some of the documents, asserting that a few of the records were covered by attorney-client privilege. In principle, however, the 2004 court said it agreed with the trial court's determination that the light rail transit system project records were presumptively public documents.[18]

Board Membership and Personnel Records

Alaska and Army National Guard Documents

Kimber Kyle served in the Guard for six years during the late 1980s and early 1990s. When she left Guard duty, she also left Alaska and moved to California where she hoped to start a new life. Instead she found herself embroiled in a long-distance dispute about access to Guard documents that she needed in order to successfully bring a paternity suit against another guardsman who had committed suicide before the baby's birth. She eventually was able to gather enough materials to secure Social Security and Veterans Administration benefits for the child, but the effort required filing dozens of FOIA requests. "I'm the best damn records clerk you ever saw," she was quoted as saying in an *Anchorage Daily News* story June 25, 1995.

Florida and Hospital Board Members

A decision by the Winter Haven Hospital board of directors in 1999 to close a family practice clinic caused a community uproar. "There's a lot of people mad in this community," Larry Lay, whose children were served by the clinic, said to a *Lakeland Ledger* reporter for a March 9, 1999, story.

When Vicki Howell, another resident served by the clinic, wanted to send signed petitions to the hospital board, her request for their names was denied. Hospital spokesman Joel Thomas said that the policy in place required that such a request be made in writing. Howell later learned that because the hospital is a not-for-profit institution the information she sought was easily available at the Florida Secretary of State's office in keeping with open records laws.

Illinois and Harassment Complaints

Nancy Moore, a member of the Carpentersville board of trustees, was the subject of a harassment complaint in April 2002. She asked to see who had filed the complaint and was denied access to that information. She continued to ask, however, over the course of several years, always receiving a denial of her request based on eight elements of the state's freedom of access laws.

In April 2005 when she was about to leave her position as trustee, she asked once again and included a four-page letter in which she challenged the exemptions used to deny her former requests. She also claimed that the denial violated her federal Sixth Amendment right to a fair trial. No punitive action was taken against Moore as a result of the complaint, but an attorney for the trustees suggested that they all might benefit from a workshop on cooperation and communication.

Bill Sarto, the new president of the trustees, told a *Chicago Daily Herald* reporter for a May 21, 2005, story that he believed the complaint and efforts to keep the complainant secret were intended to urge Moore to resign as trustee. Among his first acts as president was to release to Moore a copy of the original complaint now that she was about to leave anyway.

Washington and Social Services Records

Kathleen O'Connor wanted to find out in 1999 if her 15-year-old son had been assaulted while in the custody of state social services workers. The Department of Social and Health Services (DSHS) told her that she would have to file suit for discovery materials in order to have access to such a report.

O'Connor was surprised by this response and rather that pursue such an expensive and time-consuming route, she instead began enlisting the aid of a lawyer and other public records advocates. The group of supporters petitioned the court. "DSHS seems to have forgotten that they work for us," the petition said in part. The state's Supreme Court agreed in 2001 and found the fact for O'Connor.[19]

Criminal and Police Investigative Records

Colorado and Sheriff Department Records

Open records laws were tested when families of slain Columbine High School students needed Jefferson County sheriff department documents before the statute of limitations expired on lawsuits to be filed against the emergency responders.

James A. Rouse, who was representing the families' requests for information, said in an April 11, 2000, *Denver Post* story, "My clients have, from time to time talked with the sheriff's department, requesting information. ... To date, they have not received full disclosure and complete information."

The response they did get from the Jefferson County Attorney's office was that the requested materials were still part of an ongoing investigation, which prohibited release. Donald Fleming, one of the parents concerned with the outcome said in the same story, "When [the deadline] comes around, ... without the information, we don't know what to do. Were things done right or things done wrong?" He added that he and other families wanted, "all the information—not just some condensed report."

Colorado and Sex Offenders

In 1996, community groups distributed fliers around Denver neighborhoods that encouraged residents to ask at nearby police departments to see the public record list of sex offenders registered within the state. In an October 3, 1996, *Denver Post* story, it was reported that the Denver police department had more than 400 people on the sex offender registry but was not recording how many requests they have to see the list. Nearby communities like Aurora listed 101 parolees, and thirty-eight requests had been made during the year to see the list. Boulder had twenty-four parolees, and eleven requests to see the list. Arvada had forty-two parolees, and forty-six requests to see the list.

At the time there was concern about the accuracy of the listed addresses for the parolees. Aurora Deputy Chief Mike Stiers said, for example, that the list was not always updated quickly when offenders moved within the city. "Some innocent citizen at that address is marked as a sex offender when he is not," Stiers said. The *Denver Post* story also reported that when a check was done October 2, 1996, of the Aurora list there were several parolees on it who had moved without leaving a forwarding address.

Iowa and Prisoner Access to Records

Robert Lee Kern, convicted of first-degree murder, asked to see public records from his clemency plea. His request in 2002 included an offer to pay for copies and postage because he had no other way to view or receive the records. His request was turned down, but the state attorney general disagreed with the denial of access to public records. Attorney General Tom Miller, according to a December 10, 2002,

Associated Press story, reversed the denial decision, and the Iowa Board of Parole now must provide public records to inmates if they are unable to get to the central offices in Des Moines.

Louisiana and Investigatory Reports

District Court Judge Jewel E. Welch ruled in 1997 that the Zachary Police Department was not required to release all its files in the shooting death the previous year of a teenager. The parents of Brulin B. Brunfield III, who died from a bullet wound, claimed that because the police department was apparently not going to arrest anyone in the shooting then the investigation's files were no longer subject to open records exemptions.[20]

Michigan and Inmate Trial Records

An appeals court upheld a Wayne County Circuit Court's ruling against a state prisoner's FOIA request for his own criminal trial records. The Michigan Department of Corrections had initially refused the inmate's request and the Michigan Court of Appeals agreed in a 1997 opinion.[21]

E-mail and Technology

California and E-mail

Superior Court Justice Kevin A. Enright ordered the San Diego Community College District to surrender e-mail correspondence of employees who may have used their computer accounts to wage a political campaign that was not directly related to their jobs.

The college district policy on e-mail was that it should be used for school business and that e-mail would not be monitored. There were, however, no guarantees in the policy that message contents would be treated as confidential, according to a *San Diego Union-Tribune* April 1, 2001, story.

Connecticut and GIS

A 2004 Superior Court ruling gave public access to the Greenwich geographic information system database despite testimony from the town's police chief that thieves of all sorts might make use of the data. Stephen Whitaker, a Stamford entrepreneur, asked to purchase an electronic copy of the Greenwich database under state FOI laws and initially was turned down.

Town officials argued that the database was exempt, that terrorists might use the database, and that hackers might be able to disrupt the larger information system supporting town activities. Whitaker's lawyer argued that open government depends on the ability of citizens to review, oversee, and challenge government officials with equally good technology and records if that is what government is using.

Justice Howard T. Owens, Jr., agreed. In his opinion, "Open government is not promoted when the public is required to sift through voluminous documents in various departments (if) the municipality can counter this by push button automation." Subsequently, the Supreme Court of Connecticut also agreed with Owens in a unanimous 2005 decision.[22]

Kentucky and E-mail

Al Baker requested copies of the e-mail exchanges among Bowling Green city officials during the autumn of 2003. The city officials initially balked at his request, claiming the e-mail messages were draft documents and protected by attorney-client privilege, so not eligible for review.

Baker renewed his request and argued before a circuit court that some of the e-mail content he asked for was already reported in the newspaper, so the privacy could not be a valid claim for denial.

Warren County Circuit Judge Steve Wilson ruled that some of the city officials' e-mail was privileged and that unauthorized leaks did not waive that privilege. The city, however, did release to Baker some e-mail messages that were thought to be discussion in preparation for a commission decision.[23]

Financial Records

Arizona and Taxpayers

A taxpayer advocacy group said in a January 23, 2002, Associated Press story that it used the state freedom of access laws all the time. "I go by the rule that if there are three or more public officials together, you should not take your eyes off of them," Mary Schuh was reported as saying. Schuh also said that the group requested state financial reports for Kino Community Hospital to learn how money was spent there, and for similar reports concerning the Tucson Unified School District, Northwest Fire District, and Amphitheater Public Schools. "People, the average citizen, should use the act when they need it. How can people speak to something when the bureaucracy keeps it a secret document?" Schuh asked.

Connecticut and Sewer Connection Fees

Robin Maheu requested a waiver for sewer connection fees on two lots that he bought in Bristol because others in the neighborhood had received such waivers. His request was denied, and he asked for an explanation. Documents that the city provided him gave no reason for the denials, so Maheu filed FOI petitions for complete information about the decision process. Maheu was so persistent with his FOI requests that, according to a *Hartford Courant* July 21, 1997, story, Bristol's mayor, Frank N. Nicastro, asked the state's FOI commission to fine Maheu for filing nuisance requests. The FOI commission denied Nicastro's request.

Florida and Bail Money

Jonathan M. Sabghir, a south Florida lawyer investigating the trail of bail money, asked each county's clerks, sheriffs, and county commissioners for relevant records. Many of the responses were satisfactory, but when Hermando County's clerk of the circuit court refused to send materials, Sabghir filed suit. "If they give me an unlawful response to a records request, I have no choice but to file a lawsuit," he told a reporter for the *St. Petersburg Times* for an April 3, 2004, story.

Sabghir wanted the information so that he could persuade the state's legislature to force all counties to publish lists of inmates and those cleared after a court appearance who have unclaimed bail money still in county offices at the end of each year. "With 67 clerks, 67 sheriffs and 67 county commissioners, I do not have the resources to keep asking for the records," Sabghir said.

Georgia and the Tax Commissioner's Office

Denise Taylor was a candidate for the Camden County tax commissioner but claimed she was denied access to public records in that office as a way to thwart her campaign in 2004. What she wanted was an audit report, but what she got was a three-sentence balance summary of expenditures.

Taylor also said she asked for several lists of county tax information including a list of the twenty largest private landowners, as well as who the timber companies were, and what amounts of taxes they paid. The tax commission office said the records were not available, according to a June 2, 2004, *Florida Times-Union* story.

Taylor then filed a FOI complaint with the Camden County Commission. David Rainer, chairman, said "[Taylor's] entitled to anything she asks for." Taylor later speculated that the tax commission office may need to update its record-keeping practices if it could not comply with her simple requests for information.

Nevada and Federal Property Acquisition Laws

The Nevada Supreme Court ruled in 2003 that the state's public records laws did not apply when the requested information was part of a local transaction related to railway property. In 2002, a request was made to the Reno city property manager for documents concerning the appraisal value of thirty-two parcels of land recently purchased by the city to provide easement and railroad right-of-ways, as well as a breakdown of the $17,760,000 property-acquisition budget. The city denied the request.

An appeal to a district court for a writ of mandamus yielded an initial compliance order. But subsequent city appeals resulted in the state's supreme court determining that the applicable law in the case was not the Nevada public records act, but the federal Uniform Relocation Assistance and Real Property Acquisistion Policy Act which deemed the requested records were confidential.[24]

New Jersey and Medical Center Finance Reports

An appeals court found that annual financial statements of a local medical center were public documents, though propriety information might be part of those reports. The Bergan Regional Medical Center was required to provide certified audit reports of its annual financial activities to the Bergen County Improvement Authority.

Though the initial public request for these reports was denied in 2004 on the grounds of exemptions found in the state's Open Public Records Act, an appeal of that decision found that the common law right of access in New Jersey supported enforcement of providing the reports. The court said that "the common law definition of 'public record' is broader than the statutory definition of 'government record' contained in the N.J.S.A. 47:1A-1.1."[25]

Sanctions for Violations

California and Access Violations

Superior Court Judge William C. Pate ruled in 2001 that the San Diego Port District had unlawfully denied the public access to documents that showed a $21 million contribution to the Padres stadium project. The only sanction, however, for the violation was to pay legal fees required to bring the law suit.

Stanley Zubel, attorney for the client who asked to see the contribution documents, told a reporter for the *San Diego Union-Tribune*, "It's secret government in blatant violation of the law," according to an April 21, 2001, story. Zubel added, "But no commissioner will be sanctioned, and the port will pay my fees with public money."

In a similar case, Monterey County Superior Court Judge Susan Dauphine ordered the city of Monterey in 2005 to pay more than $100,000 in legal fees to Michael Stamp who represented Patricia Bernardi in an open records request spanning several years.

Florida and Public Records Used for Harassment

A circuit court judge in 1999 ordered Paul Curry, then of Jensen Beach, not to seek any more public records about Jacqueline DiCarlo after the court determined that Curry was using the documents as a form of harassment. Circuit Judge Larry Schack said that Florida's open records laws were "not intended as a tool of harassment … to place another individual's life under a microscope," and he sentenced Curry to three years of prison, and two years of house arrest after his release.

Curry admitted he "tried to find every bit of information on her I could," and then he used it in complaints to local officials claiming DiCarlo had falsified information on her drivers' license and that she provided psychic services without the proper license. Curry also asserted that he had done all this only as a way to defend himself against her accusations that had resulted in a restraining order to keep him away from her.

The prosecutor in the case had requested that the court consider community service as part of Curry's sentence, but the judge demurred. "I don't want to impose him on anybody else," Judge Schack was reported to have said, in an Associated Press story July 29, 1999.

Student and School Records

Georgia and Student Discipline Records

Two parents of middle school students decided that they needed to know more about what kinds of dangers their children faced from other students in the classroom. Cindi Wilson and Shannon Sanderson began filing requests for discipline records when their sons told them that a classmate had been suspended for just a few days after bringing a knife to the Snellville Middle School in 2001.

School administrators initially told the parents that the disciplinary action records were confidential, but Wilson and Sanderson learned that the Gwinnett school system judiciary panel filed monthly reports of disciplinary incidents and actions taken at each school, blanking out the student's name, and that these reports were public records. They began collecting these reports and compiling them so that they could compare them with an annual report that school systems were required to supply to the state education office.

When Wilson asked the state education department for a copy of the Gwinnett school system report, she said she knew right away that the school system's report had grossly understated the number of incidents. According to a March 13, 2005, *Atlanta Journal-Constitution* story, the county had reported 4,258 disciplinary actions, while Wilson and Sanderson counted more than ten times that number.

Illinois and Student Test Records

Tim Kassel, a statistician by trade, asked to see students' reading test scores, with names stripped out, at the Fox River Grove Elementary District 3 school in 2005. He wanted to understand why slow readers were not catching up to their peers, as generally reported in a school district study. He was not alone in his desire to see the raw data. At least seven other parents made similar requests.

The school board was unwilling to provide the information, according to a June 28, 2005, *Chicago Daily Herald* story, because Kassel, the board said, didn't have the education background to understand the data. School district officials did say, however, they might ask Kassel to help with a new study of the issue.

Illinois and School Contruction Contracts

Asbestos removal cost the Calument Park Elemetary School District 132 nearly twice the original estimate when an unlicensed contractor began the project that later required a new contractor to complete. FOIA documents revealed that school administrators had simply tried to save some money.[26] An initial estimate of the abatement job was about $7,000, but after the asbestos had been spread around the school site by the first contractor, the lowest bit for cleanup was nearly $13,000.

Louisiana and School Board Meeting Documents

Ruth Klopf wanted a packet of materials that were provided to reporters and board members at a St. Tammany Parish School Board meeting in 1997. School Superintendent Lenny Monteleone told her she was not entitled to the information.

School board members disagreed. Board member Mary K. Lynch said, "What point do we have in asking for public input when they don't have the information?" Another member, Don Villere said, "We do have a responsibility to provide whatever information a person is looking for," according to an October 10, 1997, *Times-Picayune* story. "That's not just our responsibility, it's what we should be doing."

Missouri and University Basketball

During the 1999 through 2004 University of Missouri basketball seasons, the NCAA suspected that the men's team coach was providing meals and gifts to players and violating recruiting rules. Requests by Associated Press, citing state open records laws, moved the university to provide copies of the allegations.[27]

Voting Records

Illinois and Ballots

Scott Kobort asked the DuPage Election Commission to let him review ballots in 2005 in order to see why there were anomalies in the municipal election. His request was denied and so Kobort filed suit in June of that year to gain access, he said, under the state's freedom of information laws.

"It makes you think 'What are they trying to hide?'" Kibort told a *Chicago Daily Herald* reporter for a June 30, 2005, story. "All I wanted to do was prove they're doing the best job they can." Sarah Klaper, an attorney for the Citizen Advocacy Center, said she thought the ballots are subject to FOI laws. "The burden of proof is on the election commission to show they're exempt," Klaper told *Daily Herald* reporter Marni Pyke.

Kentucky and Voter Assistance Forms

Gordon B. Long asked Magoffin County Clerk Haden Arnett to see the voter assistance forms housed in that office after the 2002 elections. The forms are used by voters who ask for help because of disabilities when casting their ballots.

Haden denied the request to inspect the forms on the grounds that they contained private information. But in a legally binding opinion of the state's Attorney General issued in March of 2003, the public interest of ensuring honest elections outweighs voter privacy concerns.

"The public's interest in the disclosure of this information is weighty, indeed," Assistant Attorney General Amye L., Bensenhaver wrote. "This is particularly true in light of the fact that a large percentage of allegations concerning voter irregularities arise in the context of fraudulent voter assistance applications and certificates."[28]

Part Three

Freedom of Information Act Tomorrow: Introduction

After forty years of public experience with the Freedom of Information Act (FOIA), there is quite a bit of evidence that it has had some effect on government information collection systems and access to them. Executive branch agencies all have FOIA officers in place with regular reporting mechanism, and though all do not work perfectly at all times there is at least a framework for review of standards and practices. The Justice Department provides ongoing advice and surveillance of information sought from and supplied by government. Its leadership has frequently offered suggestions about how to change the system, sometimes for better or worse depending on which side of the change one sits.

Also during this period of testing, amending, and retesting, civic groups have sprung up to encourage and celebrate public use of the FOIA. The National Freedom of Information Coalition, for example, serves as a clearing house for funding and organizing state-level FOIA initiatives. The Marion Brechner Citizen's Action Project serves as data resource for comparing and tracking the states' open records and open meetings statutes, court activities, and attorney generals' opinions.

The next chapter will survey the activities and resources that many FOIA service organizations made available so that anyone and everyone could explore public access into government data. The kinds of support included templates for letters of requests, contact information for all FOIA offices within federal agencies, as well as state agencies in some cases, and explanations of the points of law that may affect the sort of request made. These organizations also offered grants to fund state-level startup organizations and the costs of particular investigations.

In a few cases the granting organizations also hosted annual contests to recognize significant work that relied on FOIA-released information.

The final chapter of this book asks the inevitable question about whether FOIA has been a successful statutory empowerment of the public's need to know what government is doing. This review is offered with an eye toward identifying the costs and benefits of FOIA to future generations of the information-seeking American public. The success of FOIA, of course, rests with the public's interest in using and improving what began more than forty years ago and what was an existential concept for democracy as envisioned nearly three hundred years ago. The phrase "knowledge is power" has proven again and again to be an irascible truism. The precursor is, as we know, that information is the foundation of knowledge, and so control of information is the control of knowledge that then leads to power.

It is also evidently true that there are no quick fixes when government creeps across the contours of privacy and employs strong-arm information collection techniques to provide a supererogatory advantage. These final two chapters, then, are in aid of arming a public with the knowledge of a shared past in order to prepare for an uncertain future.

Enthusiasm, Awards, and FOIA

Web sites, handbooks, endowments, database libraries, annual awards, training workshops, and listservs were just some of the ways that groups of people dedicated to the encouragement and use of Freedom of Information Act (FOIA) helped both lay and professionals understand the law. The Investigative Reporters and Editors Inc. (IRE) hosts an extensive Web site with dozens of FOIA resources. Listed on the IRE pages are the active and relentless advocates of FOIA at both national coalition and state-level organizations. These include not only the obvious National Freedom of Information Coalition but also the larger, overarching journalists' organizations such as the Reporters Committee for Freedom of the Press and the Society of Professional Journalists. Journalists are not the only advocacy sponsors: Another group whose mission to strengthen the active use of FOIA is the Sunshine in Government Initiative. This consortium includes the American Society of Newspaper Editors (ASNE), The Associated Press, the National Newspaper Association, and the Newspaper Association of America, as well as the Radio-Television News Directors Association, along with the groups mentioned above.

Citizen Action Initiatives

Among the equally committed efforts are the university-sponsored initiatives, like the Marion Brechner Citizen Action Project (MBCAP), housed with the Brechner Center for the Freedom of Information at the University of Florida, and the Freedom of Information (FOI) Center, hosted at the University of Missouri. Both of these organizations support zealous use of FOIA and host extensive

Web resources for research and active use. Coalitions have also organized to bring together consumers and good government groups. The National Security Archive, for example, is a non-government repository for declassified documents and records. The archive was intended to serve anyone interested in reviewing government information and obtains its collection through not only FOIA but also congressional hearings and testimony, presidential papers and court records. The archive espouses a mandate to "help shed light on the decision-making process of the U.S. government and provide the historical context underlying those decisions." Another FOIA-centered coalition is OpenTheGovernment.org, which also was supported by grants from a half dozen foundations and institutes as well as individual contributions. Their 2006 "Secrecy Report Card" declared that the group's primary constituency was "Americans for less secrecy, more Democracy." The thirteen-page report detailed the evidence that members said indicated greater withholding of government information.

Annual Awards

Several of the FOIA-centered groups provide special recognition through annual contests. The winning entries have been posted for more than a decade on the respective Web sites so that others benefit from examples as well as the content of the investigations. For example, IRE has awarded FOIA-based news reports since 1979. In recent years the IRE awards contest has received about five hundred entries annually. Judging of the entries is handled by the IRE members, but in order to avoid conflicts of interest, members who work as part of an entry do not participate in the selection process.

The Brechner awards for FOIA-based news reports began in 1986. Judging of the entries is done by a panel selected by the Brechner Center director to include a journalism academic, a lawyer, and a journalist, according to the Center's Web site, with none of the panel members from the University of Florida. Winners have sometimes included multiple news organizations as was the case in 1999 when seven newspapers in Indiana won for their efforts to co-ordinate a statewide information audit and report on the way police records were handled. Similarly, the next year the Gannett newspapers in New Jersey won for their efforts at a statewide information audit across government agencies and the subsequent series of stories. What follows is a snapshot of the award-winning entries from both Brechner and IRE.

Years of investigative work resulted in a series of stories carried by the *Argus Leader* about former South Dakota Governor and U.S. Congressman Bill Janklow.

The focus of the stories was on Janklow's granting of pardons that went to former state officials, his own son-in-law, and his legal counsel before he found himself convicted of manslaughter in that state after the death of a motorcyclist in 2003. The *Asbury Park Press* in New Jersey showcased the legislature's lack of action in support of state freedom of access laws. The series of stories highlighted the wide range of differences among the state's towns and municipalities in determining what was a public record and what should be protected. The blame for this inconsistency was placed in the offices of the legislators who had for years sidelined any efforts to address the disparities of access.

The *Daily Business Review* in Miami reported on a practise discovered in Florida that allowed judges to shield even case docket numbers from public review so that the custody and detention of a suspect would not be publicly known. The case in point was of an employee of a restaurant whose patrons included some of the September 11, 2001, hijackers. Prisoner prosecution and treatment was the subject of another award-winning series by the Associated Press that focused on detainees at Guantanamo Bay since 2002. The stories reported on the tribunal proceedings as retold by the prisoners who complained that no evidence was brought against them during their incarceration.

In 2004 The Bakersfield *Californian* reported that a school assistant principal had been charged with killing five members of his family. The school board would not release the personnel record; and in the process of the legal battle that followed, the reporter learned that the school employee had a record of violence and sexual misconduct. Another series of stories that same year by the Palm Beach, Florida, *Post* revealed a system of private contractors who hired counselors to work with juveniles, but found that some of those counselors also had a history of inappropriate behavior with juveniles. A sequence of stories published in the Kansas City, Missouri, *Star* in 2004 investigated the facts around what was seen to be an unusually high rate of deaths among children in the state.

The Burlington (VT) *Free Press* published a series of stories that revealed problems in the state's reporting of suspected medical malpractice. The fault lay, apparently, with confidentiality laws that kept the records of complaints and reported problems within the domain of the profession and away from public scrutiny. In addition, a 2002 series in the *Detroit News* focused on the state's health care system that failed to stall, or even slow down, an outbreak of syphilis though there were ample warnings from the national Centers for Disease Control and Prevention.

Long before the 2007 furore over U.S. military hospital care of the Iraq and Afghanistan veterans, the *Cleveland Plain Dealer* investigated the practises found in some veterans hospitals that allowed surgeons to phone in their patient care.

The newspaper reported that some attending physicians who were salaried at the veterans hospitals were allowed to treat the patients there by telephoning instructions and diagnoses to resident doctors. In this way the salaried physicians put in the requisite hours but were also able to attend, and charge, their private, paying patients at the same time.

A 2004 series of stories published in the Louisville, Kentucky, *Courier-Journal* chronicled several years of legal battles the newspaper pursued while trying to learn the list of donors to the University of Louisville's McConnell Center for Political Leadership. The courts eventually ruled in favor of the newspaper's request for the donor list. The series included some evidence that Senator Mitch McConnell, founder of the Center, had participated in the efforts to block access to foundation documents.

The New Orleans *Times-Picayune* reported on the abuses of scholarship awards administered by public officials. The series of stories brought attention to the ways in which recipients were shielded by lax reporting and highlighted the variations in qualifications for awards. The Fort Lauderdale *Sun-Sentinel* examined a recent law that shielded pawnbroker slips from inclusion as a state public record. The result of protecting the slips, according to the investigation, was that when stolen items were recovered, the victims of those thefts could not discover who had pawned the items. Moreover, another New Jersey story reported that under new state regulations a public body could meet privately as long it kept minutes and made those available. The *Press of Atlantic City*, however, found that about one-third of the groups meeting privately either kept no minutes at all or the records were so slim as to make the meeting's activities unknowable.

In 2005 the Scripps Howard News Service detailed the system of reporting missing children and found that frequently the guidelines of the 1990 National Child Search Assistance Act were of little use. Reporters also noted that many police departments failed to notify state authorities which then delayed interjuristical tracking and support in the missing persons search.

Annual awards that recognize outstanding work are not the only way to highlight and encourage good efforts. Several groups award grants and seed money to found FOIA-interest organizations at the state and local government levels. Some of these awards have supported particular projects like statewide information audits.

Projects and Grants

The National Freedom of Information Coalition has been providing support to local organizations since its inception in 1989. As the organization, originally called the National Freedom of Information Assembly, developed a strong network among state organizations, it sought funding from foundations and advocates, like the Knight Foundation, already working the areas of free speech and open government. Recently the NFOIC began providing "pass through" grants that support or assist projects that encourage public access to government records, or that help create and grow state-level Freedom of Information coalition groups. In 2007 NFOIC offered $220,000 in grant funding for these kinds of projects.

One such recipient was the Indiana Coalition of Open Government (ICOG), which received funding support for a users' survey to assess the effectiveness of the state's Public Access Counselor's (PAC) office. The office was created by executive order and then organized by state legislative action to provide legal advice for all who sought access to government records. During the 2005–2006 fiscal year the PAC office reported receiving more than 1,800 formal and informal requests for assistance.

The survey was administered in partnership with Indiana University's journalism school and Center for Survey Research to assess whether government information requesters got the documents they sought. More specifically, the survey gathered data about the circumstances under which requesters had to resort to law suits in order to receive information they were entitled to under the law. The survey gathered feedback in a sample of about four hundred respondents who had asked the Public Access Counselor's office for advice on records laws. ICOG, a statewide nonprofit formed in 1995, posted the survey results on its Web site at www.indianacog.org and asked for changes to legislation and policy based on the survey results.

Another grant winner was the Georgia First Amendment Foundation, which produced a training guide for school administrators and reporters covering the state's education system called, "Public Schools and the Open Records Act in Georgia." The First Amendment Foundation also conducted an information audit of the school offices to see how well administrators adhere to the access laws affecting these records.

Texas also received some pass-through funding for a project that demonstrated in a "blackout" handbook how much information would have been unavailable and unpublished in daily newspapers during a single week if public information laws were not effectively administered in the state. The NFOIC funding of the Freedom of Information Foundation of Texas was also used for cooperative reporting projects that relied on FOIA-driven information access that then led to stories produced by the state's university journalism programs. A recent subject of this project's investigation concerned 254 Texas counties and 310 cities. Students requested from sheriff and police chiefs all policy statements and any documents filed in law enforcement agency offices that reported incidents of "use of force" weapons since January 2000.

Access Rhode Island used its NFOIC funding for the development of an instructional DVD on the importance of free speech, and provided the DVD to classroom teachers for free use. The producers of the DVD used three stories by reporters that had received much attention for their investigative efforts using public documents. And the Washington Coalition for Open Government used NFOIC's pass-through grant to fund a series of community workshops for local officials that featured the state's archivist, city attorneys and clerks, as well as lawyers who specialized in access law.

Another very recent FOIA support organization is the Sunlight Foundation. Established in 2006, the foundation set about immediately to provide "transparency grants" to boost the placement of government information onto the Web. The foundation supports enhancement of databases that go beyond a single subject of information collection and awarded hundreds of thousands of dollars to several startup projects. For example, the Center for Media and Democracy received support to build a Web-based reference about Congress, dubbed Congresspedia.org. The site hosts news and entries about Congress and its members. Congresspedia was set up as part of the "wiki" progeny that allows anyone to be an editor of the site.

The Center for Democracy and Technology received grant money from the Sunshine Foundation to host a Web site that posts Congressional Research Service reports. The site fit the mission of the Sunshine Foundation because it would more broadly distribute the research papers and reports that Congressional members request and use. Taxpayers for Common Sense (TCS) received a grant to assess ways that TCS might better present and support a Web-based platform for timely information about tax issues. And the Citizens for Responsibility and Ethics, based in Washington, D.C., received funding to launch its Open Community Open Document Review System. The OCODR system was designed and developed to allow Internet users to view, tag, and comment on government documents that were acquired and housed by the Citizens for Responsibility and Ethics in Washington. These online contributions in notation format were thought to be a better way to get timely feedback on government work being done far from easy public access.

Smaller grants from the Sunlight Foundation for more specific and somewhat narrower projects went to Maplight.org to provide easier tracking of campaign contributions and legislative votes, and the Center for Citizens Media for development and implementation of a test-bed Web site that captured and posted all aspects of a congressional election campaign as citizen journalists reported it. Similarly, a grant went to Connecticut Local Politics to host a Web site and post local and federal governments political activities including candidates' online question-and-answer sessions as well as interview and news about all aspects of political life.

There were grants from the Sunlight Foundation that offered real-time education as legislative bills were offered and debated. ReadTheBill.org was one such effort. Room Eight, another example, was the recipient of a grant to provide blog coverage of New York's twenty-nine congressional members. The in-depth reporting was to include these members' budget and earmarking activities, and to provide links to relevant Congressional Wire and Megabux Index references. Other small or sequential grants went to WashingtonWatchdog.org for hardware purchases, the Center for Responsive Politics for building a database containing lobbyists' financial disclosures, OMB Watch for creating and developing a database of government grants and contracts, and The Project on Government Oversight for a report on government and private sector hand-in-glove projects.

Conclusion

Though this listing of grant givers and receivers is partial, it does provide a glimpse into the extensive interest that FOIA generates beyond deadline-driven journalism and public crisis attention. The social import of government information is clearly much more than a passing fancy of a few liberals or consciousness raising do-gooders. Real money from many professionals in all parts of the country has supported the continuing pursuit of government information available to all who care to know what government has done or is about to do.

Is Less Really More?

As we approach fifty years of experience with the Freedom of Information Act (FOIA), the relationship between access and protection is still uncomfortable. Almost every day there are stories and reports of information loss that cause millions of Americans to be concerned about identity theft. In February of 2007, the Federal Bureau of Investigation (FBI) admitted that three or four laptops were lost or stolen each month from the agency. The agency's inspector general noted, too, that it was not known if the dozens of missing laptops contained classified or sensitive information and was reported as saying, "more needs to be done."[1] Some information, however, the agency is clearly capable of protecting for a very long time. As previously noted, the agency frequently held reports about many distinguished non-political residents. Among the FBI files it was clear that special attention was given to Pearl Buck, Archibald MacLeish, Carl Sandburg, Edna St. Vincent Millay, and William Faulkner.[2]

Less clear was what could be done about the FBI's use of national security letters. Though the practice was initiated in the late 1970s, these carte blanche investigative tools were used hundreds of times per year. But during 2003, the number jumped to more than 39,000 and again in 2004 climbed to more than 56,000.[3] The FBI was warned in 2007 by Congress that it could lose the power to demand from communication and banking companies their customers' telephone, email, and financial records if it did not quickly solve the problems of information loss and abuse that had been brought to the attention of the House of Representatives' Judiciary Committee.[4]

Similarly there are revelations about overprotection that gave pause to those pursuing basic information about incarceration and court proceedings. In 2005 the Justice Department reportedly told a FOIA research group that about $373,000 would have to be paid before a search would begin. People for the American Way had requested any documents about the detention of those jailed after the September 11, 2001, attacks. The estimated charge was only for the agency's search time and would not cover copying and document preparation, according to Elliot M. Mincberg, legal counsel for People for the American Way Foundation.

Steven Aftergood joked in 2004 about his waiting for Air Force historical papers. He made a request in 1990, as director of the Federation of American Scientists' Project on Government Secrecy. "You almost expect them to ask you to designate a next of kin for when the document is ultimately released, because you won't be here," the 47-year-old Aftergood told a reporter.[5]

Some agencies have chosen to subcontract their FOIA responsibilities because budgets would not allow permanent hiring of new FOIA officers. Some of these contract workers were former officials who had retired from civil service, like William Ferroggiaro, past president of a nonprofit group that encourages FOIA use particularly among those working as information access professionals. Agencies reported to have contractors handling FOIA work include departments of Defense, Energy, State, Transportation, and the Transportation Security Administration. Companies that had accepted these contracts include CACI International Inc., McNeil Technologies, and FOIA Group Inc. The problem most feared by these contract companies is divulging what should be protected. Donald Kirkley, Jr., a McNeil company representative, told a reporter, "It only takes one mistake to hit the street. ... We'll be dead in the water."[6]

The contours of that line between overprotection and information loss are still being detailed. When the Texas Air National Guard records of President George W. Bush were requested again and again, the responses became the ever-present centerpiece of late-night television comedy.[7] When bogus documents were broadcast as part of a television report, the lack of credible information among government records should have served as a wake-up call. Instead, the incident only created a buzz among politicians and served as a slap to all Americans who are dependent on careful record keeping when they act as civil servants. Similarly, after John G. Roberts, Jr. was confirmed as the Supreme Court's Chief Justice, reporters were still trying to discover what happened to some of Roberts' work papers on the issue of affirmative action while he was an associate counsel in the Reagan White House administration.[8]

When the news that the National Archives had agreed to reclassify documents that had already been through a period of declassification, some researchers were nonplussed.[9] An example offered as "silly secrecy" included a March 9, 1971, chart provided by Defense Secretary Melvin R. Laird to the House of Representatives' Armed Services Committee. The graphic display included the fact that the United States had thirty strategic bomber squadrons, fifty-four Titan intercontinental ballistic missiles, and one thousand Minuteman missiles. This public record, part of the congressional hearings material more than thirty years ago, was redacted by January of 2006 so that none of the enumeration was evident on the chart. One analyst at the archive wrote, "The Pentagon is now trying to keep secret numbers of strategic weapons that have never been classified before. … It would be difficult to find more dramatic examples of unjustified secrecy than these decisions to classify the numbers of U.S. strategic weapons," William Burr reported.[10]

While reclassification remained a problem for researchers during the George W. Bush administration, there were struggles yet to be embraced. Not only was the administration working backwards through government papers, there were also efforts to curtail access to presidential papers in the future. It was reported in 2001 that a new order by President Bush required that "members of the public seeking particular documents [among presidential papers] show at least a demonstrated, specific need for them before they would be considered for release." The order also instructed the archivists to withhold papers if possible.[11] The order also instructed that an incumbent president may independently order the withholding of records, despite the instructions of a former president to release them.

Maarja Krusten, an archivist who handled President Richard M. Nixon's historical records at the National Archives and Records Administration, had a different take on the declassification system. Her experience with pressure to delete portions of the Watergate special prosecutor tapes led her to write a letter to the *Washington Post* in 2005. "We argued for referral [of our resistance to the deletion request] to a high-level board established by regulations to consider deletions the former president wanted," she wrote, but got no relief. "We sought the protection lawmakers had provided … but we failed in our pleas. It was as if Congress had never spoken." She closed her letter with the question, "Was our experience an aberration, or will power continue to trump regulations?"[12] The question might well have been lifted from James Russell Wiggins' 1956 book, *Freedom of Secrecy.*

Though there is little to find amusing among these reports, there was some mirth on the subject, in March, of the past several years when the National Security Archives' Rosemary Awards were announced. The National Security Archive is a nonprofit research organization that hosts a database of government information for public research. In 2007, the U.S. Air Force won the unflattering title, named after Rose Mary Woods, President Richard M. Nixon's secretary who accidentally erased eighteen and one-half minutes of a key Watergate conversation tape. Recognized for "the worst Freedom of Information Act performance by a federal agency," the Air Force won on the basis of a U.S. district court opinion that cited the agency's miserable record for meeting FOIA deadlines, according to the NSA's announcement March 16, 2007. The CIA was named the 2006 recipient of the award for its creative use of a "neither confirm nor deny" response to a request for records on the relationship between Taliban leader Mullah Omar and Osama bin Laden.[13]

Standards for Success

Beyond jokes and hand-wringing, how should we evaluate the usefulness and success of FOIA? What are the grounds for deciding if the gains from making public all that government information offsets the costs to government efficiency and perhaps some citizens' privacy? While these questions must be asked and answered here, there are prior questions that must be asserted and affirmed as well. These first questions include queries about the value of a representative democracy as a government model, and if we agree upon this form of government as one to be preserved, then how best can we sustain an informed constituency which is the percolating element of a representative democracy.

This book is not, nor was it intended to be, an assessment of government forms or the evolution of representative democracies. It does not intend to argue the issue of adequate bureaucracies for sustaining government for the people, by the people, and of the people. Let us assume, then, that we are in favor of the present form of the U.S. representative democracy and move on to thinking about best practices for an electorate that is responsive and the elected who are responsible to the public. It is evident in the historical examples among the early chapters of this book that the government and public have experimented with a balance of give and take between branches of government and with the citizenry. As Clark Hoyt, a career Washington, D.C., newspaper correspondent, told a House of Representatives government reform committee in 2007, "the free flow of government information isn't a partisan issue. It isn't a liberal versus conservative issue. Regardless of party or political philosophy ... everyone can agree that the government's information is the people's information."[14]

As the British colonies in America began the hard work of forming a new kind of government, Thomas Jefferson captured the spirit of the founding framers' intentions when he wrote, "The basis of our government being the opinion of the people, the very first object should be to keep that right." The means to that end that Jefferson went on to describe was through an unfettered press. "The way to prevent these irregular interpositions of the people is to give them full information of their affairs through the channel of the public papers, and to contrive that those papers should penetrate the whole mass of the people."[15] Jefferson's reference to public newspapers here was meant to distinguish a publicly available but privately owned press from the government licensed press known in the British colonies. Nearly two hundred years later, however, even the most ardent newspaper advocates were cautious of an unfettered press even in the best of times. James Russell Wiggins wrote, "A people whose government interposes no restraints upon the freedom of any medium of information still might be informed inadequately upon the transactions of its public agencies and about the life around it."[16]

Newspapers and the Private Sector Model

Evidence of the failure of public newspapers as the central means of information dissemination was unmistakable at all times during the nation's struggle for successful leadership. Alexis de Tocqueville, a French political observer and visitor to the relatively new United States, was rather famously quoted as characterizing American newspapers. "Three quarters of the enormous sheets are filled with advertisements, and the remainder is frequently occupied by political intelligence or trivial anecdotes."[17] The relatively small measure of government news, sandwiched in among the "political intelligence or trivial anecdotes," does not suggest an outstanding forum for assessing government's performance based on reports of fact. The newspaper industry evolved in both form, such as tabloid and smaller broadsheets, and content, such as crusader journalism, beats, yellow journalism, new journalism, and community journalism.

The complaints against, and casualties of modern journalism, at every stage of American history, are legion. One need go no further than the media critics of the day, or the letters to the editor of any local newspapers to see evidence of the industry's shortcomings. Clearly media still thrive on carrying the news; it has been so in every era of America's development. When government makes information available the media usually takes advantage of distributing what seems relevant or important to subscribers and viewers. It would seem, then, that the essence of news media fulfils the general designs of a democratic politic. Why, then, does the government pushback seem to be omnipresent?

Government and the Public Sector Model

Samuel Archibald, a member of the House subcommittee staff that helped John Moss bring FOIA to life, wrote in a 1993 *Political Science and Politics* article that "the effectiveness of laws on access to government information depends upon ... the will of the government ... to make participatory democracy work in the Information Age." That government will include, by Archibald's reckoning, an executive branch that honors open records provisions, a judiciary that enforced access provisions, and a legislature that stands up for the public's right to know if the law is weakly enforced by other branches of government.[18]

Government initiatives since the tussle between President George Washington and the first congress have included a depository libraries system that provides distribution to all voting districts of the legislative activities and selected agency materials, described more fully in a previous chapter of this book. The failures of this system involve the limits of local support for the facility of the libraries and the selection of materials to be stored and accessible. Another attempt at getting government information to the governed was the Housekeeping Act and its variations, also described at length in earlier chapters. The Freedom of Information Act, though a substantial reach forward in the tussle among administrative branches of government and the electorate, is still just one means of making government information available. It has been a halting effort, lurching in fits and starts as if trying to find its way among the ruins of previous efforts to get government information out of the bureaucracy and into the electorate. The failures of FOIA particularly include the uneven administration of the law and the requirement that citizens know *what* to request among their government's information stores when asking for documents.

Less or More of What?

The shortcomings of government law efforts have been frequently chronicled in news reports and in this book. The details are instructive, but the results are not attractive. The successes may be many, but the failures are just as numerous and in some cases horrific. If public newspapers have also failed to provide for adequate information about government activities, and the law through congressional efforts has failed to open the doors of access to government records, what should be done?

Clearly there needs to be an information stream that stimulates a well-informed public that can appropriately pressure and engage its representatives in the government. What then *will* work in supporting this aspect of government life? Archibald's assertion that information access depends on the will of the government is the elephant in the room of FOIA's success or failure. Government information access should *not* depend on the willingness of government, any more than a fair trial should depend on the willingness of the sitting judge, or tax levees on the whims of an officer. The purpose of a constitution and a bill of rights is to ensure that government acts within parameters agreed to by all, rather than the druthers of a particular administration.

If, then, we agree that a representative democracy cannot succeed without a well-informed electorate, a central tenet—a right among those like free speech, a right to assemble, a fair trial, no quartering of troops, equal rights, etc.—ought to be a right to all information about government activity. This assertion of a right to government information will, of course, open the door—flood gates in fact—to all sorts of complaints leveled at all the previously listed rights. Free speech, for example, some say has led to ugly, mean, divisive language; the right to assemble has prompted labor unrest and civil rights, student protests, and antiwar demonstrations; fair trials are fraught with errors and releases where everyone knows who is guilty. The list of grievances against perpetuating a bill of rights began as the Constitution was forming and lives on today. The fact, however, is that nearly every day the need for that set of rights is brought to light where government will has proven to be an ill will.

That said, the avenues to being well-informed should not, perhaps, be left to the will of the government that might on occasion have a vested interest in keeping the electorate uninformed. Perhaps the model to be working from in supporting a well-informed constituency that sustains a vigorous representative democracy, instead, should be one that expects those in public office to push, rather than hold back, information by putting it into the hands and before the faces of those it serves. Whether it is read, evaluated, digested, and swallowed by the public should be irrelevant to the model. The public should not have to ask for, but should receive government activity reports without delay and without question, in the same way that public education does not rely on students asking for instructional materials but on teachers who are expected to provide those materials in full to all, regardless of attention span or level of interest.

The short answer, then, to this question of FOIA success is that FOIA and all the other efforts in prompting government information access have not worked because the premise for success is based on a wrong-headed model. The success of FOIA and access to government information should not be considered by the number of documents released or the speed with which requests are dispatched.

The success of FOIA ought to be based on the reduced need for requests and diminished stress on FOIA officers. The answer to the question ought to be based on a presumption of pushing government information out of the bureaucracy, rather than a model that requires citizens to pull the information out of government offices. What this means is that there should be *less* law about the way requests are to be made, to whom, and under what conditions and at what cost when citizens want to know what government has done, or has collected or is planning to do. Rather there should be more presumption that government employees must get the information to us all in a timely and useful form so that we all know and can assess this government that is supposed to be by the people, for the people, and of the people.

This expansive answer, however, does not address the specifics of the special sorts of problems with privacy and database security that the system of information collected and administered now by the government would require. The more detailed legal solutions ought to be found among the many years of FOIA experience already examined for flaws and successes in the previous chapters. Though the examples of FOIA's successes and shortcomings were framed with the current FOIA structure in mind, they serve as a template for locating many of the trouble spots that will need to be reassessed if and when a broader stance on government information access is formalized.

Among the more pronounced difficulties for FOIA use has been the concern about protecting citizens' privacy. Though not addressed specifically among these pages describing the history of FOIA, the issue does require some consideration when ciphering models for the handling of government information. A right to privacy is, in a certain way, like a right to government information access. It seems so obvious in the social contract that binds a representative democracy that the founding documents include no such language. This non-specified right has been cobbled together from court decisions and a parallel series of legislative acts and administrative initiatives, much like the FOIA history.

The handling of safeguards for privacy have been as tenuous, too, as the safeguards for government information access, though few would argue wholeheartedly for abolishment of these rights. Privacy rights, however, are already breached in many ways, just as access to information rights are breached in many ways now. It is this constant updating of exceptions, both cases, which ought to serve as a warning that the system is not as well conceived as it stands.

Many citizens give away privacy rights when they seek a loan or a credit card, deposit or withdraw large sums of money in a bank or credit union if government suspects money laundering or illegal handling. Visits to the doctor or other health care services may result in privacy surrender if government believes that there is a greater social concern to be addressed—disease or system mismanagement, for example. Surveillance by government agencies of private citizens who traverse public buildings or spaces has become so common place that it is routinely an expected component in television crime genre entertainment.

In the specific cases of FOIA requests, some researchers simply want to see what government agencies are holding about hapless citizens who find their way into the vast stores of all these collections. Often the standard for protecting these caches of individuals' identifying information, deemed as private, has been to require that when government databases are inspected under FOIA these records must be stripped of such personally identifying markers as names and faces. Data is made available in this way for use in aggregate studies or to indicate trends and patterns.

When seekers of government records want to know the details about individuals' treatment, government officers usually bar the way with claims of protecting individuals' rights of privacy. This standard is intended to keep prying eyes from creating embarrassment for those unlucky enough to find themselves among a scrutinized group. In some cases, however, researchers have convinced a few of the individuals discovered to be in such a group that having broader knowledge about the database may enhance their chances of getting the government to put right what researchers suspect is a government-administered wrong. How should the law, then, balance the citizen's right of privacy with the sometimes-competing right of access to government information?

The question need not be answered with an either/or solution if the model of access to government information just described is embraced wholly. If the premise of access to government information is to know how and what government is doing, then privacy need not be breached except in the interest of knowing that government is doing what it should be doing or what citizens expect it to do. The best interest of any individual is to be sure that he or she is treated by the government in every way at least as well as the neighbors are treated.

Laws that inhibit the circulation of information that then lead to knowledge about government activity ought to be few, and held under strict, reviewable circumstances. Otherwise, the voting public may be left with the belief that its bureaucrats are willing to accept the electorate's judgment at times of election, but untrusting of that electorate's judgment about the government's job performance—election without accountability. James Russell Wiggins closes his 1956 book, *Freedom of Secrecy*, with an apt observation. "A government that generally asserts the right to say which of its acts may be divulged and which must be concealed exercises a power that tends to tyranny whatever its outward form."

Too frequently the government office holders have engaged in public relations tactics only to highlight the benefits of a program or effort and minimize the problems or deficits. Sometimes the public finds out, sometimes it is too late, and always the country pays a price for hidden agendas. Access to government information is not a panacea for right thinking or perfect progress. But without broad distribution of all the available information, knowledge as the basis for sound government decisions is just a pipe dream and the best laid plans are a figment of political imagination.

APPENDIX A

Title 5. Government Organization and Employees

Part I. The Agencies Generally

Chapter 5. Administrative Procedure

SubChapter II. Administrative Procedure

5 Uscs § 552

Sept. 6, 1966, P.L. 89–554, § 1,80 Stat. 383;
June 5, 1967, P.L. 90–23 § 1,81 Stat. 54;
Nov. 21, 1974, P.L. 93–502, §§ 1–3,88 Stat. 1561, 1563, 1564;
Sept. 13, 1976, P.L. 94–409, § 5(b),90 Stat. 1247;
Oct. 13, 1978, P.L. 95–454, Title IX, § 906(a)(10),92 Stat. 1225;
Nov. 8, 1984, P.L. 98–620, Title IV, Subtitle A, § 402(2),98 Stat. 3357;
Oct. 27, 1986, P.L. 99–570, Title I, Subtitle N, §§ 1802, 1803,100 Stat. 3207–48, 3207–49;
Oct. 2, 1996, P.L. 104–231, §§ 3–11,110 Stat. 3049;
Nov. 27, 2002, P.L. 107–306, Title III, Subtitle B, § 312,116 Stat. 2390.

§ 552. Public information; agency rules, opinions, orders, records, and proceedings

(a) Each agency shall make available to the public information as follows:

   (1) Each agency shall separately state and currently publish in the Federal Register for the guidance of the public-

    (A) descriptions of its central and field organization and the established places at which, the employees (and in the case of a uniformed service, the members) from whom, and the methods whereby, the public may obtain information, make submittals or requests, or obtain decisions;

    (B) statements of the general course and method by which its functions are channeled and determined, including the nature and requirements of all formal and informal procedures available;

    (C) rules of procedure, descriptions of forms available or the places at which forms may be obtained, and instructions as to the scope and contents of all papers, reports, or examinations;

    (D) substantive rules of general applicability adopted as authorized by law, and statements of general policy or interpretations of general applicability formulated and adopted by the agency; and

    (E) each amendment, revision, or repeal of the foregoing.

Except to the extent that a person has actual and timely notice of the terms thereof, a person may not in any manner be required to resort to, or be adversely affected by, a matter required to be published in the Federal Register and not so published. For the purpose of this paragraph, matter reasonably available to the class of persons affected thereby is deemed published in the Federal Register when incorporated by reference therein with the approval of the Director of the Federal Register.

    (2) Each agency, in accordance with published rules, shall make available for public inspection and copying-

    (A) final opinions, including concurring and dissenting opinions, as well as orders, made in the adjudication of cases;

    (B) those statements of policy and interpretations which have been adopted by the agency and are not published in the Federal Register;

    (C) administrative staff manuals and instructions to staff that affect a member of the public;

    (D) copies of all records, regardless of form or format, which have been released to any person under paragraph (3) and which, because of the nature of their subject matter, the agency determines have become or are likely to become the subject of subsequent requests for substantially the same records; and

    (E) a general index of the records referred to under subparagraph (D);

unless the materials are promptly published and copies offered for sale. For records created on or after November 1, 1996, within one year after such date, each agency shall make such records available, including by computer telecommunications or, if computer telecommunications means have not been established by the agency, by other electronic means. To the extent required to prevent a clearly unwarranted invasion of personal privacy, an agency may delete identifying details when it makes available or publishes an opinion, statement of policy, interpretation, staff manual, instruction, or copies of records referred to in subparagraph (D). However, in each case the justification for the deletion shall be explained fully in writing, and the extent of such deletion shall be indicated on the portion of the record which is made available or published, unless including that indication would harm an interest protected by the exemption in subsection (b) under which the deletion is made. If technically feasible, the extent of the deletion shall be indicated at the place in the record where the deletion was made. Each agency shall also maintain and make available for public inspection and copying current indexes providing identifying information for the public as to any matter issued, adopted, or promulgated after July 4, 1967, and required by this paragraph to be made available or published. Each agency shall make the index referred to in subparagraph (E) available by computer telecommunications by December 31, 1999. Each agency shall promptly publish, quarterly or more frequently, and distribute (by sale or otherwise) copies of each index or supplements thereto unless it determines by order published in the Federal Register that the publication would be unnecessary and impracticable, in which case the agency shall nonetheless provide copies of such index on request at a cost not to exceed the direct cost of duplication. A final order, opinion, statement of policy, interpretation, or staff manual or instruction that affects a member of the public may be relied on, used, or cited as precedent by an agency against a party other than an agency only if-

    (i)   it has been indexed and either made available or published as provided by this paragraph; or

    (ii) the party has actual and timely notice of the terms thereof.

(3)

    (A) Except with respect to the records made available under paragraphs (1) and (2) of this subsection, and except as provided in subparagraph (E), each agency, upon any request for records which (i) reasonably describes such records and (ii) is made in accordance with published rules stating the time, place, fees (if any), and procedures to be followed, shall make the records promptly available to any person.

    (B) In making any record available to a person under this paragraph, an agency shall provide the record in any form or format requested by the person if the record is readily reproducible by the agency in that form or format. Each agency shall make reasonable efforts to maintain its records in forms or formats that are reproducible for purposes of this section.

    (C) In responding under this paragraph to a request for records, an agency shall make reasonable efforts to search for the records in electronic form or format, except when such efforts would significantly interfere with the operation of the agency's automated information system.

    (D) For purposes of this paragraph, the term "search" means to review, manually or by automated means, agency records for the purpose of locating those records which are responsive to a request.

(E) An agency, or part of an agency, that is an element of the intelligence community (as that term is defined in section 3(4) of the National Security Act of 1947 (50 U.S.C. 401a(4))) shall not make any record available under this paragraph to-

(i) any government entity, other than a State, territory, commonwealth, or district of the United States, or any subdivision thereof; or

(ii) a representative of a government entity described in clause (i).

(4)

(A)

(i) In order to carry out the provisions of this section, each agency shall promulgate regulations, pursuant to notice and receipt of public comment, specifying the schedule of fees applicable to the processing of requests under this section and establishing procedures and guidelines for determining when such fees should be waived or reduced. Such schedule shall conform to the guidelines which shall be promulgated, pursuant to notice and receipt of public comment, by the Director of the Office of Management and Budget and which shall provide for a uniform schedule of fees for all agencies.

(ii) Such agency regulations shall provide that-

(I) fees shall be limited to reasonable standard charges for document search, duplication, and review, when records are requested for commercial use;

(II) fees shall be limited to reasonable standard charges for document duplication when records are not sought for commercial use and the request is made by an educational or noncommercial scientific institution, whose purpose is scholarly or scientific research; or a representative of the news media; and

(III) for any request not described in (I) or (II), fees shall be limited to reasonable standard charges for document search and duplication.

(iii) Documents shall be furnished without any charge or at a charge reduced below the fees established under clause (ii) if disclosure of the information is in the public interest because it is likely to contribute significantly to public understanding of the operations or activities of the government and is not primarily in the commercial interest of the requester.

(iv) Fee schedules shall provide for the recovery of only the direct costs of search, duplication, or review. Review costs shall include only the direct costs incurred during the initial examination of a document for the purposes of determining whether the documents must be disclosed under this section and for the purposes of withholding any portions exempt from disclosure under this section. Review costs may not include any costs incurred in resolving issues of law or policy that may be raised in the course of processing a request under this section. No fee may be charged by any agency under this section-

  (I) if the costs of routine collection and processing of the fee are likely to equal or exceed the amount of the fee; or
  (II) for any request described in clause (ii)(II) or (III) of this subparagraph for the first two hours of search time or for the first one hundred pages of duplication.

(v) No agency may require advance payment of any fee unless the requester has previously failed to pay fees in a timely fashion, or the agency has determined that the fee will exceed $ 250.

(vi) Nothing in this subparagraph shall supersede fees chargeable under a statute specifically providing for setting the level of fees for particular types of records.

(vii) In any action by a requester regarding the waiver of fees under this section, the court shall determine the matter de novo: *Provided,* That the court's review of the matter shall be limited to the record before the agency.

(B) On complaint, the district court of the United States in the district in which the complainant resides, or has his principal place of business, or in which the agency records are situated, or in the District of Columbia, has jurisdiction to enjoin the agency from withholding agency records and to order the production of any agency records improperly withheld from the complainant. In such a case the court shall determine the matter de novo, and may examine the contents of such agency records in camera to determine whether such records or any part thereof shall be withheld under any of the exemptions set forth in subsection (b) of this section, and the burden is on the agency to sustain its action. In addition to any other matters to which a court accords substantial weight, a court shall accord substantial weight to an affidavit of an agency concerning the agency's determination as to technical feasibility under paragraph (2)(C) and subsection (b) and reproducibility under paragraph (3)(B).

(C) Notwithstanding any other provision of law, the defendant shall serve an answer or otherwise plead to any complaint made under this subsection within thirty days after service upon the defendant of the pleading in which such complaint is made, unless the court otherwise directs for good cause shown.

(D) [Repealed]

(E) The court may assess against the United States reasonable attorney fees and other litigation costs reasonably incurred in any case under this section in which the complainant has substantially prevailed.

(F) Whenever the court orders the production of any agency records improperly withheld from the complainant and assesses against the United States reasonable attorney fees and other litigation costs, and the court additionally issues a written finding that the circumstances surrounding the withholding raise questions whether agency personnel acted arbitrarily or capriciously with respect to the withholding, the Special Counsel shall promptly initiate a proceeding to determine whether disciplinary action is warranted against the officer or employee who was primarily responsible for the withholding. The Special Counsel, after investigation and consideration of the evidence submitted, shall submit his findings and recommendations to the administrative authority of the agency concerned and shall send copies of the findings and recommendations to the officer or employee or his representative. The administrative authority shall take the corrective action that the Special Counsel recommends.

(G) In the event of noncompliance with the order of the court, the district court may punish for contempt the responsible employee, and in the case of a uniformed service, the responsible member.

(5) Each agency having more than one member shall maintain and make available for public inspection a record of the final votes of each member in every agency proceeding.

(6)

(A) Each agency, upon any request for records made under paragraph (1), (2), or (3) of this subsection, shall-

(i) determine within 20 days (excepting Saturdays, Sundays, and legal public holidays) after the receipt of any such request whether to comply with such request and shall immediately notify the person making such request of such determination and the reasons therefore, and of the right of such person to appeal to the head of the agency any adverse determination; and

(ii) make a determination with respect to any appeal within twenty days (excepting Saturdays, Sundays, and legal public holidays) after the receipt of such appeal. If on appeal the denial of the request for records is in whole or in part upheld, the agency shall notify the person making such request of the provisions for judicial review of that determination under paragraph (4) of this subsection.

(B)

(i)   In unusual circumstances as specified in this subparagraph, the time limits prescribed in either clause (i) or clause (ii) of subparagraph (A) may be extended by written notice to the person making such request setting forth the unusual circumstances for such extension and the date on which a determination is expected to be dispatched. No such notice shall specify a date that would result in an extension for more than ten working days, except as provided in clause (ii) of this subparagraph.

(ii) With respect to a request for which a written notice under clause (i) extends the time limits prescribed under clause (i) of subparagraph (A), the agency shall notify the person making the request if the request cannot be processed within the time limit specified in that clause and shall provide the person an opportunity to limit the scope of the request so that it may be processed within that time limit or an opportunity to arrange with the agency an alternative time frame for processing the request or a modified request. Refusal by the person to reasonably modify the request or arrange such an alternative time frame shall be considered as a factor in determining whether exceptional circumstances exist for purposes of subparagraph (C).

(iii) As used in this subparagraph, "unusual circumstances" means, but only to the extent reasonably necessary to the proper processing of the particular requests-

   (I)   the need to search for and collect the requested records from field facilities or other establishments that are separate from the office processing the request;

   (II) the need to search for, collect, and appropriately examine a voluminous amount of separate and distinct records which are demanded in a single request; or

   (III) the need for consultation, which shall be conducted with all practicable speed, with another agency having a substantial interest in the determination of the request or among two or more components of the agency having substantial subject-matter interest therein.

(iv) Each agency may promulgate regulations, pursuant to notice and receipt of public comment, providing for the aggregation of certain requests by the same requestor, or by a group of requestors acting in concert, if the agency reasonably believes that such requests actually constitute a single request, which would otherwise satisfy the unusual circumstances specified in this subparagraph, and the requests involve clearly related matters. Multiple requests involving unrelated matters shall not be aggregated.

(C)

    (i) Any person making a request to any agency for records under paragraph (1), (2), or (3) of this subsection shall be deemed to have exhausted his administrative remedies with respect to such request if the agency fails to comply with the applicable time limit provisions of this paragraph. If the Government can show exceptional circumstances exist and that the agency is exercising due diligence in responding to the request, the court may retain jurisdiction and allow the agency additional time to complete its review of the records. Upon any determination by an agency to comply with a request for records, the records shall be made promptly available to such person making such request. Any notification of denial of any request for records under this subsection shall set forth the names and titles or positions of each person responsible for the denial of such request.

    (ii) For purposes of this subparagraph, the term "exceptional circumstances" does not include a delay that results from a predictable agency workload of requests under this section, unless the agency demonstrates reasonable progress in reducing its backlog of pending requests.

    (iii) Refusal by a person to reasonably modify the scope of a request or arrange an alternative time frame for processing a request (or a modified request) under clause (ii) after being given an opportunity to do so by the agency to whom the person made the request shall be considered as a factor in determining whether exceptional circumstances exist for purposes of this subparagraph.

(D)

    (i) Each agency may promulgate regulations, pursuant to notice and receipt of public comment, providing for multitrack processing of requests for records based on the amount of work or time (or both) involved in processing requests.

    (ii) Regulations under this subparagraph may provide a person making a request that does not qualify for the fastest multitrack processing an opportunity to limit the scope of the request in order to qualify for faster processing.

    (iii) This subparagraph shall not be considered to affect the requirement under subparagraph (C) to exercise due diligence.

(E)

    (i) Each agency shall promulgate regulations, pursuant to notice and receipt of public comment, providing for expedited processing of requests for records-

        (I) in cases in which the person requesting the records demonstrates a compelling need; and

        (II) in other cases determined by the agency.

  (ii) Notwithstanding clause (i), regulations under this subparagraph must ensure-

        (I) that a determination of whether to provide expedited processing shall be made, and notice of the determination shall be provided to the person making the request, within 10 days after the date of the request; and

        (II) expeditious consideration of administrative appeals of such determinations of whether to provide expedited processing.

  (iii) An agency shall process as soon as practicable any request for records to which the agency has granted expedited processing under this subparagraph. Agency action to deny or affirm denial of a request for expedited processing pursuant to this subparagraph, and failure by an agency to respond in a timely manner to such a request shall be subject to judicial review under paragraph (4), except that the judicial review shall be based on the record before the agency at the time of the determination.

  (iv) A district court of the United States shall not have jurisdiction to review an agency denial of expedited processing of a request for records after the agency has provided a complete response to the request.

  (v) For purposes of this subparagraph, the term "compelling need" means-

        (I) that a failure to obtain requested records on an expedited basis under this paragraph could reasonably be expected to pose an imminent threat to the life or physical safety of an individual; or

        (II) with respect to a request made by a person primarily engaged in disseminating information, urgency to inform the public concerning actual or alleged Federal Government activity.

  (vi) A demonstration of a compelling need by a person making a request for expedited processing shall be made by a statement certified by such person to be true and correct to the best of such person's knowledge and belief.

(F) In denying a request for records, in whole or in part, an agency shall make a reasonable effort to estimate the volume of any requested matter the provision of which is denied, and shall provide any such estimate to the person making the request, unless providing such estimate would harm an interest protected by the exemption in subsection (b) pursuant to which the denial is made.

(b) This section does not apply to matters that are-

   (1) (A) specifically authorized under criteria established by an Executive order to be kept secret in the interest of national defense or foreign policy and (B) are in fact properly classified pursuant to such Executive order;

   (2) related solely to the internal personnel rules and practices of an agency;

   (3) specifically exempted from disclosure by statute (other than section 552b of this title) provided that such statute (A) requires that the matters be withheld from the public in such a manner as to leave no discretion on the issue, or (B) establishes particular criteria for withholding or refers to particular types of matters to be withheld;

   (4) trade secrets and commercial or financial information obtained from a person and privileged or confidential;

   (5) inter-agency or intra-agency memorandums or letters which would not be available by law to a party other than an agency in litigation with the agency;

   (6) personnel and medical files and similar files the disclosure of which would constitute a clearly unwarranted invasion of personal privacy;

   (7) records or information compiled for law enforcement purposes, but only to the extent that the production of such law enforcement records or information (A) could reasonably be expected to interfere with enforcement proceedings, (B) would deprive a person of a right to a fair trial or an impartial adjudication, (C) could reasonably be expected to constitute an unwarranted invasion of personal privacy, (D) could reasonably be expected to disclose the identity of a confidential source, including a State, local, or foreign agency or authority or any private institution which furnished information on a confidential basis, and, in the case of a record or information compiled by criminal law enforcement authority in the course of a criminal investigation or by an agency conducting a lawful national security intelligence investigation, information furnished by a confidential source, (E) would disclose techniques and procedures for law enforcement investigations or prosecutions, or would disclose guidelines for law enforcement investigations or prosecutions if such disclosure could reasonably be expected to risk circumvention of the law, or (F) could reasonably be expected to endanger the life or physical safety of any individual;

   (8) contained in or related to examination, operating, or condition reports prepared by, on behalf of, or for the use of an agency responsible for the regulation or supervision of financial institutions; or

   (9) geological or geophysical information and data, including maps, concerning wells.

Any reasonably segregable portion of a record shall be provided to any person requesting such record after deletion of the portions which are exempt under this subsection. The amount of information deleted shall be indicated on the released portion of the record, unless including that indication would harm an interest protected by the exemption in this subsection under which the deletion is made. If technically feasible, the amount of the information deleted shall be indicated at the place in the record where such deletion is made.

(c)

    (1) Whenever a request is made which involves access to records described in subsection (b)(7)(A) and-

        (A) the investigation or proceeding involves a possible violation of criminal law; and

        (B) there is reason to believe that (i) the subject of the investigation or proceeding is not aware of its pendency, and (ii) disclosure of the existence of the records could reasonably be expected to interfere with enforcement proceedings,

the agency may, during only such time as that circumstance continues, treat the records as not subject to the requirements of this section.

    (2) Whenever informant records maintained by a criminal law enforcement agency under an informant's name or personal identifier are requested by a third party according to the informant's name or personal identifier, the agency may treat the records as not subject to the requirements of this section unless the informant's status as an informant has been officially confirmed.

    (3) Whenever a request is made which involves access to records maintained by the Federal Bureau of Investigation pertaining to foreign intelligence or counterintelligence, or international terrorism, and the existence of the records is classified information as provided in subsection (b)(1), the Bureau may, as long as the existence of the records remains classified information, treat the records as not subject to the requirements of this section.

(d) This section does not authorize withholding of information or limit the availability of records to the public, except as specifically stated in this section. This section is not authority to withhold information from Congress.

(e)

    (1) On or before February 1 of each year, each agency shall submit to the Attorney General of the United States a report which shall cover the preceding fiscal year and which shall include-

        (A) the number of determinations made by the agency not to comply with requests for records made to such agency under subsection (a) and the reasons for each such determination;

(B)

    (i)   the number of appeals made by persons under subsection (a)(6), the result of such appeals, and the reason for the action upon each appeal that results in a denial of information; and

    (ii)   a complete list of all statutes that the agency relies upon to authorize the agency to withhold information under subsection (b)(3), a description of whether a court has upheld the decision of the agency to withhold information under each such statute, and a concise description of the scope of any information withheld;

(C)   the number of requests for records pending before the agency as of September 30 of the preceding year, and the median number of days that such requests had been pending before the agency as of that date;

(D)   the number of requests for records received by the agency and the number of requests which the agency processed;

(E)   the median number of days taken by the agency to process different types of requests;

(F)   the total amount of fees collected by the agency for processing requests; and

(G)   the number of full-time staff of the agency devoted to processing requests for records under this section, and the total amount expended by the agency for processing such requests.

(2)   Each agency shall make each such report available to the public including by computer telecommunications, or if computer telecommunications means have not been established by the agency, by other electronic means.

(3)   The Attorney General of the United States shall make each report which has been made available by electronic means available at a single electronic access point. The Attorney General of the United States shall notify the Chairman and ranking minority member of the Committee on Government Reform and Oversight of the House of Representatives and the Chairman and ranking minority member of the Committees on Governmental Affairs and the Judiciary of the Senate, no later than April 1 of the year in which each such report is issued, that such reports are available by electronic means.

(4)   The Attorney General of the United States, in consultation with the Director of the Office of Management and Budget, shall develop reporting and performance guidelines in connection with reports required by this subsection by October 1, 1997, and may establish additional requirements for such reports as the Attorney General determines may be useful.

(5)   The Attorney General of the United States shall submit an annual report on or before April 1 of each calendar year which shall include for the prior calendar year a listing of the number of cases arising under this section,

the exemption involved in each case, the disposition of such case, and the cost, fees, and penalties assessed under subparagraphs (E), (F), and (G) of subsection (a)(4). Such report shall also include a description of the efforts undertaken by the Department of Justice to encourage agency compliance with this section.

(f) For purposes of this section, the term-

(1) "agency" as defined in section 551(1) of this title [5 USCS § 551(1)] includes any executive department, military department, Government corporation, Government controlled corporation, or other establishment in the executive branch of the Government (including the Executive Office of the President), or any independent regulatory agency; and

(2) "record" and any other term used in this section in reference to information includes any information that would be an agency record subject to the requirements of this section when maintained by an agency in any format, including an electronic format.

(g) The head of each agency shall prepare and make publicly available upon request, reference material or a guide for requesting records or information from the agency, subject to the exemptions in subsection (b), including-

(1) an index of all major information systems of the agency;

(2) a description of major information and record locator systems maintained by the agency; and

(3) a handbook for obtaining various types and categories of public information from the agency pursuant to chapter 35 of title 44 [44 USCS §§ 3501 et seq.], and under this section.

1966 Act

5 USC Sec. 1002, June 11, 1946, ch 324, Sec. 3,60 Stat. 238.

In subsection (b)(3), the words "formulated and" are omitted as surplusage. In the last sentence of subsection (b), the words "in any manner" are omitted as surplusage since the prohibition is all inclusive.

Standard changes are made to conform with the definitions applicable and the style of this title as outlined in the preface to the report.

1967 Act

Section 1 [of Pub. L. 90-23] amends section 552 of title 5, United States Code, to reflect-Public Law 89-487.

In subsection (a)(1)(A), the words "employees (and in the case of a uniformed service, the member)" are substituted for "officer" to retain the coverage of Public Law 89-487 and to conform to the definitions in 5 U.S.C. 2101, 2104, and 2105.

In the last sentence of subsection (a)(2), the words "A final order ... may be relied on ... only if" are substituted for "No final order ... may be relied upon ... unless"; and the words "a party other than an agency" and "the party" are substituted for "a private party" and "the private party", respectively, on authority of the definition of "private party" in 5 App. U.S.C. 1002(g).

In subsection (a)(3), the words "the responsible employee, and in the case of a uniformed service, the responsible member" are substituted for "the responsible officers" to retain the coverage of ◆ Public Law 89-487 and to conform to the definitions in 5 U.S.C. 2101, 2104, and 2105.

In subsection (a)(4), the words "shall maintain and make available for public inspection a record" are substituted for "shall keep a record ... and that record shall be available for public inspection."

In subsection (b)(5) and (7), the words "a party other than an agency" are substituted for "a private party" on authority of the definition of "private party" in 5 App. U.S.C. 1002(g).

In subsection (c), the words "This section does not authorize" and "This section is not authority" are substituted for "Nothing in this section authorizes" and "nor shall this section be authority," respectively.

5 App. U.S.C. 1002(g), defining "private party" to mean a party other than an agency, is omitted since the words "party other than an agency" are substituted for the words "private party" wherever they appear in revised 5 U.S.C. 552.

5 App. U.S.C. 1002(h), prescribing the effective date, is omitted as unnecessary. That effective date is prescribed by section 4 of this bill.

Amendments

1967. Act June 5, 1967 (effective 7/4/67, as provided by § 3 of such Act, which appears as a note to this section) substituted this section for one which read:

§ 552. Publication of information, rules, opinions, orders, and public records

(a) This section applies, according to the provisions thereof, except to the extent that there is involved-

   (1) a function of the United States requiring secrecy in the public interest; or

   (2) a matter relating solely to the internal management of an agency.

(b) Each agency shall separately state and currently publish in the Federal Register-

   (1) descriptions of its central and field organizations, including delegations of final authority by the agency, and the established places at which, and methods whereby, the public may obtain information or make submittals or requests;

(2) statements of the general course and method by which its functions are channeled and determined, including the nature and requirements of the formal or informal procedures available and forms and instructions as to the scope and contents of all papers, reports, or examinations; and

(3) substantive rules adopted as authorized by law and statements of general policy or interpretations adopted by the agency for public guidance, except rules addressed to and served on named persons in accordance with law.

A person may not be required to resort to organization or procedure not so published.

(c) Each agency shall publish or, in accordance with published rule, make available to public inspection all final opinions or orders in the adjudication of cases (except those required for good cause to be held confidential and not cited as precedents) and all rules.

"(d) Except as otherwise required by statute, matters of official record shall be made available, in accordance with published rule, to persons properly and directly concerned, except information held confidential for good cause found.

1974. Act Nov. 21, 1974 (effective as provided by § 4 of such Act, which appears as a note to this section), in subsec. (a), in para. (2), substituted "Each agency shall also maintain and make available for public inspection and copying current indexes providing identifying information for the public as to any matter issued, adopted, or promulgated after July 4, 1967, and required by this paragraph to be made available or published. Each agency shall promptly publish, quarterly or more frequently, and distribute (by sale or otherwise) copies of each index or supplements thereto unless it determines by order published in the Federal Register that the publication would be unnecessary and impracticable, in which case the agency shall nonetheless provide copies of such index on request at a cost not to exceed the direct cost of duplication." for "Each agency also shall maintain and make available for public inspection and copying a current index providing identifying information for the public as to any matter issued, adopted, or promulgated after July 4, 1967, and required by this paragraph to be made available or published." substituted para. (3) for one which read: "Except with respect to the records made available under paragraphs (1) and (2) of this subsection, each agency, on request for identifiable records made in accordance with published rules stating the time, place, fees to the extent authorized by statute, and procedure to be followed, shall make the records promptly available to any person. On complaint, the district court of the United States in the district in which the complainant resides, or has his principal place of business, or in which the agency records are situated, has jurisdiction to enjoin the agency from withholding agency records and to order the production of any agency records improperly withheld from the complainant. In such a case the court shall determine the matter de novo and the burden is on the agency to sustain its action. In the event of noncompliance with the order of the court, the district court may punish for contempt the responsible employee, and in the case of a uniformed service, the responsible member. Except as to causes the court considers of greater importance, proceedings before the district court, as authorized by this paragraph, take precedence on the docket over all other causes and shall be assigned for hearing and trial at the earliest practicable date and expedited in every way." redesignated para. (4) as para. (5) and added new paras. (4) and (6); in subsec. (b), substituted para. (1) for one which read: "specifically required by Executive order to be kept secret in the interest of the national defense or foreign policy;" substituted para. (7) for one which read: "investigatory files compiled for law enforcement purposes except to the extent available by law to a party other than an agency;" and added the concluding matter; and added subsecs. (d) and (e).

1976. Act Sept. 13, 1976 (effective 180 days after enactment, as provided by § 6 of such Act, which appears as 5 USCS 552b note) substituted subsec. (b)(3) for one which read: "specifically exempted from disclosure by statute."

1978. Act Oct. 13, 1978 (effective 90 days after enactment as provided by § 907 of such Act, which appears as 5 USCS § 1101 note), in subsec. (a)(4)(F), substituted "Special Counsel" for "Civil Service Commission", and substituted "his" for "its."

1984. Act Nov. 8, 1984 (applicable as provided by § 403 of such Act, which appears as 28 USCS § 1657 note), deleted subsec. (a)(4)(D), which read: "Except as to cases the court considers of greater importance, proceedings before the district court, as authorized by this subsection, and appeals there from, take precedence on the docket over all cases and shall be assigned for hearing and trial or for argument at the earliest practicable date and expedited in every way."

1986. Act Oct. 27, 1986 (effective on enactment and applicable as provided by § 1804(a) of such Act, which appears as a note to this section), in subsec. (b), substituted para. (7) for one which read: "investigatory records complied for law enforcement purposes, but only to the extent that the production of such records would (A) interfere with enforcement proceedings, (B) deprive a person of a right to a fair trial or an impartial adjudication, (C) constitute an unwarranted invasion of personal privacy, (D) disclose the identity of a confidential source and, in the case of a record compiled by a criminal law enforcement authority in the course of a criminal investigation, or by an agency conducting a lawful national security intelligence investigation, confidential information furnished only by the confidential source, (E) disclose investigative techniques and procedures, or (F) endanger the life or physical safety of law enforcement personnel;" redesignated subsecs. (c)-(e) as subsecs. (d)-(f), respectively, and added a new subsec. (c).

Such Act further (effective 180 days after enactment and applicable as provided by § 1804(b) of such Act, which appears as a note to this section), in subsec. (a), substituted para. (4)(A) for one which read: "In order to carry out the provisions of this section, each agency shall promulgate regulations, pursuant to notice and receipt of public comment, specifying a uniform schedule of fees applicable to all constituent units of such agency. Such fees shall be limited to reasonable standard charges for document search and duplication and provide for recovery of only the direct costs of such search and duplication. Documents shall be furnished without charge or at a reduced charge where the agency determines that waiver or reduction of the fee is in the public interest because furnishing the information can be considered as primarily benefiting the general public."

1996. Act Oct. 2, 1996 (effective 180 days after enactment, as provided by § 12 of such Act, which appears as a note to this section), in subsec. (a), in para. (2), in subpara. (B), deleted "and" after the concluding semicolon, added subparas. (D) and (E) and, in the concluding matter, inserted the sentence beginning "For records created on or after November 1, 1996 …," substituted "staff manual, instruction, or copies of records referred to in subparagraph (D)" for "or staff manual or instruction", inserted "and the extent of such deletion shall be indicated on the portion of the record which is made available or published, unless including that indication would harm an interest protected by the exemption in subsection (b) under which the deletion is made", and inserted the sentences beginning "If technically feasible, the extent …" and "Each agency shall make the index …" in para. (3), designated the existing provisions as subpara. (A), redesignated cls. (A) and (B) as cls. (i) and (ii), respectively, and added subparas. (B)-(D), and, in para. (4)(B), added the sentence beginning "In addition to any other matters …" in subsec. (b)(9), in the concluding matter, added the sentences beginning "The amount of information deleted …" and "If technically feasible …" substituted subsecs. (e) and (f) for ones which read:

(e)

(1) the number of determinations made by such agency not to comply with requests for records made to such agency under subsection (a) and the reasons for each such determination;

(2) the number of appeals made by persons under subsection (a)(6), the result of such appeals, and the reason for the action upon each appeal that results in a denial of information;

(3) the names and titles or positions of each person responsible for the denial of records requested under this section, and the number of instances of participation for each;

(4) the results of each proceeding conducted pursuant to subsection (a)(4)(F), including a report of the disciplinary action taken against the officer or employee who was primarily responsible for improperly withholding records or an explanation of why disciplinary action was not taken;

(5) a copy of every rule made by such agency regarding this section;

(6) a copy of the fee schedule and the total amount of fees collected by the agency for making records available under this section; and

(7) such other information as indicates efforts to administer fully this section.

The Attorney General shall submit an annual report on or before March 1 of each calendar year which shall include for the prior calendar year a listing of the number of cases arising under this section, the exemption involved in each case, the disposition of such case, and the cost, fees, and penalties assessed under subsections (a)(4)(E), (F), and (G). Such report shall also include a description of the efforts undertaken by the Department of Justice to encourage agency compliance with this section.

(f) For purposes of this section, the term 'agency' as defined in section 551(1) of this title includes any executive department, military department, Government corporation, Government controlled corporation, or other establishment in the executive branch of the Government (including the Executive Office of the President), or any independent regulatory agency." and added subsec. (g).

Such Act further (effective one year after enactment, as provided by § 12 of such Act, which appears as a note to this section), in subsec. (a)(6), in subpara. (A)(i), substituted "20 days" for "ten days", substituted subpara. (B) for one which read:

(B) In unusual circumstances as specified in this subparagraph, the time limits prescribed in either clause (i) or clause (ii) of subparagraph (A) may be extended by written notice to the person making such request setting forth the reasons for such extension and the date on which a determination is expected to be dispatched. No such notice shall specify a date that would result in an extension for more than ten working days. As used in this subparagraph, 'unusual circumstances' means, but only to the extent reasonably necessary to the proper processing of the particular request-

(i) the need to search for and collect the requested records from field facilities or other establishments that are separate from the office processing the request;

(ii) the need to search for, collect, and appropriately examine a voluminous amount of separate and distinct records which are demanded in a single request; or

(iii) the need for consultation, which shall be conducted with all practicable speed, with another agency having a substantial interest in the determination of the request or among two or more components of the agency having substantial subject-matter interest therein."

in subpara. (C), designated the existing provisions as cl. (i), and added cls. (ii) and (iii), and added subparas. (D)–(F).

2002. Act Nov. 27, 2002, in subsec. (a)(3), in subpara. (A), inserted "and except as provided in subparagraph (E)," and added subpara. (E).

APPENDIX B

Contact Information for FOIA Offices of Federal Offices, Departments and Agencies

Agency for International Development
FOIA Coordinator, Room 2.07C, RRB
Washington, D.C. 20523-2701
telephone number: (202) 712-1217
fax number: (202) 216-30 70

Air Force
HAF/ICIOD (FOIA)
1000 Air Force Pentagon
Washington, D.C. 20330-1000
telephone number: (703) 696-7263
fax number: (703) 696-7273
e-mail address: haffoia.workflow@pentagon.af.mil

American Battle Monuments Commission
FOIA Assistant, Suite 500
2300 Clarendon Blvd.
Arlington, VA 22201

Amtrak (National Railroad Passenger Corporation)
FOIA Officer
60 Massachusetts Avenue, N.E.
Washington, D.C. 20002
telephone number: (202) 906-2728
fax number: (202) 906-2169

Army
Freedom of Information and Privacy Acts Division
Attn: AHRC-PDD-FP

7701 Telegraph Road
Alexandria, VA 22315-3860
telephone number: (703) 428-6508
fax number: (703) 428-6522
e-mail address: FOIA@rmda.belvoir.army.mil

Broadcasting Board of Governors
FOIA/PA Officer, Office of the General Counsel
Suite 3349
330 Independence Avenue, S.W.
Washington, D.C. 20237
telephone number: (202) 260-4395
fax number: (202) 260-4394

Bureau of Customs and Border Protection
Chief, Disclosure Law Branch
1300 Pennsylvania Avenue, N.W.
Washington, D.C. 20229
telephone number: (202) 572-8720
fax number: (202) 572-8755

Centers for Medicare & Medicaid Services
Director, Freedom of Information Group
Room N2-20-16
7500 Security Boulevard
Baltimore, MD 21244-1850
telephone number: (410) 786-5353
fax number: (410) 786-0474

Central Intelligence Agency
Information and Privacy Coordinator
Washington, D.C. 20505
telephone number: (703) 613-1287

Chemical Safety and Hazard Investigation Board
FOIA Officer, Suite C-100
2175 K Street, N.W.
Washington, D.C. 20037
telephone number: (202) 261-7600
fax number: (202) 261-7650

Commission on Civil Rights
FOIA Officer, Room 730
624 9th Street, N.W.

Washington, D.C. 20425
telephone number: (202) 376-7700
fax number: (202) 376-1163

Committee for Purchase from People who Are Blind or Severely Disabled
General Counsel, Suite 10800
1421 Jefferson Davis Highway
Arlington, VA 22202-3259
telephone number: (703) 603-7740
fax number: (703) 603-0655

Commodity Futures Trading Commission
Assistant Secretary of the Commission
1155 21st Street, N.W.
Washington, D.C. 20581
telephone number: (202) 418-5096
fax number: (202) 418-5543

Comptroller of the Currency
Disclosure Officer
Washington, D.C. 20219
telephone number: (202) 874-4700
fax number: (202) 874-5274
e-mail address: foia-pa@occ.treas.gov

Consumer Product Safety Commission
FOIA Officer
4330 East West Highway
Bethesda, MD 20814
telephone number: (301) 504-7923
fax number: (301) 504-0127

Corporation for National Service
FOIA/PA Officer
1201 New York Avenue, N.W., Room 8200
Washington, D.C. 20525
telephone number: (202) 606-6671
fax number: (202) 565-2796

Council on Environmental Quality
Deputy General Counsel
722 Jackson Place, N.W.
Washington, D.C. 20503
telephone number: (202) 395-5750

Court Services and Offender Supervision Agency

FOIA Officer, Room 1254
633 Indiana Avenue, N.W.
Washington, D.C. 20004-2902
telephone number: (202) 220-5355
fax number: (202) 220-5350

Defense Contract Audit Agency

8725 John J. Kingman Road, Suite 2135
Fort Belvoir, VA 22060-6219
telephone number: (703) 767-1002
fax number: (703) 767-1011

Defense Contract Management Agency

P.O. Box 151300
Alexandria, VA 22315-9998
telephone number: (703) 428-1453
fax number: (703) 428-3580

Defense Finance and Accounting Service

FOIA/PA Program Manager, DFAS-HAC/DE
6760 East Irvington Place
Denver, CO 80279-8000
telephone number: (303) 676-6045
fax number: (303) 676-7710

Defense Information Systems Agency

Code R/GC, 701 South Courthouse Road
Arlington, VA 22204-2199
telephone number: (703) 607-6515
fax number: (703) 607-4344

Defense Intelligence Agency

Chief, FOIA Staff, DAN-1A
Washington, D.C. 20340-5100
telephone number: (202) 231-3916
fax number: (202) 231-3909
e-mail address: foia@dia.mil

Defense Logistics Agency

FOIA/PA Officer, Stop 2533
8725 John J. Kingman Road
Fort Belvoir, VA 22060-6221
telephone number: (703) 767-6183
fax number: (703) 767-6312

Defense Nuclear Facilities Safety Board
FOIA Director
625 Indiana Avenue, N.W., Suite 700
Washington, D.C. 20004
telephone number: (202) 694-7088
fax number: (202) 208-6518

Defense Security Service
Chief, Office of FOIA and Privacy, GCF
1340 Braddock Place
Alexandria, VA 22314-1651
telephone number: (703) 325-5991
fax number: (703) 325-5341

Defense Threat Reduction Agency
COSMI (FOIA)
8725 John J. Kingman Road
Fort Belvoir, VA 22060-6201
telephone number: (703) 767-1792
fax number: (703) 767-3623
e-mail address: efoia@dtra.mil

Department of Agriculture
FOIA/PA Coordinator
Room 440AA, Whitten Building
Washington, D.C. 20250-1300
telephone number: (202) 720-8164

Department of Commerce
FOIA/PA Officer, Room 5327
14th Street and Constitution Avenue, N.W.
Washington, D.C. 20230
telephone number: (202) 482-3707
fax number: (202) 219-8979
e-mail address: EFoia@doc.gov

Department of Defense
Office of Freedom of Information
1155 Defense Pentagon
Washington, D.C. 20301-1155
telephone number: (703) 696-4689
fax number: (703) 696-4506
e-mail address: foia@whs.mil

Department of Education
Chief, FOIA Office, PCP-9156
550 12th Street, S.W.
Washington, D.C. 20202-4700
telephone number: (202) 245-6651

Department of Energy
Director, FOIA/PA Division, ME-73
1000 Independence Avenue, S.W.
Washington, D.C. 20585
telephone number: (202) 586-5955
fax number: (202) 586-0575

Department of Health and Human Services
Director, FOIA/Privacy Division
Room 5416, Mary E. Switzer Building
330 C Street, S.W.
Washington, D.C. 20201
telephone number: (202) 690-7453
fax number: (202) 690-8320

Department of Homeland Security
Director, Departmental Disclosure, D-3
601 South 12th Street
Arlington, VA 22202
telephone number: (571) 227-3813
fax number: (571) 227-1125

Department of Housing and Urban Development
Assistant General Counsel, Room 10248
451 7th Street, S.W.
Washington, D.C. 20410
telephone number: (202) 708-3866
fax number: (202) 401-7901
e-mail address: foia_hud@hud.gov

Department of Labor
Office of the Solicitor, Room N-2428
200 Constitution Avenue, N.W.
Washington, D.C. 20210
telephone number: (202) 693-5500
fax number: (202) 693-5538

Department of State
Director, Office of IRM Programs and Services, SA-2
5th Floor
Washington, D.C. 20522-6001
telephone number: (202) 261-8484
fax number: (202) 261-8579

Department of the Interior
Departmental FOIA Officer (MS-5312 MIB)
Office of Information Resources Management
1849 C Street, N.W.
Washington, D.C. 20240
telephone number: (202) 208-5342
fax number: (202) 501-2360

Department of the Treasury
Director, Disclosure Services
1500 Pennsylvania Avenue, N.W.
Washington, D.C. 20220
telephone number: (202) 622-0930
fax number: (202) 622-3895

Department of Transportation
FOIA Officer, Office of General Counsel (C-12/5432)
400 7th Street, S.W.
Washington, D.C. 20590
telephone number: (202) 366-4542
fax number: (202) 366-8536

Department of Veterans Affairs
Records Management Service (005E3)
810 Vermont Avenue, N.W.
Washington, D.C. 20420
telephone number: (202) 565-8014
fax number: (202) 565-6950

Environmental Protection Agency
National FOIA Officer, Mail Code 2822T
1200 Pennsylvania Avenue, N.W.
Washington, D.C. 20460
telephone number: (202) 566-1667
fax number: (202) 566-2147
e-mail address: hq.foia@epamail.epa.gov

Equal Employment Opportunity Commission
Assistant Legal Counsel/FOIA
1801 L Street, N.W., 6th Floor
Washington, D.C. 20507
telephone number: (202) 663-4640

Export-Import Bank
Deputy Treasurer Controller
811 Vermont Avenue, N.W., Room 1053
Washington, D.C. 20571
telephone number: (202) 565-3241
fax number: (202) 565-3294

Farm Credit Administration
FOI Officer
1501 Farm Credit Drive
McLean, VA 22102-5090
telephone number: (703) 883-4022
fax number: (703) 790-0052
e-mail address: foiaofficer@fca.gov

Farm Credit System Insurance Corporation
FOI Officer
1501 Farm Credit Drive
McLean, VA 22102-5090
telephone number: (703) 883-4022
fax number: (703) 790-0052
e-mail address: foiaofficer@fca.gov

Federal Aviation Administration
Manager, National FOIA Staff, ARC-40
800 Independence Avenue, S.W.
Washington, D.C. 20591
telephone number: (202) 267-9165
fax number: (202) 493-5032
e-mail address: 7-AWA-ARC-FOIA@faa.gov

Federal Communications Commission
FOIA Officer, Room 5C406
445 12th Street, S.W.
Washington, D.C. 20554
telephone number: (202) 418-1379
fax number: (202) 418-0521

Federal Deposit Insurance Corporation
    Supervisory Counsel, Room H-3039
    550 17th Street, N.W.
    Washington, D.C. 20429
    telephone number: (202) 898-7021
    fax number: (202) 736-0547
    e-mail address: efoia@fdic.gov

Federal Election Commission
    Press/FOIA Officer
    999 E Street, N.W.
    Washington, D.C. 20463
    telephone number: (202) 694-1220
    fax number: (202) 501-3283

Federal Emergency Management Agency
    FOI/PA Specialist, Room 840
    500 C Street, S.W.
    Washington, D.C. 20472
    telephone number: (202) 646-3051
    fax number: (202) 646-4536

Federal Energy Regulatory Commission
    Director, Office of External Affairs
    888 1st Street, N.E.
    Washington, D.C. 20426
    telephone number: (202) 502-8004
    fax number: (202) 208-2106

Federal Housing Finance Board
    FOIA Officer
    1777 F Street, N.W.
    Washington, D.C. 20006
    telephone number: (202) 408-2511
    fax number: (202) 408-2580
    e-mail address: foia@fhfb.gov

Federal Labor Relations Authority
    FOIA Officer, Office of the General Counsel
    Suite 210
    607 14th Street, N.W.
    Washington, D.C. 20424
    telephone number: (202) 218-7743
    fax number: (202) 482-6608

Federal Law Enforcement Training Center
Building 94, OBP
Glynco, GA 31524
telephone number: (912) 261-4524
fax number: (912) 267-3113

Federal Maritime Commission
Secretary of the Commission
800 North Capitol Street, N.W., Room 1046
Washington, D.C. 20573
telephone number: (202) 523-5725

Federal Mediation and Conciliation Service
General Counsel
2100 K Street, N.W.
Washington, D.C. 20427
telephone number: (202) 606-5444
e-mail address: foia@fmcs.gov

Federal Mine Safety and Health Review Commission
Executive Director
601 New Jersey Avenue, N.W.
Washington, D.C. 20001-2021
telephone number: (202) 434-9905
fax number: (202) 434-9906
e-mail address: info@fmshrc.gov

Federal Open Market Committee
Secretariat Assistant
20th Street and Constitution Avenue, N.W., Mail Stop 55
Washington, D.C. 20551
telephone number: (202) 452-3255
fax number: (202) 452-2921

Federal Reserve System
FOIA Manager
20th and C Streets, N.W., Room MP500
Washington, D.C. 20551
telephone number: (202) 452-2407
fax number: (202) 872-7565

Federal Retirement Thrift Investment Board
Associate General Counsel and FOIA Officer
1250 H Street, N.W., 2nd Floor
Washington, D.C. 20005-3952

telephone number: (202) 942-1630
fax number: (202) 942-1676

Federal Trade Commission
FOIA/PA Officer
6th Street and Pennsylvania Avenue, N.W.
Washington, D.C. 20580
telephone number: (202) 326-2013
fax number: (202) 326-2477
e-mail address: foia@ftc.gov

Food and Drug Administration
Acting Director, FOI Staff
5600 Fishers Lane (HFI-30)
Rockville, MD 20857
telephone number: (301) 827-6567
fax number: (301) 443-1726

General Services Administration
FOIA Officer, Information Management and Administrative Policy Division
Room 7123
1800 F Street, N.W.
Washington, D.C. 20405
telephone number: (202) 501-2262
fax number: (202) 501-2727
e-mail address: gsa.foia@gsa.gov

Institute of Museum and Library Services
Office of the General Counsel
Room 802
1100 Pennsylvania Avenue, N.W.
Washington, D.C. 20506
telephone number: (202) 653-4642
fax number: (202) 653-4625

Inter-American Foundation
Assistant General Counsel
10th Floor
901 North Stuart Street
Arlington, VA 22203
telephone number: (703) 306-4301

Internal Revenue Service
Director, Disclosure, Office of Disclosure
1111 Constitution Avenue, N.W.

Washington, D.C. 20224
telephone number: (202) 927-7425

Legal Services Corporation

FOIA Officer
3333 K Street, N.W.
Washington, D.C. 20007
telephone number: (202) 295-1625
fax number: (202) 337-6519
e-mail address: info@smtp.lsc.gov

Marine Corps

FOIA/PA Coordinator
Headquarters, U.S. Marine Corps [CMC (ARSF)]
2 Navy Annex
Washington, D.C. 20380-1775
telephone number: (703) 614-4008/3685
fax number: (703) 614-6287

Merit Systems Protection Board

FOIA/PA Officer, Office of the Clerk
1615 M Street, N.W.
Washington, D.C. 20419
telephone number: (202) 653-7200, ext. 1162
fax number: (202) 653-7130
e-mail address: mspb@mspb.gov

Millennium Challenge Corporation

Assistant General Counsel for Administration
875 15th Street, N.W.
Washington, D.C. 20005
telephone number: (202) 521-3863

National Aeronautics and Space Administration

FOIA Officer (Code PS)
300 E Street, S.W.
Washington, D.C. 20546
telephone number: (202) 358-0068
fax number: (202) 358-4345
e-mail address: foia@hq.nasa.gov

National Archives and Records Administration

FOIA Officer, Office of the General Counsel
Room 3110

8601 Adelphi Road
College Park, MD 20740-6001
telephone number: (301) 837-2024

National Capital Planning Commission
General Counsel
North Lobby, Suite 500
401 9th Street, N.W.
Washington, D.C. 20004
telephone number: (202) 482-7200

National Credit Union Administration
Staff Attorney
1775 Duke Street
Alexandria, VA 22314
telephone number: (703) 518-6540
fax number: (703) 518-6569
e-mail address: foia@ncua.gov

National Endowment for the Arts
FOIA Officer
1100 Pennsylvania Avenue, N.W., Room 518
Washington, D.C. 20506
telephone number: (202) 682-5505
fax number: (202) 682-5572
e-mail address: foia@arts.endow.gov

National Endowment for the Humanities
Deputy General Counsel
1100 Pennsylvania Avenue, N.W., Room 529
Washington, D.C. 20506
telephone number: (202) 606-8322
fax number: (202) 606-8600
e-mail address: foia@neh.gov

National Geospatial-Intelligence Agency
Office of the General Counsel
4600 Sangamore Road (D-10)
Bethesda, MD 20816
telephone number: (301) 227-2268
fax number: (301) 227-2035

National Indian Gaming Commission
FOIA/PA Officer
Suite 9100

1441 L Street, N.W.
Washington, D.C. 20005
telephone number: (202) 632-7003
fax number: (202) 632-7066

National Institutes of Health
FOIA Officer, Building 31, Room 5B35
9000 Rockville Pike
Bethesda, MD 20892
telephone number: (301) 496-5633
fax number: (301) 402-4541

National Labor Relations Board
Assistant General Counsel
Room 10612
1099 14th Street, N.W.
Washington, D.C. 20570
telephone number: (202) 273-3840

National Mediation Board
FOIA Officer
1301 K Street, N.W., Suite 250 East
Washington, D.C. 20572
telephone number: (202) 692-5040
fax number: (202) 692-5085

National Oceanic and Atmospheric Administration
FOIA/PA Officer, Room 10641, SSMC-3
1315 East West Highway
Silver Spring, MD 20910-3281
telephone number: (301) 713-3540, ext. 209
fax number: (301) 713-1169

National Reconnaissance Office
Information Access and Release Center
14675 Lee Road
Chantilly, VA 20151-1715
telephone number: (703) 227-9128
fax number: (703) 227-9198
e-mail address: foia@nro.mil

National Science Foundation
FOIA Officer, Room 1265
Office of the General Counsel
4201 Wilson Boulevard

Arlington, VA 22230
telephone number: (703) 292-8060
fax number: (703) 292-9041
e-mail address: foia@nsf.gov

National Security Agency
Chief, FOIA/PA Services
Office of Information Policy, DC321
Ft. George G. Meade, MD 20755-6248
telephone number: (301) 688-6527
fax number: (301) 688-6198

National Transportation Safety Board
FOIA Officer
490 L'Enfant Plaza East, S.W.
Washington, D.C. 20594
telephone number: (202) 314-6551
fax number: (202) 314-6132

Navy
Head, DONPA/FOIA Policy Branch
CNO (DNS-36)
2000 Navy Pentagon
Washington, D.C. 20350-2000
telephone number: (202) 685-6545
fax number: (202) 685-6580
e-mail address: foia@mail.navy.mil

Nuclear Regulatory Commission
FOIA/PA Officer
Washington, D.C. 20555
telephone number: (301) 415-7169
fax number: (301) 415-5130
e-mail address: foia@nrc.gov

Occupational Safety and Health Review Commission
Attorney-Advisor
1120 20th Street, N.W., 9th Floor
Washington, D.C. 20036-3419
telephone number: (202) 606-5410

Office of Executive Branch Administration
FOIA Officer
5001 New Executive Office Building
Washington, D.C. 20503

telephone number: (202) 395-2273
fax number: (202) 456-7921

Office of Federal Housing Enterprise Oversight
FOIA Officer
1700 G Street, N.W., 4th Floor
Washington, D.C. 20552
telephone number: (202) 414-6425
fax number: (202) 414-8917
e-mail address: FOIAOffice@ofheo.gov

Office of Government Ethics
Senior Associate General Counsel
1201 New York Avenue, N.W., Suite 500
Washington, D.C. 20005-3917
telephone number: (202) 482-9245
fax number: (202) 482-9237

Office of Inspector General
245 Murray Drive, Building 410
Mail Stop 2600
Washington, D.C. 20528-0001
telephone number: (202) 254-4002
fax number: (202) 254-4287

Office of Management and Budget
FOIA Officer
9026 New Executive Office Building
Washington, D.C. 20503
telephone number: (202) 395-3642
fax number: (202) 395-3504

Office of National Drug Control Policy
Assistant General Counsel
Washington, D.C. 20503

Office of Personnel Management
FOIA/PA Coordinator
Room 5415
1900 E Street, N.W.
Washington, D.C. 20415
telephone number: (202) 606-2150
fax number: (202) 418-3251
e-mail address: foia@opm.gov

Office of Science and Technology Policy
Associate General Counsel
431 Eisenhower Executive Office Building
Washington, D.C. 20502
telephone number: (202) 456-6125
fax number: (202) 456-6027

Office of Special Counsel
FOIA/PA Specialist
1730 M Street, N.W., Suite 201
Washington, D.C. 20036-4505
telephone number: (202) 254-3600

Office of the Director of National Intelligence
Director, Information Management Office
Washington, D.C. 20511
telephone number: (703) 482-1707

Office of the Inspector General
Chief, FOIA/PA Office
400 Army Navy Drive, Room U-226
Arlington, VA 22202-2885
telephone number: (703) 604-9775
fax number: (703) 602-0294
e-mail address: foia@dodig.osd.mil

Office of the United States Trade Representative
FOIA Officer
600 17th Street, N.W.
Washington, D.C. 20508
telephone number: (202) 395-3419
fax number: (202) 395-9458

Office of Thrift Supervision
Program Specialist (FOIA), Dissemination Branch
1700 G Street, N.W.
Washington, D.C. 20552
telephone number: (202) 906-5922
fax number: (202) 906-7755
e-mail address: public.info@ots.treas.gov

Overseas Private Investment Corporation
FOIA Director
1100 New York Avenue, N.W.

Washington, D.C. 20527
telephone number: (202) 336-8418
fax number: (202) 408-0297
e-mail address: info@opic.gov

Peace Corps

FOIA Officer
1111 20th Street, N.W.
Washington, D.C. 20526-0001
telephone number: (202) 692-1186
fax number: (202) 692-1121

Pension Benefit Guaranty Corporation

Disclosure Officer, Room 240
1200 K Street, N.W.
Washington, D.C. 20005
telephone number: (202) 326-4040

Postal Regulatory Commission

Secretary, Suite 200
901 New York Avenue, N.W.
Washington, D.C. 20268
telephone number: (202) 789-6840
fax number: (202) 789-6886

Privacy and Civil Liberties Oversight Board

Deputy Executive Director and Counsel
1724 F Street, N.W.
Washington, D.C. 20502
telephone number: (202) 456-1240
fax number: (202) 456-1066

Public Health Service

FOIA Officer, Room 17A46
5600 Fishers Lane
Rockville, MD 20857
telephone number: (301) 443-5252
fax number: (301) 443-0925

Railroad Retirement Board

General Counsel
844 Rush Street
Chicago, IL 60611
telephone number: (312) 751-4935
fax number: (312) 751-7102

Securities and Exchange Commission
FOIA/Privacy Act Branch Chief
Mail Stop 5100
100 F Street, N.E.
Washington, D.C. 20549
telephone number: (202) 551-7900
fax number: (202) 772-9337
e-mail address: foia/pa@sec.gov

Selective Service System
FOIA Officer
1515 Wilson Boulevard
Arlington, VA 22209-2425
telephone number: (703) 605-4100
fax number: (703) 605-4106

Small Business Administration
Chief, Office of FOI/PA
409 3rd Street, S.W.
Washington, D.C. 20416
telephone number: (202) 401-8203
fax number: (202) 205-7059
e-mail address: foia@sba.gov

Social Security Administration
FOIA Office, Room 3-A-6 Operations
6401 Security Boulevard
Baltimore, MD 21235
telephone number: (410) 966-6645
fax number: (410) 966-4304

Surface Transportation Board
FOIA/PA Officer, Room 1263
395 E Street, S.W.
Washington, D.C. 20423-0001
telephone number: (202) 245-0269
fax number: (202) 245-0460
e-mail address: FOIA.Privacy@stb.dot.gov

Tennessee Valley Authority
FOIA Officer
400 West Summit Hill Drive
Knoxville, TN 37902
telephone number: (865) 632-6945

fax number: (865) 632-6901
e-mail address: foia@tva.gov

Transportation Security Administration
Associate Director, Office of Security
West Building, 4th Floor, Room 432-N, TSA-20
601 South 12th Street
Arlington, VA 22202-4220
telephone number: (571) 227-2300
fax number: (571) 227-1406

United States Citizenship and Immigration Services
FOIA/PA Program
111 Massachusetts Avenue, N.W., 4th Floor
ULLICO Building
Washington, D.C. 20529
telephone number: (202) 272-8269
fax number: (202) 272-8331

United States Coast Guard
HQ USCG Commandant, CG-611
Washington, D.C. 20593-0001
telephone number: (202) 475-3519
fax number: (202) 475-3926

United States Copyright Office
Supervisory Copyright Information Specialist
P.O. Box 70400
Southwest Station
Washington, D.C. 20024
telephone number: (202) 707-6800
fax number: (202) 707-6859

United States Immigration and Customs Enforcement
FOIA Section Chief, Room 4038
425 "I" Street, N.W.
Washington, D.C. 20536
telephone number: (202) 616-7498
fax number: (202) 616-7612

United States International Trade Commission
Secretary to the Commission
500 E Street, S.W., Room 112A

Washington, D.C. 20436
telephone: (202) 205-2000
fax number: (202) 205-2104

United States Postal Service
Manager, Records Office
475 L'Enfant Plaza West, S.W.
Washington, D.C. 20260-5202
telephone number: (202) 268-2608
fax number: (202) 268-5353

United States Secret Service
Disclosure Officer, Bldg. 410
245 Murray Drive
Washington, D.C. 20223
telephone number: (202) 406-5838
fax number: (202) 406-5154

United States Trade and Development Agency
Attorney-Advisor, Suite 1600
1000 Wilson Blvd.
Arlington, VA 22209-3901
telephone number: (703) 875-4357
fax number: (703) 875-4009

US-VISIT
FOIA Officer
Washington, D.C. 20528
telephone number: (202) 298-5200
fax number: (202) 298-5201

Notes

Part 1 Government Information and News : Introduction

1. Richard Saul Wurman, *Information Anxiety* (Doubleday: New York, 1989).
2. Anne Wells Branscomb, *Who Owns Information?* (Basic Books: New York, 1994), p. 3.
3. Frank Hayes, "Number Control," *Computerworld*, June 9, 2006, p. 56.
4. Leslie Cauley, "NSA has massive database of Americans' phone calls," *USA Today*, www.usatoday.com/news/washington/2006-05-10-nsa_x.htm, viewed June 16, 2006.
5. Kathleen Burge, "Mayors Demand Phone Inquiry," *The Boston Globe*, May 25, 2006, p. B1.
6. Cauley.
7. Arshad Mohammed and Sara Kehaulani Goo, "Government Increasingly Turning to Data Mining," *The Washington Post*, June 15, 2006, p. D3.
8. Linda Rosencrance, "GAO: U.S. Agencies Need to Better Account for IT Investments," Computerworld, February 15, 2006.
9. Grant Gross and Robert McMillan, "Feds Again Score Low on IT Security," *Computerworld*, March 17, 2006, p. 1.
10. U.S., First Session, First Congress, Ch. 14 (1789).
11. See, for example, negotiations of the John Jay Treaty, 1794, and the dismissal by Washington of congressionally approved appointments of three foreign ministers, two consuls, as well as Secretary of State Edmund Randolph.

Chapter 1 Information and Government

1. Constitution.
2. U.S. Constitution, Article 1, Sec. 8.
3. *Acts of the First Session of the First Congress,* Ch. 14 @2, 1 Stat. 68 (1789).

4. Sian Lewis, *News and Society in the Greek Polis* (Chapel Hill: University of North Carolina Press, 1996); Anthony Smith, *The Newspaper, An International History* (London: Thames and Hudson, 1979).

5. Margaret Blanchard, *Revolutionary Sparks* (New York: Oxford University Press, 1992).

6. *Journals*, ed. in the Library of Congress, Vol. 5 (September 26, 1776): p. 829; Vol. 8 (June 2, 1777): p. 412.

7. Sarah Jordan Miller, "The Depository Library System" (unpublished dissertation: Columbia University, 1980), p. 36.

8. Miller, p. 29.

9. Miller, p. 46ff.

10. Annals, 4 (3d Cong., 2d sess., December 1, 1794): 951.

11. Miller, p. 50ff.

12. The Printing Act, 28 Stat. 601 (1895).

13. System of Library Distribution, 28 Stat. 624 (1895).

14. Depository Library Act of 1962, Pub.L. No.87-579, 76 Stat. 352 (1962).

15. U.S. Code, Title 44 sec.1903.

16. 44 U.S.C. sec.1909.

17. OMB Management of Federal Information Resources, 50 Fed. Reg. 52,730, and 52,736 (1985).

18. For example, see 5 U.S.C. 552, 552a, 552b, 701; 11 U.S.C. 1125(a)(1); 13 U.S.C. 9; 15 U.S.C. 796, 2054; 18 U.S.C. 1905; 19 U.S.C. 2155; 20 U.S.C. 1221; 22 U.S.C. 2403; 26 U.S.C. 274; 41 U.S.C. 423 and 50 U.S.C. 823.

19. *The Compact Edition of the Oxford English Dictionary*, Vol. 1 (New York: Oxford University Press, 1971), p. 1432.

20. Chaucer, *Melibee*, 904, "Whanne Melibee hadde herd the grete skiles and reasons of Dame Prudence, and hire wise informacions and techynges" (1386).

21. 5 U.S.C. sec.3111(D).

22. 13 U.S.C. sec.91.

23. 26 U.S.C. sec.6103b.

24. 15 U.S.C. sec.2055.

25. 5 U.S.C. sec.552.

26. *Black's Law Dictionary* defines "information" as an accusation exhibited against a person for some criminal offense, without an indictment and grand jury hearing. (St. Paul, MN: West Publishing, 1983), p.398.

27. 26 U.S.C. sec.274(II)(iii).

28. 26 U.S.C. sec.6103(2).

29. 5 U.S.C. sec.552a.

30. 5 U.S.C. sec.552(b)(1–9).

31. Fritz Machlup, *The Study of Information: Interdisciplinary Messages* (New York: John Wiley & Sons, 1983), pp. 641–656.

32. Evidence of information science as a distinct discipline can be found as early as 1945, described by Glynn Harmon, "Opinion Paper on the Evolution of Information

Science," *Journal of American Society of Information Science*, Vol. 22, No. 4 (1971): p. 235, and S.C. Bradford's examination of the characteristics of documentation, which allowed for a transition to and separation of information science, as described by him, *Documentation* (London: Crosby Lockwood & Son, 1948); See also Dorothy B. Lilley and Ronald W. Trice, *A History of Information Science 1945–1985* (New York: Academic Press, 1989).

33. Vannevar Bush, "As We May Think," *Atlantic Monthly*, Vol. 176, No. 1 (July 1954): p. 101

34. Gordon Miller, "The Concept of Information," *Information and Behavior*, Vol. 2, Brent D. Ruben, ed. (New Brunswick, NJ: Transaction, 1988), p. 28.

35. Miller, pp. 32–33.

36. Miller, p. 37.

37. Miller, p. 40.

38. "Feds Start to Pull Net Information," *Library Journal* (November 15, 2001): p. 16.

39. List of Federal Database Web sites Restricted after 9/11 Attacks, www.ombwatch. org/info/2001/access.html, viewed January 10, 2002.

40. Gary Bass, "A Post-Sep tember 11 Attach on Right to Know," October 2, 2001, www. ombwatch.org/article/articleview/212/1/254?TopicID=1, viewed November 1, 2006.

Chapter 2   Government and News Media

1. David A. Copeland, *Colonial American Newspapers: Character and Content* (Newark: University of Delaware Press, 1997), p. 264.

2. Copeland, p. 11.

3. Copeland, pp. 288–290.

4. Copeland, p. 119.

5. *London Universal Daily Register*, January 1, 1785.

6. Charles E. Clark, *The Public Prints: The Newspaper in Anglo-American Culture, 1665–1740* (New York: Oxford University Press, 1994), p. 252.

7. Clark, pp. 77–79.

8. Clark, p. 79.

9. Announced in 1740, but published January 1741, Philadelphia, Pennsylvania.

10. See examples of the magazine pages in Frank Luther Mott, *A History of American Magazines, 1741–1850*, Vol. 1 (Appleton: New York, 1930), pp. 71–73.

11. *American Magazine and Monthly Chronicle*, Vol. 1 (October, 1757): pp. 5–6 [Emphasis original.]

12. Cited in Frank L. Mott and Ralph D. Casey, *Interpretations of Journalism* (New York: Crofts, 1937), p. 52.

13. "…and were it left to me to decide whether we should have a government without newspapers or newspapers without government, I should not hesitate to prefer the latter."

14. Michael Emery and Edwin Emery, *The Press and America* (Englewood Cliffs, NJ: Prentice Hall, 1988), pp. 37–44.

15. See, for example, George Boyce, James Curran, and Pauline Wingate, *Newspaper History: From the 17th Century to the Present Day* (Beverly Hills, CA: Sage, 1978); Edwin Emery and Henry Ladd Smith, *The Press and America* (New York: Prentice Hall, 1954); Thomas C. Leonard, *News for All* (New York: Oxford, 1995); Thomas C. Leonard, *The Power of the Press* (New York: Oxford, 1986); Leonard Levy, *Emergence of a Free Press* (New York: Oxford, 1985); Frank Luther Mott, *American Journalism* (New York: Macmillan, 1941); Richard N. Rosenfeld, *American Aurora* (New York: St. Martin's Press, 1997); Jeffery A. Smith, *Printers and Press Freedom* (New York: Oxford, 1988).

16. *Absence of Malice*, 1981, newspaper reporter, movie character played by Sally Field, demands information about a government investigation. When questioned about where this assertion and her job to get information emanates, Field replies, "There's a sign on my desk."

17. Leonard, *News for All*, p. xiii.

18. See, for example, Aurora Wallace, *Newspapers and the Making of Modern American: A History* (Westport, CT: Greenwood Press, 2005).

19. Robert M. Hutchins, *A Free and Responsible Press: A General Report on Mass Communication* (Chicago, IL: University of Chicago Press, 1947), pp. 90–94.

20. Herbert Brucker, Freedom of Information (New York: Macmillan, 1949), pp. 9–70.

21. Walter Lippmann, *Public Opinion* (New York: Macmillan, 1922), pp. 364–365.

22. Thomas Erskine, defending Thomas Paine, *The Federalist and Other Constitutional Papers*, (Chicago: Albert, Scott, 1894), No. LXXXIV, pp. 469–470.

23. Brucker, *Freedom of Information*, p. 36.

24. S. Warren and L. Brandeis, "The Right to Privacy," *Harvard Law Review*, Vol. 4 (1890–1891): pp. 193–220.

25. Mary Louis Ramsey, American Law Section, memo "Control of Government Information," dated November 8, 1951, to Frances Case and Robert C. Albrook, James Russell Wiggins Collection, Fogler Library, University of Maine, Orono, Maine.

26. Administrative Procedure Act, 5 U.S.C. 1002, sec. 3(c) 1951.

27. Mary Louis Ramsey, American Law Section, memo "Control of Government Information" dated November 8, 1951, to Frances Case and Robert C. Albrook, pp. 6–18, James Russell Wiggins Collection, Fogler Library, University of Maine, Orono, Maine.

28. "Constitutional and Legal Aspects of S. 2190," Senate Committee on Expenditures in the Executive Departments, Staff Memo No. 82–1–60, Eli E. Nobleman and Walter L. Reynolds, November 29, 1951, James Russell Wiggins Collection, Fogler Library, University of Maine, Orono, Maine.

29. Contained in private correspondence between Ralph A. Dunham, Attorney General of South Dakota, and James S. Pope, editor, *Louisville Times & Courier-Journal*, November 17, 1952, James Russell Wiggins Collection, Fogler Library, University of Maine, Orono, Maine.

30. V.M. Newton, Jr., *Tampa Morning Tribune* managing editor, personal correspondence with James Russell Wiggins, Dec. 8, 1951, James Russell Wiggins Collection, Fogler Library, University of Maine, Orono, Maine.

31. V.M. Newton, Jr., personal correspondence, January 11, 1952, with James Russell Wiggins. James Russell Wiggins Collection, Fogler Library, University of Maine, Orono, Maine.

32. George E. Clapp, personal correspondence, with Victor Hackler, copied to V.M. Newton Jr., and James Russell Wiggins, March 12, 1952, James Russell Wiggins Collection, Fogler Library, University of Maine, Orono, Maine.

33. James S. Pope, managing editor of the *Louisville Courier-Journal & Times*, personal correspondence May 28, 1952, with William W. Vosburgh Jr., Waterbury, Connecticut, copied to James Russell Wiggins, James Russell Wiggins Collection, Fogler Library, University of Maine, Orono, Maine.

34. James S. Pope, managing editor of the *Louisville Courier-Journal & Times*, personal correspondence March 7, 1952, with Charles F. Brannan, Secretary of Agriculture, copied to James Russell Wiggins and Harold Cross, James Russell Wiggins Collection, Fogler Library, University of Maine, Orono, Maine.

35. Private correspondence between James Russell Wiggins and Frank J. Starzel, December 19, 1952, James Russell Wiggins Collection, Fogler Library, University of Maine, Orono, Maine.

36. James Russell Wiggins, *Freedom or Secrecy* (New York: Oxford University Press, 1956), p. viii.

37. *Grosjean v. American Press Co.*, 297 U.S. 233 (1936).

38. *Minneapolis Star & Tribune v. Minneapolis Commissioner of Revenue*, 460 U.S. 575 (1983).

39. 283 U.S. 697 (1931).

40. *The New York Times Company v. U.S. & U.S. v. The Washington Post Company*, 403 U.S. 713 (1971).

41. Wiggins, *Freedom or Secrecy*, pp. 3–4.

42. *New York Sun*, May 2, 1898.

43. Reuters News Service, April 25, 1944.

44. Shannon E. Martin, "U.S. Media Pools and Military Interventions in the 1980s and 1990s," *Journal of Peace Research*, Vol. 43, No. 5 (2006): pp. 607–608.

45. Martin, pp. 607–608.

Chapter 3   How News Media Report About Government-held Information

1. Francis Williams, *The Right to Know: The Rise of the World Press* (Longmans: London, 1969), p. 2.

2. The Missouri Group, News Reporting and Writing, 6th ed. (Boston and New York: Bedford/St. Martin's, 1999).

3. Gerry Keir, Maxwell McCombs, Donald L. Shaw, *Advanced Reporting: Beyond News Events* (New York: Longman, 1986).

4. William Gaines, *Investigative Reporting for Print and Broadcast* (Chicago: Nelson-Hall Publishers, 1994).

5. Henry H. Schulte, *Reporting Public Affairs* (New York: Macmillan, 1981).

6. John Ullmann and Jan Colbert, eds., *The Reporter's Handbook: An Investigator's Guide to Documents and Techniques*, 2nd ed. (New York: St. Martin's Press, 1991), p. xi.

7. See, for example, Donald Lewis Shaw, Maxwell McCombs, and Gerry Keir, *Advanced Reporting: Beyond News Events* (Long Grove, IL: Waveland Press Inc.), pp. 205–209.

8. See, for example, www.gao.gov and www.gpoaccess.gov/gaoreports/index.html for reports, viewed November 9, 2006. For the federal depository library system see, www.access.gpo.gov/su_docs/fdlp/pr/keepam.html, viewed November 9, 2006.

9. P.L. 104–13, 44 U.S.C. 35 (1996).

10. Robert W. Houk, "GPO/2001: Vision for a New Millennium" U.S. Government Printing Office: Washington D.C., 1991, p. 35.

11. See, for example, Judy Andrews, "Government Information in an Electronic Age," www.ala.org/ala/acrlbucket/nashville1997pap/andrews.htm, viewed November 15, 2006.

12. OMB Watch "Questions Surround Handling of FirstGov" December 10, 2001, www.ombwatch.org/article/articleview/415/-1/254, viewed November 15, 2006.

13. Executive Order 10290, Establishing Minimum Standards for the Classification Transmission, and Handling by Departments and Agencies of the Executive branch, of Official Information which Requires Safeguarding in the Interest of the Security of the United States, September 24, 1951, reported in 3 *Code of Federal Regulations*, 789–790.

14. See, for example, Executive Order 13292, March 25, 2003, Federal Register Vol. 68, No. 60, March 28, 2003, 15315.

15. See "2005 Report to the President," Information Security Oversight Office, pp. 13–15, available at www.archives.gov/isoo/ and Scott Shane, "Since 2001, Sharp Increase in the Number of Documents Classified by the Government," *New York Times*, July 3, 2005.

16. 60 Stat. 766 (1946).

17. Personal correspondence of V.M. Newton, Jr., with James R. Wiggins, January 11, 1952, James Russell Wiggins Collection, Fogler Library, University of Maine, Orono, Maine.

18. Personal correspondence of V.M. Newton, Jr., with James R. Wiggins, January 11, 1952.

19. P.L. 1975, Ch. 758 Sec.1.

20. 1 M.R.N.A. Ch.13 sec.402.3 (2005).

21. 1 M.R.N.A. Ch.13 sec.401–521 (2005).

22. 7 M.R.N.A. Ch.604–A sec.2998–B (2005).
23. 38 M.R.N.A. Ch. 26 sec.2309.1 (2005).
24. 1980 Alas. AG LEXIS 652; 1980 Op. (Inf) Atty Gen. Alas., April 10.
25. *Southwestern Bell Telephone Company v. The State Corporation Commission of the State of Kansas*, 6 Kan. App. 2d 444, 629 P. 2d 1174 (1981).
26. Senate Bill 5581, Chapter 424, 2005 Wa. ALS 424.
27. *Weston v. Carolina Research and Development Foundation*, 303 S.C. 398, 401 S.E. 2d 161 (1991).
28. *In Defense of Animals v. Oregon Health Sciences University*, 199 Ore. App. 160 (2005).
29. *Dorson v. Louisiana State University*, 657 S. 2d 755 (1995).
30. Alabama, Code of Ala. sec.36–12–40 (2003); Arkansas, ARK. Code Ann. sec.25–19–105(a)(2003); Delaware, 29 Del. Code Ann. sec.10003(a)(2003); Georgia, Ga. Code Ann. sec.50–18–70(b)(2002); Montana, Mont. Code Ann. sec.2–6–102(1)(2003); New Jersey, N.J. Stat. Ann. sec.47:1A–1(2003); South Dakota, S.D. Codified Laws sec.1–18C–5(2003); Tennessee, Tenn. Code Ann. sec.10–7–503(a)(2003); Virginia, Va. Code Ann. sec.2.2–370(a)(2003). Other states with confusing language are Alaska, "Every person in the state has the right to inspect public records" Alaska Statsec.40.25.120(a)(2003); Nebraska, "all state citizens, and all other persons interested in the examination of public records" Neb. Rev. Stat. sec.84–712(1)(2002); New Hampshire, "every citizen" has the right to inspect public records, N.H. Rev. Stat. Ann. sec.91–A:4(i)(2002).
31. Birmingham, Alabama, Associated Press, "Suspect in 1963 Bombing Says he Needs his Full FBI File," August 25, 2000.
32. Chanda Temple, "Third Attempt Will Be Made to Find Grave of Girl Killed in '63 Bombing," *Birmingham News*, March 20, 1998, p. 7B.
33. Gardiner Harris, "Inner Circle Taking More of C.D.C Bonuses," *New York Times*, September 17, 2006, p. 20.
34. Miles Moore, "NHTSA Delays Warning Data Release," *Tire Business*, October 25, 2004, p. 53; also see, Jeffrey McCracken, "U.S. Keeping Crash Data Secret," *Detroit Free Press*, September 24, 2004.
35. Ann Parks, "USPS Can Keep Contract Details a Secret," *The Daily Record*, February 3, 2004, reporting on *Wickwire Gavin, P.C. v. USPS*, US 4th Dist., No. 02-2310, January 30, 2004.

Chapter 4   Government Housekeeping

1. First Congress, Session I, Chapter XIV, September 15, 1789, p. 68.
2. Abraham D. Sofaer, "Executive Power and the Control of Information: Practice Under the Framers," *Duke Law Journal* (March 1977): pp. 1–57.
3. U.S. Constitution, Article II, Sec. 3.

4. 3 Annals of Congress 493 (1792).
5. Paul Leicester Ford, ed., *The Writings of Thomas Jefferson*, 12 vols. (New York: Putnam, 1904), 3:189–190; www.constitution.org/tj/jeff01.txt, viewed November 30, 2006.
6. 4 Annals of Congress 250 (1794).
7. 4 Annals of Congress 56 (1794).
8. "The President's Message, on the Treaty Papers," *Centinel-Office,* Boston: Benjamin Russell, April 7, 1796.
9. 8 Annals of Congress 1374–5 (1798).
10. Letter to Robert Livingston, in Ford, *The Writings of Thomas Jefferson*, 8:143–144.
11. Communication from Jefferson to George Hay, in Ford, *The Writings of Thomas Jefferson*, 9: notes 55–64.
12. *Marbury v. Madison*, 5 U.S. 137 (1803).
13. See, for example, "The Power of the President to Withhold Information from the Congress," Memoranda of the Attorney General, Complies by the Subcommittee on Congressional Rights of the Senate Committee on the Judiciary, 85th Congress, 2d Session, February 6 and October 31, 1958.
14. See, for example, Mark J. Rozell, Congressional Testimony, November 6, 2001, and Rozell, *Executive Privilege: The Dilemma of Secrecy and Democratic Accountability* (Baltimore: Johns Hopkins University Press, 1994).
15. Fred I. Greenstein, *The Hidden-Hand Presidency: Eisenhower as Leader* (New York: Basic Books, 1982), p. 205.
16. Executive Privilege, U.S. Senate, 92nd Congress, 1st session, Hearings Before the Subcommittee on Separation of Powers of the Committee on the Judiciary, 1971, p. 35.
17. Memorandum from President Richard M. Nixon to Executive Department Heads, March 24, 1969, "Executive Privilege" White House Staff Files, Nixon Presidential Materials Project, Alexandra, Virginia.
18. *United States v. Nixon*, 418 U.S. 683 (1974).
19. Debate on Articles of Impeachment, Hearings Before the House Committee on the Judiciary, 93rd Congress, 2d Session, 449 (1974).
20. Memorandum from President Reagan to Heads of Executive Departments and Agencies, "Procedures Governing Responses to Congressional Requests for Information," November 4, 1982.
21. Memorandum from Lloyd Cutler to all Executive Department and Agency General Councils, September 28, 1994, cited in Mark J. Rozell, "Congressional Testimony on the Presidential Records Act," November 6, 2001.
22. 5 U.S.C. 1002, 60 Stat. 238 (1946).
23. See, for example, Walter Gellhorn, "The Administrative Procedure Act: The Beginnings," *Virginia Law Review,* Vol. 72 (1986): p. 219.

24. See, for example, Martin Shapiro, "APA, Past, Present, Future," *Virginia Law Review,* Vol. 72 (1986): p. 447; Edward Rubin, "Its Time to Make the Administrative Procedures Act Administrative," *Cornell Law Review,* Vol. 89 (2003): p. 95

25. Administrative Procedures Act, 79th Congress, 2nd Session, Senate Doc. 248 (July 26, 1946): p. 198.

26. "Replies from Federal Agencies to Questionnaire Submitted by the Special Subcommittee on Government Information," 84th Congress, 1st Session, November 1, 1955.

27. Executive Order 10290 Prescribing Regulations Establishing Minimum Standards for the Classification, Transmission and Handling by Departments and Agencies of the Executive Branch, of Official Information Which Requires Safeguarding in the Interest of the Security of the United States. (1951).

28. Francis E. Rourke, "Administrative Secrecy: A Congressional Dilemma," *The American Political Science Review*, Vol. 54 , No. 3, (September 1960): p. 686.

29. Executive Order 10,501, 10,964, 11,652, 12,065, 12,356, 12,958, and 13,292.

30. Scott Shane, "U.S. Reclassifies Many Documents in Secret Review," *New York Times,* February 21, 2006.

31. Public Law No. 100–235, 101 Stat. 1724 (1987).

32. 101 Stat. 1724 Sec. 3.

33. Memorandum for Heads of Executive Departments and Agencies from Andrew H. Card, "Action to Safeguard Information Regarding Weapons of Mass Destruction and Other Sensitive Documents Related to Homeland Security," March 19, 2002.

34. See *FOIA Post*, "New Attorney General FOIA Memorandum Issued," posted 10/15/01, at www.usdoj.gov/oip/foiapost/2001foiapost19.htm.

35. Nathan Winegar, "Secret but not classified," *The News Media & the Law*, Vol. 30, No. 4 (Fall 2006): p. 20.

Chapter 5   The Paper Curtain

1. 273 U.S. 135 at 161 (1927).

2. Bernard Schwartz, "Executive Privilege and Congressional Investigatory Power," *California Law Review,* Vol. 47, No. 1 (March 1959): pp. 3–50, at 31 quoting C.S. Potts, "Power of Legislative Bodies to Punish for Contempt," *University of Pennsylvania Review*, Vol. 74, No. 7 (1926): pp. 691–725, at 708.

3. See, for example, a 1934 American Bar Association report in which lawyers detailed complaints about the difficulty of those seeking government documents in defense of their clients.

4. James Russell Wiggins, *Freedom or Secrecy* (New York: Oxford University Press, 1956), p. 101.

5. George A. Brandenburg, "Sigma Delta Chi Opposes Security Rule," *Editor & Publisher*, November 24, 1951, p. 12.

6. See, for example, "Administrative Order No. 46, Revised," General Services Administration, September 18, 1950; "Compliance and Security Order No. 2," General Services Administration, November 14, 1950; "Security Regulations" U.S. Department of Agriculture," April 6, 1950; "Security Regulations" U.S. Department of the Interior, January 20, 1950, all in the James Russell Wiggins Collection, Fogler Library, University of Maine, Orono, Maine.

7. Correspondence between Cross and Wiggins, James Russell Wiggins, James Russell Wiggins Collection, Fogler Library, University of Maine, Orono, Maine.

8. Correspondence between Canham and Wiggins, July 7, 1951, July 9, 1951, and July 11, 1951, in James Russell Wiggins Collection, Fogler Library, University of Maine, Orono, Maine.

9. "Classification Survey," December 20, 1951, in James Russell Wiggins Collection, Fogler Library, University of Maine, Orono, Maine.

10. Freedom of Information Committee Report, APME, February 15, 1952, in James Russell Wiggins Collection, Fogler Library, University of Maine, Orono, Maine.

11. FOI Committee Report, p. 2.

12. Correspondence between Wiggins and Cleavinger, April 1952, in James Russell Wiggins Collection, Fogler Library, University of Maine, Orono, Maine.

13. Letter from V.M. "Red" Newton, Jr., managing editor of the *Tampa Morning Tribune*, to John Marshall Butler, U.S. Senate, January 19, 1954, in James Russell Wiggins Collection, Fogler Library, University of Maine, Orono, Maine.

14. Second Commission on Organization of the Executive Branch of the Government, chaired by former President Herbert C. Hoover, established by act of July 10, 1953 (67 Stat. 142), and extended by act of May 23, 1955 (69 Stat. 64). Report to Congress, June 29, 1955, published in two volumes.

15. Letter from William L. Dawson to John E. Moss, U.S. House Subcommittee on Government Information, June 9, 1955, Folder 1, File 84A–F.7.34, Record Group 233, National Archives, Washington, D.C.

16. Letter from Harold L. Cross to J.R. Wiggins, July 19, 1955, in the personal papers of James Russell Wiggins, James Russell Wiggins Collection, Fogler Library, University of Maine, Orono, Maine.

17. Letter from James Russell Wiggins to Harold L. Cross, July 22, 1955, in the personal papers of James Russell Wiggins, James Russell Wiggins Collection, Fogler Library, University of Maine, Orono, Maine.

18. Letter from James S. Pope, managing editor of the *Louisville Courier-Journal* to John E. Moss, Jr., August 12, 1955, in James Russell Wiggins Collection, Fogler Library, University of Maine, Orono, Maine.

19. Letter from Harold L. Cross to James Russell Wiggins, September 28, 1955, in the personal papers of James Russell Wiggins, James Russell Wiggins Collection, Fogler Library, University of Maine, Orono, Maine.

20. 5 U.S.C. 301, P.L. 85-619, 72 Stat. 547 (August 12, 1958).

21. "The Growth of Executive Privilege," report for the Government Information Subcommittee of the Committee on Government Operations, John Moss, chairman, October 1959.

22. Excerpts from a Talk by Samuel J. Archibald, Staff Administrator, House Government Information Subcommittee, October 17, 1959, in the personal papers of James Russell Wiggins, James Russell Wiggins Collection, Fogler Library, University of Maine, Orono, Maine.

23. Excerpts from a Talk by Archibald, p. 2.

24. Excerpts from a Talk by Archibald, pp. 3–4.

25. James S. Pope, ASNE 1952 Committee Report, p. 108, in James Russell Wiggins Collection, Fogler Library, University of Maine, Orono, Maine.

26. James S. Pope, ASNE 1953 Committee Report, p. 130.

27. Harold L. Cross, "Access to Public Records," ASNE Annual Meeting Remarks, 1951, in James Russell Wiggins Collection, Fogler Library, University of Maine, Orono, Maine.

28. "Moss Has Hand on Knob to Open More Doors," *Editor & Publisher*, April 28, 1956, p. 56.

29. Schwartz, p. 5.

30. "Brownell Memorandum on Testimony," *New York Times*, May 18, 1954, p. 24.

31. Schwartz, p. 5.

32. Schwartz, pp. 45–46, quoting Jackson's concurring opinion in *Youngstown Sheet Tube Co., v. Sawyer*, 343 U.S. 579, 654 (1952).

33. Schwartz, p. 46.

34. Elliot's Debates, Vol. 3, p. 170.

35. See, for example, Jerry Walker, "Editors Would Rip Curtain that Shields New York Officials," *Editor & Publisher*, October 21, 1950, p. 5; Hanson W. Baldwin, American Society of Newspaper Editors Annual Meeting Proceedings, 1948, pp. 191–196, in James Russell Wiggins Collection, Fogler Library, University of Maine, Orono, Maine; John B. Oakes, "The Paper Curtain of Washington," *Nieman Reports,* Vol. 12, No. 4 (October 1958): pp. 3–5; Samuel J. Archibald, "The Early Years of the Freedom of Information Act. 1955 to 1974." *PS: Political Science and Politics*, Vol. 26, No. 4 (December, 1993): pp. 726–731; Samuel J. Archibald, "The Freedom of Information Act Revisited" *Public Administration Review*, Vol. 39, No. 4 (July– August, 1979): pp. 311–318.

Chapter 6   The Freedom of Information Act

1. S. 1160.

2. 5 U.S.C. sec.552 (1966).

3. July 4, 1966, Statement by the President, The White House.

4. Acts of the First Session, First Congress, Ch. 14, 1 Stat. 68 (1789).

5. List of World War I and World War II cases, and Lincoln's cases.

6. Reporters committee background cases.

7. President's classification and Washington's disclosure trail.

8. 5 U.S.C. sec.1002 (1946).

9. S.Rep.No.752, 79th Cong., 1st Sess. 198 (1945).

10. Attorney General's Manual on the Administrative Procedure Act 24 (1947).

11. 16 Fed. reg. 9795(1951). Executive Order No. 10,290.

12. "Younger, Congressional Investigations and Executive Secrecy: A Study in the Separation of Powers," *University of Pittsburg Law Review,* Vol. 20 (1959): p. 755.

13. Withholding Information the Public and the Press, A Survey of Federal Departments and Agencies, Senate Committee on the Judiciary, Subcommittee on Constitutional Rights, 86th Cong., 1st Sess. (1959).

14. Report of the Special Committee on Legal Services and Procedure to the 1956 Midyear Meeting of the House of Delegates, 42 A.B.A.J. 372 (1956).

15. U.S. Commission on Organization of the Executive Branch of the Government, Legal Services and Procedures: A Report to Congress (1955).

16. A Legislative Measure to Augment the Free Flow of Public Information, *American University Law Review,* Vol. 8 (1959): pp. 19, 22.

17. S.Rep.No.813, 89th Cong., 1st Sess. (1965), 3.

18. 5 U.S.C. sec.22.

19. 5 U.S.C. sec.22, later to be sec.301.

20. H.R. 2767 and S. 91(1957).

21. PubL. No. 85-619, 2 Stat. 547 (1958).

22. Availability of Information from Federal Departments and Agencies: Progress of Study, August 1958–July 1959, H.R. Rep.No.1137, 86th Congress, 1st Sess. 367–370 (1959).

23. S.2148, 85th Cong., 1st Sess. (1957).

24. Hearings on the Administrative Procedure Act Before the Subcommittee on Administrative Practice and Procedure of the Senate Committee on the Judiciary, 88th Cong, 2d Sess. (1964).

25. Hearings on S.1160, S.1336, S.1758, and S.1879 Before the Senate Committee on Judiciary, Subcommittee on Administrative Practice and Procedure, 89th Cong., 1st Sess.1 (1965).

26. Hearings on H.R.5012 and Other Bills to Amend the Federal Public Records Law, Hearings Before the House of Common. On Government Operations, Subcommittee On Foreign and Government Information, 89th Cong., 1st Sess. (1965).

27. 112 Cong. Rec. 13,661 (1966).

28. PubL.No.89-487, 80 Stat.250 (1966).

29. U.S. Department of Justice, Attorney General's Memorandum on the Public Information Section of the Administrative Procedure Act, A Memorandum for

the Executive Departments and Agencies Concerning sec.3 of the Administrative Procedure Act as Revised Effective July 4, 1967 (June 1967).

30. Brandenburg, Information Requests Under the FOI Act, *Food, Drug, Cosmetic, Law Journal*, Vol. 30 (1975): p. 321.

31. *Barceloneta Shoe Corp v. Compton*, 271 F. Supp. 591 (D.P.R. 1967), decided July 20, 1967.

32. *Benson v. General Serv. Admin.*, 298 F. Supp. 590, 595 (W.D.Wash. 1968); *Vaughn v. Rosen*, 523 F. 2d 1136 (D.C. Cir. 1975).

33. U.S. Government Information Policies and Practices, Hearings Before the House Committee on Government Operations, Subcommittee On Foreign Operations and Government Information, Part 4, 92d Cong., 2d Sess. 1177 (1972).

34. Ralph Nader, "Freedom from Information: The Act and the Agencies," *Harvard Civil Rights.-Civil Liberties Law Review*, Vol. 5, No. 1 (1970): p. 14.

35. 118 Cong. Rec. 9949-53 (1972).

36. The Freedom of Information Act, Hearings Before the Subcommittee on Foreign Operations and Government Information of the House Comm. On Government Operations, 93d Cong., 1st Sess. (1973); H.R. Rep. No. 876, 93d Cong., 2d Sess. (1974); S. Rep.No. 854, 93d Cong., 2d Sess. (1974).

37. 120 Cong. Rec. 33,300-01; 120 Cong.Rec. 34,161-68; 120 Cong.Rec. 34,810 (1974).

38. 410 U.S. 73 (1973).

39. Memo to John S. Warmer, September 23, 1974, "Veto Action on H.R. 12471.

40. "Enrolled Bill H.R. 12471—Freedom of Information Act Amendments," Memorandum to the President, Executive Office of the President, Office of Management and Budget, October 16, 1974.

41. 120 Cong.Rec. 36243-44 (1974).

42. 120 Cong. Rec. 36,865 (1974).

43. 120 Cong.Rec. 36,622-23 (1974).

44. 120 Cong.Rec. 36,865-82 (1974).

45. Attorney General's Memorandum Re. Preliminary Guidance Concerning the 1974 Freedom of Information act Amendments, Pub.L.No. 93-502, Enacted November 21, 1974 (December 11, 1974).

46. U.S. Department of Justice Attorney General's Memorandum on the 1974 Amendments to the Freedom of Information Act (February, 1975).

47. Agency Implementation of the 1974 Amendments to the Freedom of Information Act: Report on Oversight Hearings, Staff of the Subcommittee on Administrative Practice and Procedure, Senate Comm. on the Judiciary, 95th Cong., 2d Sess. (1980).

48. May 5, 1977, letter part of the Agency Implementation of the 1974 Amendments to the Freedom of Information Act: Report on Oversight Hearings, Staff of the Subcommittee on Administrative Practice and Procedure, Senate Committee of the Judiciary, 95th Cong., 2d Sess. 1980.

49. Oversight of the Freedom of Information Act, Hearings Before the Subcommittee on Administrative Practice and Procedure of the Senate Judiciary Committee, 95th Cong., 1st Sess. (1977).

50. Department of Justice Order No. 97382, 47 Fed. Reg. 10,809 (1982).

51. "FOIA Exemption 3 and the CIA: An Approach to End the Confusion and Controversy," *Minnesota Law Review*, Vol. 68 (1984): p. 1231.

52. "Computer Tapes Are Public Information," *The News Media & the Law*, September/October (1983): p. 30.

53. S. 1730, 97th Cong., 1st Sess. (1981).

54. S. 774, 98th Cong., 2d Sess. (1984); 130 Cong. Rec. S. 1822 (February 27, 1984).

55. PubL. No. 99-570, secs.1801–1804, 100 Stat. 3207–48 (1986).

56. PubL. No. 99-570, 100 Stat. 3207 (1986).

57. Report to the Chairman, Subcommittee on the Constitution, Senate Committee on the Judiciary United States Senate, General Accounting Office, GAO/GGD-83-71, (June 22, 1983): cover page.

58. Report to the Chairman, Subcommittee on the Constitution, Senate Committee on the Judiciary United States Senate, General Accounting Office, GAO/GGD-83-71, (June 22, 1983): p. 5.

59. Letter from L. Nye Stevens to Rep. Glenn English, Chairman of the Subcommittee on Government Information, Justice and Agriculture, Committee on Government Operations, House of Representatives (April 7, 1987).

60. Cost of Collecting and Processing Fees, Fact Sheet for the Chairman of the Subcommittee on Government Information, Justice and Agriculture, Committee on Government Operations, House of Representatives, General Accounting Office, (April 1987): p. 4

61. State Department Request Processing, Report to the Chairman, Subcommittee on Government Information, Justice and Agriculture, Committee on Government Operations, House of Representatives, General Accounting Office, GAO/GGD-89-23, (January 1989), p. 3.

62. State Department Request Processing, p. 13.

63. State Department Request Processing, p. 15.

64. State Department Request Processing, p. 17.

65. 5 U.S.C. sec.552(a)(4)(A)(i)(1986 Supp.IV).

66. Uniform Freedom of Information Act Fee Schedule and Guidelines, 52 Fed.Reg. 10,017-8 (1987).

67. Uniform Freedom of Information Act Fee Schedule and Guidelines, 52 Fed.Reg. 10,018 (1987).

68. 5 U.S.C. sec.552(a)(4)(A)(iii)(1986 Supp.IV).

69. PubL.100-235, 101 Stat. 1724 (1987).

70. PubL.100-235, sec.8 (1987).

71. Decision and Order of the Department of Energy on Motion for Clarification, 17 Energy Mgmt (CCH), 80,121 (May 26, 1988).

72. Exec.Order No. 12,600, 52 Fed. Reg. 23,781 (1987).

73. See H.R. 4862, 99th Cong., 2d Sess. (1986); S.150, 99th Cong., 1st Sess. (1985); H.R. 1882, 99th Cong., 1st Sess. (1985).

74. 489 U.S. 749 (1989).

75. 489 U.S. 749, 752 (1989).

76. 110 S.Ct. 471, 477 (1989).

77. Department of Justice, Exemption 6 and Exemption 7(C): Step-by-Step Decision Making, FOIA Update, Spring 1989.

78. Department of Justice Report on "Electronic Record" Issues under the Freedom of Information Act, Office of Information and Privacy, Department of Justice, October 1990.

79. Survey Regarding "Electronic Record" Issues, Memorandum from the Office of Information and Privacy, Department of Justice, May 1, 1989.

80. Justice Department Guide to the Freedom of Information Act, September 1988, 351; *Yeager v. Drug Enforcement Administration*, 678 F.2d 315 (D.C. Circ. 1982).

81. Department of Justice Report on "Electronic Record," p. 5.

82. Department of Justice Report on "Electronic Record," pp. 6–11.

83. Report from the FOIA Front: A Study of Journalists' Usage of the Freedom of Information Act, The Society of Professional Journalists, December 1989.

84. Report from the FOIA Front, Appendix A, 2.

85. Henry H. Perritt, Electronic Public Information and the Public's Right to Know, Benton Foundation and the Bauman Family Foundation, Washington DC, 1990.

86. Perritt, pp. 39–42.

87. Memorandum for Heads of Departments and Agencies, The Freedom of Information Act, William J. Clinton, October 4, 1993.

88. A Bill to Amend FOIA to Provide for Public Access to Information in an Electronic Format, H.R. 4917, Cong.Rec. H7194, August 8, 1994; Electronic Freedom of Information Improvement Act, S. 1782, Cong.Rec. S12646, August 25, 1994.

89. J. Kevin O'Brien, Federal Bureau of Investigation, statement before the H.R. Subcommittee on Government Management, Information and Technology of the Committee on Government Reform and Oversight, June 13, 1996.

90. O'Brien, pp. 1–4.

91. Martin Campbell-Kelly and William Aspray, *Computer: A History of the Information Machine* (New York: BasicBooks, 1996); see also for current statistical reports, Source: Internet Software Consortium, www.isc.org/ds/host-count-history.html, viewed November 30, 2000.

92. H.R.3802, An Act to amend section 552 of title 5, United States Code, popularly known as the Freedom of Information Act, to provide for public access to information in an electronic format, and for other purposes, 104 Cong. 2nd Sess. (1996).

93. Darrell M. West, *Assessing e-Government: The Internet, Democracy, and Service Delivery by State and Federal Governments* (Providence: Brown University, 2000); OMB Watch,

Plugged In, Tuning Up: An Assessment of State Legislative Websites (Washington, DC: March 2001); Shannon E. Martin, Bill F. Chamberlin, and Irina Dmitrieva, "State Laws Requiring World Wide Web Dissemination of Information: A Review of State Government Mandates for Documents Online," *Information & Communication Technology Law*, Vol. 10 (2001): p. 169.

94. OMB Watch.
95. West.
96. Martin, et al., *State Laws Requiring World Wide Web*, pp. 169–180.
97. Information Management: Progress in Implementing the 1996 Electronic Freedom of Information Act Amendments, U.S. General Accounting Office Report to Congressional Requesters, March 2001.
98. Briefing on Implementation of EFOIA Amendments, Appendix I, U.S. General Accounting Office. December 19, 2000,p. 9.
99. Information Management: Update on Implementation of the 1996 Electronic Freedom of Information Act Amendments, U.S. General Accounting Office Report to Congressional Requesters, August 2002.
100. Results of OMB Watch FOIA Request on Information Withheld 05/15/2002, www.ombwatch.org/article/archive/253/30?TopicID=1, viewed November 2, 2006.
101. OMB Watch list with descriptions of what was withdrawn from government Web sites, www.ombwatch.org/article/articleview/213/1/104, viewed November 2, 2006.
102. Federal Register: September 20, 2006 (Vol. 71, No.182) [Notices][Page 54986], "Notification of Closure of the EPA Headquarters Library."
103. Brian Wingfield, "Unions for Border Workers Criticize Rules on Disclosure," *New York Times*, November 30, 2004.

PART 2 Freedom of Information Act in Practice: Introduction

1. American Society of Access Professionals' Statement of Principles, www.accesspro.org/principles.html, viewed January 11, 2007.
2. Mark Tapscott and Nicole Taylor, "Few Journalists Use the Federal Freedom of Information Act: A Study by the Center for Media and Public Policy, The Heritage Foundation," www.heritage.org/Press/MediaCenter/FOIA.cfm, viewed November 2, 2006.
3. "Open Government: Gains and Losses: How Freedom of Information Act is Working Out," *U.S. News & World Report*, May 5, 1975, p. 30.
4. *Kissinger v. Reporters Committee*, 445 U.S. 136 (1980); *Forsham v. Harris*, 445 U.S. 169 (1980).
5. Linda Greenhouse, "Agencies Get New Power to Withhold Investigative Reports," *New York Times*, October 29, 1986, Sec. A, p. 18.

6. John Markoff, "Computers Challenge Freedom of Information Act," *New York Times*, June 18, 1989, Sec.1, p. 25.

7. Markoff, p. 25.

8. Gloria Borger, "Practicing the Art of Secrecy," *U.S. News & World Report*, Vol. 132, No. 8 (March 18, 2002): p. 24.

Chapter 7   Federal Agencies through the Lens of FOIA

1. See, for example, www.foia.cia.gov/new_releases.asp, viewed February 2007.

2. Darrell M. West, *Assessing e-government: The Internet, Democracy, and Service Delivery by State and Federal Governments*, Brown University, 2000; OMB Watch, *Plugged In, Tuning Up: An Assessment of State Legislative Websites*, Washington, DC, March 2001; Shannon E. Martin, Bill F. Chamberlin, Irina Dmitrieva, "State Laws Requiring World Wide Web Dissemination of Information: A Review of State Government Mandates for Documents Online," 10 *Information & Comm. Tech. L.* 169 (2001).

3. Peter Montgomery and Peter Overby, "The Fight to Know," *Common Cause*, Summer 1991.

4. Mark Silva, "Bush Team Imposes Thick Veil of Secrecy," *Chicago Tribune,* April 30, 2006, p. C1.

5. Kathleen Day, "Ex-Hostage's FOI Quest Takes a Ludicrous Turn," October 3, 1994, A17.

6. Christopher H. Schmitt and Edward T. Pound, "Keeping Secrets," *U.S. News & World Report*, Vol. 135, No. 22 (December 22 2003): p. 18.

7. Ed Bruske, "Atomic Waste Shipping Routes Are Disclosed," *Washington Post,* September 29, 1980, p. B1.

8. Sara Kehaulani Goo, "Northwest Gave U.S. Data on Passengers," *Washington Post,* January 18, 2004, p. A1.

9. Schmitt and Pound, p. 18 .

10. Walter Pincus and Vernon Loeb, *Washington Post,* August 9, 1999, p. A13.

11. Nicholas M. Horrock, "CIA Documents Tell of 1954 Project to Create Involuntary Assassins," *New York Times*, February 9, 1978.

12. John Marks, *The Search for the "Manchurian Candidate": The CIA and Mind Control* (TimesBooks: New York, 1979), p. vii.

13. Bill Richards and John Jacobs, "3 Area College Used by CIA in Behavior Testing," *Washington Post*, August 18, 1977, A1; John Jacobs, "CIA Papers Detail Secret Experiments on Behavior Control," *Washington Post*, July 21, 1977, p. A5.

14. "CIA Linked to Mind-Control Drug Experiments," *New York Times*, December 4, 1980.

15. Andrew Curry, et al., "Hoaxes of the Ages," *U.S. News & World Report,* Vol. 129, No. 4 (June 24 & July 31, 2000): Cover Package.

16. George Lardner Jr. and William Claiborne, "CIA's Glomar Game Plan," *Washington Post,* October 23, 1977, Al; Harriet Phillippi, "The Story Behind The Story," *Washington Post,* November 20, 1977, magazine, p. 5.

17. Anna Mulrine, et al., "Ask the CIA," *U.S. News & World Report,* Vol. 139, No. 21 (December 5, 2005): p. 18.

18. Stephen Schlesinger, "Preserving bitter fruit," *Harvard International Review,* Vol. 21, No. 4 (Fall 1999): p. 24.

19. "Documents Reveal CIA Hit Lists in the '50s. Assassins Trained for Guatemalan Coup," *Dallas Morning News,* May 24, 1997, A12.

20. Associated Press Service, "National Archives Agreed to Documents Coverup", *Los Angeles Times,* April 12, 2006, p. A13.

21. Athan Theoharis, *Spying on Americans: Political Surveillance from Hoover to the Huston Plan* (Philadelphia, PA : Temple University Press, 1978), p. xiii.

22. Theoharis, p. xiv.

23. Angus Mackenzie, *Secrets: The CIA's War at Home* (Berkeley, CA: University of California Press, 1997), p. 203.

24. Mackenzie, p. 207.

25. Michael Dobbs, "The FBI's Pas de Duh," *Washington Post,* July 16, 1999, C1.

26. Al Kamen, "Moscow Clears Release of 1962 Correspondence," *Washington Post,* April 11, 1991, p. A15.

27. Tracy Thompson, "State Pressed for Papers on Cuban Crisis," *Washington Post,* October 11, 1990, p. A4.

28. *National Security Archives v. FBI,* 759 F. Supp. 872 (Washington D.C. Cir. 1991).

29. Alexander Charns, "FBI Kept a File on Supreme Court," *New York Times,* August 21, 1988, p. A29.

30. New York Times News Service, "Kennedy Report Splits Warren, Hoover," *Chicago Tribune,* December 5, 1985, p. 38 .

31. Sanford J. Ungar, "The FBI on the Defensive Once Again," *New York Times* May 15, 1988, p. 46.

32. Seth Rosenfeld, "Keeping Secrets: The FBI's Information Bottleneck," *Columbia Journalism Review,* Vol. 31, No. 6 (March/April 1992): p.14.

33. Scott Simon, National Public Radio, Weekend Edition, January 17, 1998, Transcript # 98011713-214.

34. Edward Walsh and Richard Leiby, "FBI Tape Includes Tear Gas Decision," *Washington Post,* September 3, 1999, p. A1.

35. Karlyn Barker & Walter Pincus, "Watergate Revisited," *Washington Post,* June 14, 1992, p. A1.

36. Linda Greenhouse, "NASA Told to Release Challenger Disaster Tape," *New York Times,* July 30, 1988, p. A31.

37. *New York Times v. NASA,* 782 F. Supp. 628, 19 Media L. Rep. 1688 (1991).

38. Justin Blum, "Theft of Experimental Money Exposes Weak Spots in Engraving Bureau Security," *Washington Post,* September 24, 1994, p. C1.

39. Toni Locy, "Commerce Told to Act on Documents' Release," *Washington Post*, May 9, 1995, p. D3.
40. Carol D. Leonnig, Jo Becker & David Nakamura, "Lead Levels in Water Misrepresented Across U.S.," *Washington Post*, October 5, 2004, p. A1.
41. Nell Henderson, "Federal Report Cites Metro in Green Line Delay," *Washington Post*, August 7, 1990, p. B1.
42. Malcolm Gladwell, "In Two Years, Almost 100 FOIA Requests," *Washington Post*, August 17, 1990, p. A8.
43. Fred Hiatt, "Pentagon Ignored Own Rules in Giving Names, GAO Says," *Washington Post*, March 21, 1986, p. A2.
44. Dobbs, "Decoded Cables," p. A1.
45. Dexter Filkins, for the *Los Angeles Times*, "U.S. Allegedly Abandoned Vietnamese Commands," *Washington Post*, June 9, 1996, p. A10.
46. Jeff Gerth, "Kemp is canceling another program linked to abuses," *New York Times*, June 30, 1989, p. A1.
47. Gerth, p. A10.
48. Philip Shenon, "Washington Talk; Public Record," *New York Times*, August 28, 1989, p. A13.

Chapter 8   The Famous, the Not-So-Famous, and FOIA

1. "Educators Assail U.S. Curbs on Access to Data," *New York Times*, September 14, 1988, p. B9.
2. Richard Chang, "Professor Awaits Final Lennon Papers," *Orange County Register*, October 18, 2004.
3. Orr Kelly, "The Secret Files of J. Edgar Hoover," *U.S. News & World Report*, December 19, 1983, p. 45.
4. Kelly, p. 46.
5. Kelly, p. 47.
6. Kelly, p. 48.
7. Linda P. Campbell, "North's Diaries May Aid Noriega in Drug Case," *Chicago Tribune*, May 19, 1990, p. C3.
8. Vernon Loeb, "NSA Admits to Holding Secret Information on Princess Diana," *Washington Post*, December 12, 1998, p. A13.
9. Kevin Sullivan and Walter Pincus, "NSA Denies Monitoring Calls of Princess Diana," *Washington Post*, December 12, 2006, p. A22.
10. Michael Kilian, "Machine-gun Kelley," *Chicago Tribune*, April 14, 1991, Tempo C1.
11. David J. Garrow, *Bearing the Cross: Martin Luther King, Jr., and the Southern Christian Leadership Conference* (William Morrow: New York, 1986), p. 627.
12. Garrow, 1981, p. 9.

13. George Lardner, Jr., "'60s Files on King Confidant: Still Under FBI Lock," *Washington Post*, November 30, 1987, p. A13.

14. Lardner, p. A13.

15. James Campbell, "Baldwin's Biographer Wins Decision on Files," *Washington Post*, December 30, 1998, p. A17.

16. Karl Evanzz, "Deadly Crossroads: Farrakhan's Rise and Malcolm X's Fall," *Washington Post*, December 10, 1995, p. C3.

17. Devlin Barrett, "Sinatra Hoped to 'Sing' of Commies," *New York Post*, December 9, 1998, p. A6.

18. Associated Press, "Julian Bond Obtains FBI File on Him," *New York Times*, September 6, 1975.

19. Michael Tackett, "Spying on the Boss," *Chicago Tribune*, August 31, 1997, p. C1.

20. Associated Press, "Justice Fortas Told President About Case, Researcher Says," *New York Times*, January 23, 1990, p. A19.

21. Richard Halloran, "Papers Link Bank to K.CIA Aide I Stock Disposal," *New York Times*, November 2, 1977.

22. Philip Shenon, "Documents Show Active Pierce Role on Fund Requests," *New York Times*, July 23, 1989, p. A1.

23. Philip Shenon with Leslie Maitland, "Files Show Pierce Helped Friends and the G.O.P.," *New York Times*, August 4, 1989, p. A1.

24. David Johnston, "North's Notes Show He Met Bush Soon After Lying to Congress in '86," *New York Times*, May 9, 1990, p. A14.

25. "Spy Probed Liberals for FBI," *New York Post*, July 29, 2001, p. 29; Jonathan Dann and J. Michael Kennedy, "Admitted traitor was Bigwig in FBI Anti-subversive Unit," *Chicago Tribune*, July 29, 2001, p. C8.

26. Peter Wallsten, "Amid Strife, Abramoff Had Pal at White House," *Los Angeles Times*, May 11, 2006, p. A4.

27. James Gerstenzang, "2 Tied to Abramoff Paid White House 100 Visits," *Los Angeles Times*, September 21, 2006, p. A29.

28. Carol J. Williams, "Decision Time on Cuban Detention," *Los Angeles Times*, November 7, 2006, p. A12.

29. Alexander Charns, "How the FBI Spied on the High Court," *Washington Post*, December 3, 1989, p. C1.

30. Charns, p. C1.

31. Charns, p. C1.

32. Frank J. Prial, "Big Growth Disclosed in List of Barred Aliens," *New York Times*, June 23, 1990, p. A24.

33. *U.S. Department of State v. Ray*, 502 U.S. 164 (1991).

34. William Glaberson, "Challenging the Cold War Today," *New York Times*, May 21, 1991, p. A1.

35. Seymour M. Hersh, "CIA Papers Indicate Broader Surveillance Than Was Admitted," *New York Times*, March 90, 1979.

36. Associated Press, "FBI Lists 110 in a Socialist Party as Threats," *New York Times*, December 18, 1975.
37. Kathleen Teltsch, "FBI Accused of Keeping Files on Foundation," *New York Times*, November 28, 1990, p. A16.
38. Associated Press, "CIA Documents Reveal Presence of Agents on 'Problem' Campuses," *New York Times*, December 18, 1977.
39. Associated Press, "CIA Documents."
40. Steven Emerson, "Secret Warriors," *U.S. News & World Report*, March 21, 1988, Cover Story, p. 24.
41. Joseph L. Galloway, "A Soldier's Story," *U.S. News & World Report*, May 31, 1999, Cover Story, p. 42.
42. Caryle Murphy, "Vindication Rewards a Six-Year Struggle," *Washington Post*, October 20, 1983, p. C1.
43. Wayne King, "An FBI Inquiry Fed by Informer Emerges in Analysis of Documents," *New York Times*, February 13, 1988, p. A33.
44. Wallace Turner, "CIA Is Blamed for Career Problems of Ex-Source," *New York Times*, February 21, 1978.
45. Nicholas M. Horrock, "Files of FBI Showed it Harassed Teacher," *New York Times*, January 29, 1975.
46. Leo H. Carney, "New Findings on '34 Ship Disaster," *New York Times*, November 6, 1988, Section New Jersey, p. 14.
47. Lewis H. Diuguid, "Excluded," *Washington Post Magazine*, January 3, 1999, p. W14.
48. Associated Press, "Widow: U.S. Hid Execution," *Chicago Tribune*, June 4, 1995, p. C7.
49. R. Jeffrey Smith, "U.S. Documents Confirm Skepticism on Nun's Rape," *Washington Post*, May 7, 1996, p. A14.
50. Lisa Leff, "Frank Perdue's Life in the Fast Lane," *Washington Post*, August 16,1989, p. B1.
51. Connie Cass, "Army Probe Cleared McCaffrey," *Washington Post*, May 12, 2000, p. A41.
52. Sheldon Himelfarb, "A Writer's Adventures in Red-Tape Land," *New York Times*, September 14, 1987, p. A19.
53. Howard Witt, "To Him, Murrah Blast Isn't Solved," *Chicago Tribune*, December 10, 2006, p. C3.
54. Lisa Anderson and Kirsten Scharnberg, "WTC Transcripts Reveal Anguish," *Chicago Tribune*, August 29, 2003, p. C1.

Chapter 9 The Business of Government, Consumers, and FOIA

1. Pete Earley, "EPA Lets Trade Secret Loose in Slip-Up," *Washington Post*, September 18, 1982, p. A1.

2. Pete Earley, "Trade Secret Blunders Make FDA a Target on Hill," *Washington Post*, January 10, 1983, p. A11.

3. Michael Dobbs, "Kissinger Offered China Satellite Data in 1973," *Washington Post*, January 10, 1999, p. A2.

4. Michael Isikoff, "Modified Versions of Banned Assault Weapons Cleared for Import," *Washington Post*, July 23, 1990, p. A4.

5. "Report Documents Poor Shape of Area's Urban Highways," *Washington Post*, September 17, 1997, p. B3.

6. John Chase and Bruce Japsen, "Illinois Targets 48 Drug Firms," *Chicago Tribune*, February 8, 2005, p. C1.

7. Associated Press, "LaRouche Followers Claim Secret Agency Investigated Group," *Chicago Tribune*, August 13, 1987, p. C21.

8. "Sellers of Government Data Thrive," *New York Times*, December 26, 1991, p. D2.

9. Peter Baker and D'Vera Cohn, "Builder, Fairfax County Can't Find Any Source of Damage to Pipeline," *Washington Post*, April 9, 1993, p. B2.

10. Florence Graves and Sara Kehaulani Goo, "Boeing Parts and Rules Bent, Whistle-Blowers Say," *Washington Post*, April 17, 2006, p. A1.

11. Bill Richards, "AID Arm Buckled Under to Hill Pressure in Funding Projects," *Washington Post*, May 13, 1978, p. A2; Bill Richards and Dan Morgan, "AID Gave Passman Assurances," *Washington Post*, February 24, 1978, p. A1.

12. Associated Press, "U.S. Grants to Venezuelans Sow Deep Suspicion," *Los Angeles Times*, August 27, 2006, p. A7.

13. Patrick Tyler, "$25 Million Bonuses for U.S. Workers," *Washington Post*, December 23, 1979, p. A1.

14. Alison Muscatine, "Congress' Pensions Can Top Salaries," *Washington Post*, July 16, 1984, p. D1.

15. Jane Cawley, "$7 Million to Heirs of 4 on Shuttle," *Chicago Tribune*, March 8, 1988, p. C3.

16. Stuart Diamond, "NASA Wasted Billions, Federal Audits Disclose," *New York Times*, April 23, 1986, p. A1.

17. Jeff Gerth, "NASA's Reliance on Contractors Is Seen as Eroding Its Capabilities," *New York Times*, September 28, 1989, p. A1.

18. Christopher Byron, "Black Hawk Clown: United Technologies Wants to Hide Copter Program Flaws," *New York Post*, June 5, 2006, p. 33.

19. Charles R. Babcock and Renae Merle, "A Contractor's Purchase on Power," *Washington Post*, March 20, 2006, p. D1.

20. Dana Priest, "Pentagon to Review Hill Fellowships," *Washington Post*, October 10, 1996, p. A19.

21. Jeff Gerth, "Kemp Is Canceling Another Program Linked to Abuses," *New York Times*, June 30, 1989, p. A1.

22. Chicago Tribune wires, "Pierce Backed Project After Plea," *Chicago Tribune,* October 6, 1989, p. C5.

23. Associated Press, "Documents Detail Collapse of Sand Linked to Whitewater," *Chicago Tribune*, April 5, 1994, p. N7.

24. Cindy Skrzycki, "A Rif-and-Ready Approach at the Seething FDIC," *Washington Post*, August 16, 1996, p. D1.

25. Don Phillips, "FAA Gets a 'Wake-up Call' on Safety," *Washington Post*, July 27, 1994, p. A25.

26. Julian E. Barnes and Peer Spiegel, "Expanding the Military, without a Draft," *Los Angeles Times,* December 24, 2006, p. A18.

27. Associated Press, "Marshals Service Chief's Perks Questioned," *Chicago Tribune*, July 29, 1991, p. M5.

28. Associated Press, "Agriculture Aide Eludes Prosecution," *Chicago Tribune*, June 7, 1985, p. C22.

29. Sharon LaFraniere and Susan Schmidt, "Espy Billed U.S. for Monthly Trips Home," *Washington Post*, September 17, 1994, p. A1.

30. Mike Allen, "HUD Files Detail Martinez's Fla. Trips," *Washington Post*, March 17, 2004, p. A6.

31. Dana Milbank, "Bush Averts Showdown with Congress," *Washington Post*, July 28, 2001, p. A4.

32. Dana Milbank and Ellen Nakashima, "Energy Dept. Ordered to Release Documents," *Washington Post,* February 28, 2002, p. A1; Jeff Zeleny, "Cheney Papers Ordered Released," *Washington Post*, March 6, 2002, p. N10; Mike Allen, "Energy Dept. Says It Tried to Engage Green Groups," *Washington Post,* March 22, 2002, p. A25; Dana Milbank and Mike Allen, "Energy Contacts Disclosed," *Washington Post*, March 26, 2002, p. A1; Dana Milbank and Mike Allen, "Energy Task Force Belatedly Consulted Environmentalists," *Washington Post*, March 27, 2002, p. A2.

33. Naftali Bendavid, "Heavy Editing of Energy Papers Criticized," *Washington Post*, March 27, 2002, p. N7.

34. Dana Milbank and Paul Blustein, "White House Aided Enron in Dispute," *Washington Post*, January 19, 2002, p. A1; Dana Milbank and Alan Sipress, "NSC Aided Enron's Efforts," *Washington Post*, January 25, 2002, p. A18.

35. Kathleen Day and James V. Grimaldi, "Lay's Lobbing Reached the Top of Treasury," *Washington Post,* February 21, 2002, p. E1.

36. Hanna Rosin, "Lay's Letters to Bush Show Personal Ties," *Washington Post*, February 16, 2002, p. A12.

37. Jo Becker and Michael Grunwald, "In Private Practice Robert's Record Is Mixed," *Washington Post,* August 5, 2005, p. A2; Jo Becker, "Roberts Papers Being Delayed," *Washington Post,* August 10, 2005, p. A1; Jo Becker and R. Jeffrey Smith, "In '81 Roberts Offered Counsel to O'Connor," *Washington Post,* August 11, 2005, p. A7;

R. Jeffrey Smith and Charles Babington, "Roberts Memo Urged Laws Prohibiting Busing, Quotas," *Washington Post,* August 30, 2005, p. A2.

38. Jo Becker and Amy Goldstein, "'86 Alito Memo Argues Against Foreigners' Rights," *Washington Post,* November 29, 2005, p. A4.

39. Michael Dobbs, "Papers Illustrate Negroponte's Contra Role," *Washington Post,* April 12, 2005, p. A4.

40. Peter Baker, "Privilege at State With Nominees," *Washington Post,* August 2, 2005, p. A6.

41. Dan Eggen, "CIA Acknowledges 2 Interrogation Memos," *Washington Post,* November 14, 2006, p. A29.

42. Josh White and Julie Tate, "4 Men Cleared of Terrorism Links but Still Detained," *Washington Post,* May 20, 2006, p. A18.

43. Michael L. Millenson, "LyphoMed Again Draws FDA Fire," *Chicago Tribune,* March 15, 1988, Business, p. C1.

44. Martha Mendoza and Christopher Sullivan, "Federal Fines Often Go Unpaid or Get Sharply Reduced," *Washington Post,* April 16, 2006, p. A4.

45. Cass Peterson, "Oak Ridge Guarded a Secret," *Washington Post,* August 17, 1983, p. A6.

46. Matthew L. Wald, "Report Assails Safety of Nuclear Waste Storage at Carolina Plant," *New York Times,* July 24, 1986, p. A11.

47. Keith Schneider, "DuPont Asserts It Fully Disclosed Reactor Problems," *New York Times,* October 3, 1988, p. A1.

48. Thom Shanker, "Public Outcry on the Rise Over Nuclear Plant Hazards," *Chicago Tribune,* November 28, 1988.

49. Keith Schneider, "U.S. Studies Health Problems Near Weapon Plant," *New York Times,* October 17, 1988, p. A1.

50. Keith Schneider, "U.S. Admits Peril of 40's Emission at A-Bomb Plant," *New York Times,* July 12, 1990, p. A1.

51. Amanda Covarrubias, "Study Says Lab Meltdown Caused Cancer," *Los Angeles Times,* October 6, 2006, p. A1.

52. New York Times News Service, "U.S. Atomic Plant Leaked High Doses," *Chicago Tribune,* July 12, 1990, p. C1.

53. Joby Warrick, "Plant Hid Risk from Workers," *Washington Post,* December 23, 1999, p. A1.

54. Warrick, "Maps Reveal Scattering of KY. Plutonium," *Washington Post,* October 1, 2000, p. A1.

55. Mark J. Rauzon, "Live Ammo: The Pacific Project Exposed U.S. Sailors to Biowarfare and Chemical Agents," *Los Angeles Times,* November 19, 2006, West Magazine, p. 18.

56. Associated Press, "In Korean War, U.S. POWs Told Soviets Much, Documents Reveal," *Chicago Tribune,* January 28, 1997, p. N9.

57. David Jackson, "School Lunches; Illness on Menu," *Chicago Tribune*, December 9, 2001, p. C1.

58. Associated Press News Service, "N.Y. Attack Site Released Contaminants," *Washington Post*, October 27, 2001, p. A11.

59. Katherine Boo, "Residents Languish," *Washington Post*, March 15, 1999, p. A1; Katherine Boo, "Invisible Deaths," *Washington Post*, December 5, 1999, p. A1.

60. Gene Kuleta, "St. Charles Water Plant Compliant, Leaders Say," *Chicago Tribune*, July 24, 1997, p. D1.

61. John Crewdson, "Everybody in the Pool," *Chicago Tribune*, November 19, 1989, p. C11.

62. John Crewdson, "Report: AIDS Patient Died in Vaccine Trial," *Chicago Tribune*, July 19, 1991, p. C1.

63. John Crewdson, "Documents May Hurt U.S. Effort to Share Patent, Cut AZT Price," *Chicago Tribune*, October 4, 1992, p. C3.

64. Larry Kramer, "Nixon's War against Public TV," *Washington Post*, February 24, 1979, p. A12.

65. Eric Brace, "ACLU Appeals Denial of Grants," *Washington Post*, November 14, 1994, p. D7.

66. Charles Leroux, "Spreading the Wealth; Public Art, Hidden Agendas," *Chicago Tribune*, June 21, 2002, p. C1.

67. James Warren, Maurice Possley, and Joseph Tybor, "Fed-up Judges Put Jailhouse Lawyer's Career on Rocks," *Chicago Tribune*, April 30, 1985, Business, p. C1.

68. Peter Carlson, "International Man of Mystery," *Washington Post*, June 22, 2004, p. C1.

69. Vernon Loeb, "Government Misconduct Is Alleged," *Washington Post* October 2, 1999, p. A3.

Chapter 10 States and Freedom of Information

1. *Miller v. Sovereign*, 17 Neb. 173, 22 N.W. 353 (1885).

2. *Spielman v. Flynn*, 19 Neb. 342, 27 N.W. 244 (1886).

3. Burns Ind. Code Ann. sec. 5-14-3-2 (2001).

4. N.C. Gen. Stat. sec. 132-6(b) (2003).

5. Ohio Rev. Code Ann. sec. 149.43(B)(3) (2003).

6. See, for example, *Clement V. Graham*, 78 Vt. 290 (1906); *Nowack v. Auditor Gen.*, 243 Mich. 200, 219 N.W. 749 (1928); *Holloran v. McGath*, 104 Mont. 490 (1937); *Nolan v. McCoy*, 77 R.I. 96 (1950); *State ex rel. Chartleston Mail Ass'n. v. Kelly*, 149 W.Va. 766, 143 S.E. 2d 136 (1965).

7. See, for example, *Payne v. Staunton*, 55 W.Va. 202, 46 S.E. 2d 927 (1904); *Holcombe v. State ex rel Chandler*, 240 Ala. 590, 200 S. 739 (1941); *People ex rel. Better Broadcasting Council, Inc., v. Keane*, 17 Ill. App. 3d 1090, 309 N.E.2d 362 (1973).

8. Tenn. Code Ann. sec. 10-7-503(c)(1-2) (2003).

9. See, for example, *Pressman v. Elgin*, 187 Md. 446, 50 A. 2d 560 (1947); *Beckon v. Emery*, 36 Wis. 2d 510, 153 N.W. 2d 501 (1967).

10. See, for example, *Butcher v. Civil Service Commission*, 163 Pa. Super. 348, 61 A. 2d 367, (1948).

11. *Parker v. Clary Lakes Recreation Association, Inc.*, Cobb Superior Court, A00A0116 (2000).

12. Ofelia Casillas, "School Leaders' Tactics Are Hit," *Chicago Tribune*, December 18, 2003, p. C3.

13. Ted Gregory, "Butterfield Park Board Accused of Skirting Law," *Chicago Tribune*, June 22, 2000, p. D1.

14. *Indianapolis Convention & Visitors Association, Inc., v. Indianapolis Newspapers, Inc.*, 577 N.E. 2d 208; 19 Media L. Rep. 1488 (1991).

15. *Brian D. Lamy v. New Hampshire Public Utilities Commission*, 872 A. 2d 1006 (2005).

16. *Walter C. Ervin, Jr. v. Southern Tier Economic Development Inc.*, 782 N.Y.S. 2d 903 (2004) at 904-905.

17. *Michael Farrimond v. State of Oklahoma, et al.*, 8 P. 3d 872, 71 O.B.A.J. 1769 (2000) at 874.

18. *Rick Hangartner v. City of Seattle, et al.* 151 Wn2d 439, 90 P. 3d 26 (2004).

19. Mike Lee, "Watergate Scandal Helped Pry Open Government Records," *Associated Press*, October 8, 2001.

20. James Minton, "Judge Rules Probe Records Not Public," *The Advocate*, October 21, 1997.

21. Tribune News Service, "Inmate Can't Get Records," *Chicago Tribune*, August 5, 1997, p. M3.

22. *Director, Department of Information Technology of the Town of Greenwich v. Freedom of Information Commission et al.*, 274 Conn. 179; 874 A. 2d 785; 33 Media L. Rep. 2128 (2005).

23. Jim Gaines, "One Citizen's Pursuit of Open Records," *Associated Press*, February 3, 2005.

24. *City of Reno, v. Reno Gazette-Journal*, 63 P. 3d 1147, 119 Nev. Adv. Rep. 6 (2003).

25. *Bergen County Imporvement Authority v. North Jersey Media Group, et al.*, 370 N.J. Super. 504; 851 A. 2d 731 (2004), at 510.

26. Tom Rybarczyk, "School Asbestos Cleanup Costs Soar," *Chicago Tribune*, April 5, 2006, p. SSW7.

27. Scott Charton, "Mizzou Coach at Center of Probe," *Chicago Tribune*, May 16, 2004, p. C16.

28. "Magoffin Clerk Can't Withhold Voter Assistance Forms," *Associated Press*, March 4, 2003.

Chapter 12   Is Less Really More?

1. Associated Press News Service, "F.B.I. Laptops Regularly Reported Lost, Stolen," February 13, 2007.

2 Charles Trueheart, "Documents Show F.B.I. Kept Files on Leading U.S. Writers," *Washington Post*, September 30, 1987, p. A1.

3 U.S. Department of Justice Inspector Generals', March 2007 Report.

4 Scott Shane, "F.B.I. Gets Bipartisan Warning on Its Misuse of Data Collection," *New York Times*, March 21, 2007, p. A17.

5 Christopher Lee, "On FOIA Front, More Agencies Contract Out," *Washington Post*, June 8, 2004, p. A21.

6 Lee, p. A21.

7 Tribune News Service, "Pentagon: Bush Guard Records Destroyed," *Chicago Tribune*, July 10, 2004, p. C16; Matt Kelley, "Suit Yields More Bush Air Guard Records," *Chicago Tribune*, September 8, 2004, p. C12; Michael Dobbs, "Assembling Full War Records a Challenge," *Washington Post*, September 30, 2004. p. A7.

8 Christopher Lee, "The Case of Roberts's Missing Papers," *Washington Post*, May 11, 2006, p. A25.

9 Michael Dobbs, "Still Secret After All These Years," *Washington Post*, March 12, 2006, p. B2.

10 Christopher Lee, "Cold War Missiles Target of Blackout," *Washington Post*, August 21, 2006, p. A1.

11 George Lardner, Jr., "Bush Clamping Down on Presidential Papers," *Washington Post*, November 1, 2001, p. A33.

12 Maarja Krusten, "Pressures Archivists Face," *Washington Post*, February 22, 2005, p. A14.

13 Al Kamen, "Who Gets the Not-So-Coveted Rosemary?" *Washington Post*, March 13, 2006, p. A13.

14 Clark Hoyt, testimony before the House of Representatives Committee on Oversight and Government Reform, Subcommittee on Information Policy, Census and National Archives, February 14, 2007.

15 Thomas Jefferson letter to Edward Carrington, July 16, 1787.

16 James Russell Wiggins, *Freedom of Secrecy* (New York: Oxford University Press, 1956), p. 199.

17 Alexis de Tocqueville, *Democracy in America* (New York: Alfred A. Knopf, 1945), Vol. 1, p. 185.

18 Sam Archibald, "The Early Years of the Freedom of Information Act—1955 to 1974," *Political Science and Politics* (December 1993): 731.

Bibliography

Books and Research Journal Articles

Archibald, Samuel J. "The Early Years of the Freedom of Information Act—1955 to 1974," *PS: Political Science and Politics*, Vol. 26, No. 4 (December, 1993).

Archibald, Samuel J. "The Freedom of Information Act Revisited," *Public Administration Review*, Vol. 39, No. 4 (July–August, 1979).

Ashman, Charles R. and Pamela Trescott. *Diplomatic Crime: Drugs, Killings, Thefts, Rapes, Slavery & Other Outrageous Crimes*, Washington, D.C.: Acropolis Books, 1987.

Blanchard, Margaret. *Revolutionary Sparks*, New York: Oxford University Press, 1992.

Branscomb, Anne Wells. *Who Owns Information?*, New York: BasicBooks, 1994.

Brucker, Herbert. *Freedom of Information*, New York: Mcmillan, 1949.

Bush, Vannevar. "As We May Think," *Atlantic Monthly*, Vol. 176, No. 1 (July, 1954): p. 101.

Clark, Charles E. *The Public Prints: The Newspaper in Anglo-American Culture, 1665–1740*, New York: Oxford, 1994.

Copeland, David A. *Colonial American Newspapers: Character and Content*, Newark: University of Delaware Press, 1997.

Cross, Harold L. *The People's Right to Know*, New York: Columbia University Press, 1953.

Davis, Charles N. and Sigman L. Splichal (eds.). *Access Denied: Freedom of Information in the Information Age*, Ames: Iowa State University Press, 2000.

Emery, Michael and Edwin Emery. *The Press and America*, Englewood Cliffs, New Jersey: Prentice Hall, 1988.

Evanzz, Karl. *The Judas Factor: The Plot to Kill Malcolm X*, Emeryville, California: Thunder's Mouth Press, 1993.

Evanzz, Karl. *The Messenger: The Rise and Fall of Elijah Muhammad,* New York: Pantheon, 1999.

Foerstel, Herbert N. *Freedom of Information and the Right to Know,* Westport, Connecticut: Greenwood Press, 1999.

"FOIA Exemption 3 and the CIA: An Approach to End the Confusion and Controversy," *Minnesota Law Review,* Vol. 68 (1984): p. 1231-1263.

Garrow, David J. *Bearing the Cross,* New York: William Marrow, 1986.

Garrow, David J. *The FBI and Martin Luther King, Jr.,* New York: W.W. Norton, 1981.

Gellhorn, Walter. "The Administrative Procedure Act: The Beginnings," *Virginia Law Review,* Vol. 72 (1986): p. 219.

Greenstein, Fred I. *The Hidden-Hand Presidency: Eisenhower as Leader,* New York: Basic Books, 1982.

Hardy, David T. *This Is Not an Assault,* New York: Xlibris, 2001.

Hayes, Frank. "Number Control," *Computerworld,* June 9, 2006, p. 56.

Hendricks, Evan. *Former Secrets: Government Records Made Public Through the Freedom of Information Act,* Washington, D.C.: Campaign for Political Rights, May 1982.

Houk, Robert. "GPO/2001: Vision for a New Millennium," Washington, D.C.: U.S. Government Printing Office, 1991.

Hutchins, Robert M. *A Free and Responsible Press: A General Report on Mass Communication,* Chicago, Illinois: University of Chicago Press, 1947.

Lax, Stephen (ed.). *Access Denied in the Information Age,* New York: Palgrave, 2001.

"A Legislative Measure to Augment the Free Flow of Public Information," *American University Law Review,* Vol. 8 (1959): pp. 19, 22.

Lewis, Sian. *News and Society in the Greek Polis,* Chapel Hill: University of North Carolina Press, 1996.

Lilley, Dorothy B. and Ronald W. Trice. *A History of Information Science, 1945–1985,* New York: Academic Press, 1989.

Machlup, Fritz. *The Study of Information: Interdisciplinary Messages,* New York: John Wiley & Sons, 1983.

Mackenzie, Angus. *Secrets: The CIA's War at Home,* Berkeley: University of California Press, 1997.

Marks, John. *The Search for the "Manchurian Candidate": The CIA and Mind Control,* New York: TimesBooks, 1979: p.601-616

Martin, Campbell-Kelly and William Aspray. *Computer: A History of the Information Machine,* New York: BasicBooks, 1996.

Martin, Shannon E. "U.S. Media Pools and Military Interventions in the 1980s and 1990s," *Journal of Peace Research,* Vol. 43, No. 5 (2006).

Martin, Shannon E., Bill F. Chamberlin, and Irina Dmitrieva. "State Laws Requiring World Wide Web Dissemination of Information: A Review of State Government Mandates for Documents Online," *Information & Communication Technology Law,* Vol. 10 (2001): p. 169.

Miller, Gordon. "The Concept of Information," *Information and Behavior,* Vol. 2, Brent D. Ruben, Ed. New Brunswick, New Jersey: Transaction, 1988.

Miller, Sarah Jordan. "The Depository Library System," Unpublished dissertation: Columbia University, 1980.

Mott, Frank L. *A History of American Magazines, 1741–1850,* Vol.1, New York: Appleton, 1930.

Mott, Frank L. and R.D. Casey. *Interpretations of Journalism,* New York: Crofts, 1937.

Moynihan, Daniel P. *Secrecy,* New Haven, Connecticut: Yale University Press, 1998.

Nader, Ralph. "Freedom from Information: The Act and the Agencies," *Harvard Civil Rights—Civil Liberty Law Review,* Vol. 5, No. 1 (1970): p. 14.

Rourke, Francis E. "Administrative Secrecy: A Congressional Dilemma," *The American Political Science Review,* Vol. 54 , No. 3 (September, 1960): p. 686.

Rozell, Mark J. *Executive Privilege,* Lawrence: University of Kansas Press, 2002.

Rubin, Edward. "Its Time to Make the Administrative Procedures Act Administrative," *Cornell Law Review,* Vol. 89 (2003): p. 95.

Schlesinger, Stephen and Stephen Kinzer. *Bitter Fruit: The Story of the American Coup in Guatemala,* Cambridge, Massachusetts: Harvard University Press, 1999.

Schwartz, Bernard. "Executive Privilege and Congressional Investigatory Power," *California Law Review,* Vol. 47, No. 1 (March, 1959): pp. 3–50.

Shapiro, Martin. "APA, Past, Present, Future," *Virginia Law Review,* Vol. 72 (1986): p. 447.

Smith, Anthony. *The Newspaper, an International History,* London: Thames and Hudson, 1979.

Sofaer, Abraham D. "Executive Power and the Control of Information: Practice under the Framers," *Duke Law Journal* Durham, NC, Duke University Law School (March, 1977): pp.1–57.

Theoharis, Athan. *Spying on Americans: Political Surveillance from Hoover to the Huston Plan,* Philadelphia: Temple University Press, 1978.

Wallace, Aurora. *Newspapers and the Making of Modern American: A History,* Westport, Connecticut: Greenwood Press, 2005.

Warren, Samuel D. and Louis D. Brandeis. "The Right to Privacy," *Harvard Law Review,* Vol. 4 (1890–1891): pp. 193–220.

Weisberg, Harold. *Whitewash: The Report on the Warren Report,* Mary Ferrell Foundation Press, 1965.

Weisberg, Harold. *Whitewash II: The FBI-Secret Service Cover-up,* New York: Dell Pubishing, 1966.

Wiggins, James Russell. *Freedom or Secrecy,* New York: Oxford University Press, 1956.

Williams, Francis. *The Right to Know: The Rise of the World Press,* London: Longmans, 1969.

Wurman, Richard Saul. *Information Anxiety,* New York: Doubleday, 1989.

Government Documents

"Enrolled Bill H.R. 12471—Freedom of Information Act Amendments," Memorandum to the President, Executive Office of the President, Office of Management and Budget, October 16, 1974.

"Replies from Federal Agencies to Questionnaire Submitted by the Special Subcommittee on Government Information," 84th Congress, 1st Session, November 1, 1955.

"The Growth of Executive Privilege," report for the Government Information Subcommittee of the Committee on Government Operations, John Moss, chairman, October 1959.

120 Cong.Rec. 33,300-01; 120 Cong.Rec. 34,161-68; 120 Cong.Rec. 34,810 (1974).

3 Annals of Congress 493 (1792).

4 Annals of Congress 250 (1794).

4 Annals of Congress 56 (1794).

8 Annals of Congress 1374-5 (1798).

A Bill to Amend FOIA to Provide for Public Access to Information in an Electronic Format, H.R. 4917, Cong.Rec. H7194, August 8, 1994.

Acts of the First Session, First Congress, Ch. 14, 1 Stat. 68 (1789).

Administrative Procedures Act, 79th Congress 2d Session, Senate Doc. 248, July 26, 1946.

Agency Implementation of the 1974 Amendments to the Freedom of Information Act: Report on Oversight Hearings, Staff of the Subcommittee on Administrative Practice and Procedure, Senate Comm. On the Judiciary, 95th Cong., 2d Sess. (1980).

Atomic Energy Commission, 60 Stat. 766 (1946).

Attorney General's Memorandum Re Preliminary Guidance Concerning the 1974 Freedom of Information Act Amendments, Pub.L.No. 93-502, Enacted November 21, 1974 (December 11, 1974).

Availability of Information From Federal Departments and Agencies: Progress of Study, August 1958–July 1959, H.R. Rep.No.1137, 86th Congress, 1st Sess. 367–370 (1959).

Barceloneta Shoe Corp v. Compton, 271 F. Supp. 591(D.P.R. 1967), decided July 20, 1967.

Benson v. General Serv. Admin., 298 F. Supp. 590, 595 (W.D.Wash. 1968); *Vaughn v. Rosen*, 523 F. 2d 1136 (D.C. Cir. 1975).

Briefing on Implementation of e-FOIA Amendments, Appendix I, U.S. General Accounting Office, December 19, 2000.

Computer Security Act of 1987, Public Law No. 100-235, 101 Stat. 1724 (1987).

Cost of Collecting and Processing Fees, Fact Sheet for the Chairman of the Subcommittee on Government Information, Justice and Agriculture, Committee on Government Operations, House of Representatives, General Accounting Office, (April 4, 1987).

Debate on Articles of Impeachment, Hearings Before the House Committee on the Judiciary, 93rd Congress 2d Session, 449 (1974).

Department of Justice Order No. 973-82, 47 Fed. Reg. 10,809 (1982).

Department of Justice Report on "Electronic Record" Issues under the Freedom of Information Act, Office of Information and Privacy, Department of Justice, October 1990.

Depository Library Act of 1962, Public Law No.87-579, 76 Stat. 352 (1962).

Dorson v. Louisiana State University, 657 S. 2d 755 (1995).

Electronic Freedom of Information Improvement Act, S. 1782, Cong.Rec. S12646, August 25, 1994.

EPA v. MINK, 410 U.S. 73 (1973).

Executive Order 10290, Establishing Minimum Standards for the Classification Transmission, and Handling by Departments and Agencies of the Executive branch, of Official Information which Requires Safeguarding in the Interest of the Security of the United States, September 24, 1951, reported in 3 Code of Federal Regulations 789–790.

Executive Privilege, U.S. Senate, 92nd Congress, 1st session, Hearings Before the Subcommittee on Separation of Powers of the Committee on the Judiciary, 1971.

First Congress, Session I, Chapter XIV, September 15, 1789, p. 68.

Freedom of Information Act, 5 U.S.C. sec.552 (1966), and July 4, 1966, Statement by the President, The White House.

Grosjean v. American Press Co., 297 U.S. 233 (1936).

Hearings on H.R.5012 and Other Bills to Amend the Federal Public Records Law, Hearings Before the House Comm. On Gov't Operations, Subcomm. On Foreign and Government Information, 89th Cong., 1st Sess. (1965).

Hearings on S.1160, S.1336, S.1758 and S.1879 Before the Senate Committee on Judiciary, Subcommittee on Administrative Practice and Procedure, 89th Cong., 1st Sess.1 (1965).

Hearings on the Administrative Procedure Act Before the Subcommittee on Administrative Practice and Procedure of the Senate Committee on the Judiciary, 88th Cong. 2d Sess. (1964).

In Defense of Animals v. Oregon Health Sciences University, 199 Ore. App. 160 (2005).

Information Management: Progress in Implementing the 1996 Electronic Freedom of Information Act Amendments, U.S. General Accounting Office Report to Congressional Requesters, March 2001.

J. Kevin O'Brien, Federal Bureau of Investigation, Statement Before the H.R. Subcommittee on Government Management, Information and Technology of the Committee on Government Reform and Oversight, June 13, 1996.

Justice Department Guide to the Freedom of Information Act, September 1988.

Letter from L. Nye Stevens to Rep. Glenn English, chairman of the Subcommittee on Government Information, Justice and Agriculture, Committee on Government Operations, House of Representatives (April 7, 1987).

Marbury v. Madison, 5 U.S. 137 (1803).

Agency Implementation of the 1974 Amendments to the Freedom of Information Act: Report on Oversight Hearings, Staff of the Subcommittee on Administrative Practise and Procedure, Senate Committee of the Judiciary, 95th Cong., 2d Sess. (1980).

McGrain v. Daugherty, 273 U.S. 135 at 161 (1927).

Memo to John S. Warmer, September 23, 1974, Veto Action on H.R. 12471.

Memorandum for Heads of Executive Departments and Agencies from Andrew H. Card, "Action to Safeguard Information Regarding Weapons of Mass Destruction and Other Sensitive Documents Related to Homeland Security," March 19, 2002.

Memorandum from Lloyd Cutler to All Executive Department and Agency General Councils, September 28, 1994, Cited in Mark J. Rozell, Congressional Testimony on the Presidential Records Act, November 6, 2001.

Memorandum from President Reagan to Heads of Executive Departments and Agencies, "Procedures Governing Responses to Congressional Requests for Information," November 4, 1982.

Memorandum from President Richard M. Nixon to Executive Department Heads, March 24, 1969, "Executive Privilege" White House Staff Files, Nixon Presidential Materials Project, Alexandra, Virginia.

Minneapolis Star & Tribune v. Minneapolis Commissioner of Revenue, 460 U.S. 575 (1983).

National Security Archives v. FBI, 759 F. Supp. 872 (D.C. Cir., 1991).

Near v. Minnesota, 283 U.S. 697 (1931).

New York Times v. NASA, 782 F. Supp. 628, 19 Media L. Rep. 1688 (1991).

Oversight of the Freedom of Information Act, Hearings Before the Subcommittee on Administrative Practise and Procedure of the Senate Judiciary Committee, 95th Cong., 1st Sess. (1977).

Paperwork Reduction Act, P.L. 104-13, 44 U.S.C. 35 (1996).

Report to the Chairman, Subcommittee on the Constitution, Senate Committee on the Judiciary, United States Senate, General Accounting Office, GAO/GGD-83-71, cover page (June 22, 1983).

Report to the Chairman, Subcommittee on the Constitution, Senate Committee on the Judiciary United States Senate, General Accounting Office, GAO/GGD-83-71, 5 (June 22, 1983).

Second Commission on Organization of the Executive Branch of the Government, Chaired by Former President Herbert C. Hoover, Established by act of July 10, 1953 (67 Stat. 142), and Extended by Act of May 23, 1955 (69 Stat. 64). Report to Congress, June 29, 1955.

Southwestern Bell Telephone Company v. The State Corporation Commission of the State of Kansas, 6 Kan. App. 2d 444, 629 P. 2d 1174 (1981).

State Department Request Processing, Report to the Chairman, Subcommittee on Government Information, Justice and Agriculture, Committee on Government Operations, House of Representatives, General Accounting Office, GAO/GGD-89-23, (January 1989).

Survey Regarding "Electronic Record" Issues, Memorandum from the Office of Information and Privacy, Department of Justice, May 1, 1989.

System of Library Distribution, 28 Stat. 624 (1895).

The Freedom of Information Act, Hearings Before the Subcommittee on Foreign Operations and Government Information of the House Comm. On Government Operations, 93d Cong., 1st Sess. (1973); H.R. Rep. No. 876, 93d Cong., 2d Sess. (1974); S. Rep. No. 854, 93d Cong., 2d Sess. (1974).

The New York Times Company v. U.S. & U.S. v. The Washington Post Company, 403 U.S. 713 (1971).

The Printing Act, 28 Stat. 601 (1895).

U.S. Commission on Organization of the Executive Branch of the Government, Legal Services and Procedures: A Report to Congress (1955).

U.S. Constitution, Article 1, Sec. 8.

U.S.Constitution, Article II, sec.3.

U.S. Department of Justice, Attorney General's Memorandum on the 1974 Amendments to the Freedom of Information Act (February 1975).

U.S. Department of Justice, Attorney General's Memorandum on the Public Information Section of the Administrative Procedure Act, A Memorandum for the Executive Departments and Agencies Concerning sec.3 of the Administrative Procedure Act as Revised Effective July 4, 1967 (June 1967).

U.S. Department of State v. Ray, 502 U.S. 164 (1991).

U.S. Government Information Policies and Practices, Hearings Before the House Comm. on Government Operations, Subcomm. On Foreign Operations and Government Information, Part 4, 92d Cong., 2d Sess. 1177 (1972).

United States v. Nixon, 418 U.S. 683 (1974).

Weston v. Carolina Research and Development Foundation, 303 S.C. 398, 401 S.E. 2d 161 (1991).

Yeager v. Drug Enforcement Administration, 678 F. 2d 315 (D.C. Circ. 1982).

Index

Abramoff, Jack, x, 103
Access Rhode Island, 158
access to government information. See public access to information
Adams, John, 43
Administrative Procedures Act (APA) (1946), 45, 60, 61
Advanced Reporting: Beyond News Events (Keir/McCombs/Shaw), 31–32
Afghanistan, 29, 88
Aftergood, Steven, 162
Agency for Internal Development, 116
"agency record" definition, 72
Ahmed, Mohammed Ali, 85
AIDS vaccine, 128
airline cargo regulations, 48
Alaska, 38, 134–35, 139
Alito, Samuel Jr., 123
Alyeska Pipeline Service Company, 38
American Bar Association, 57, 61, 62
American Civil Liberties Union (ACLU), 62, 78, 105–6, 123
American Committee on Africa/Africa Fund, 89–90
American Library Association (ALA), 91

American Magazine and Monthly Chronicle (magazine), 19
American Magazine or a Monthly View of the Political State of the British Colonies, The (magazine), 19
American Newspapers Publishers Association, 46
American Schools and Hospitals Abroad Program, 116
American Society of Access Professionals (ASAP), 77
American Society of Newspaper Editors (ASNE), 46, 50, 57, 61, 153
Anchorage Daily News (newspaper), 139
Anderson, Terry, 84
annual awards, for FOIA-based news, 154–56
Antonelli, Michael, 129
Archibald, Samuel, 56, 166, 167
Argus Leader, 154–55
Aristotle, 15
Arizona, 143–44
Arizona State University, 108
"Armed Forces Medical Library, 1-9," 23
Army Chemical Corps., 57

Army National Guard documents, 139
Army, the. See U.S. Army
Arnett, Haden, 148–49
Art Censorship Project, 129
art, government spending on, 129
"Artichoke," 86
asbestos removal, 147
Asbury Park Press, 155
Ashcroft, John, 47
ASNE. See American Society of
    Newspaper Editors (ASNE)
Associated Press Managing Editors
    (APME)
    "Censorship at the Source" resolution of,
        50–51
    fight for the Freedom of Information
        Act by, 24
    on improvements in access to
        government information, 52
    on information security classification
        system, 46
    report on lack of information access
        by, 34–36
Associated Press, the
    FOIA-related documents to, 127
    and reclassification of documents, 88
    stories by, 35–36, 124, 134–36,
        143–44, 146
    in the Sunshine Government
        Initiative, 153
    support for the FOIA by, 153
Atlanta Journal-Constitution (newspaper),
    135, 147
Atomic Energy Commission (AEC), 34
audits/self-studies, 117–21
Aurora, Colorado, 141
Authority for Employment (Title 5), 12
automobiles, product safety and, 114–15
awards, FOIA-based news, 154–56
AZT treatment, 128

bail money, 144
Baker, Al, 143
Baldwin, James, 100–1
ballots, access to voting, 148
Baltimore, Maryland, 39
Bamford, James, 115
BATF (Bureau of Alcohol, Tobacco, and
    Firearms), 114
*Bearing the Cross: Martin Luther King, Jr.,
    and the Southern Christian Leadership
    Conference* (Garrow), 100
"beat" reporting, 31–32
Bensenhaver, Amye L., 137, 149
Bergan Regional Medical Center (New
    Jersey), 145
Berman, Jerry J., 72
Bernstein, Carl, 92–93
bin Laden, Osama, 164
biological warfare testing, 126–27
Birmingham, Alabama church bombing,
    38–39
*Bitter Fruit: The Story of the American
    Coup in Guatemala* (Schlesinger/
    Kinzer), 88
Black Hawk helicopters, 118
Black, Hugo, 104
Black's Law Dictionary, 12, 13
Black Student Communications
    Organizing Network, 90
blood bank errors, 124
board membership records, 139–40
Boeing airplanes, 116, 120
Bolton, John, 123
Bond, Julian, 101
Bonner, Raymond, 102
Boston News-Letter (newspaper), 19
Boulder, Colorado, 125, 141
Bowling Green, Kentucky, 143
Bradford, Andrew, 19
Bradford, William, 19

Branch Davidian standoff, 92
Branch, Taylor, 100
Brandeis, Louis D., 9, 22
Brannan, Charles F., 25
Branscomb, Anne, 1–2
Brechner Center for the Freedom of
    Information (FOI) Center, 153–54
Breitman, Richard, 95
Brenner, Philip, 90
Brownell, Herbert, 57
Brown, Ronald H., 93
Brucker, Herbert, 21
Brunfield, Brulin B., III, 142
Buck, Pearl, 161
Bureau of Alcohol, Tobacco, and Firearms
    (BATF), 114
Bureau of Engraving and Printing, 93
Burke, John R., 110
Burlington, Vermont, 155
Burr, Aaron, 43–44
Burroughs Welcome, 128
Burton, Harold, 104
Bush, George W.
    and executive privilege, 44
    and FOIA compliance, 80–81
    government secrecy under, 83–85,
        121–23, 163
    information availability under, 34
    information classification system
        under, 47
    request for military in Iraq and
        Afghanistan under, 120
    Texas Air National Guard records of,
        162
    withholding of work papers, 121–23
Bush, George W.H., 128
Bush, Vannevar, 14–15
business community
    information requested by, 78
    mishandling of information by, 113

business of government, 113–14
    agency self-studies, 119–21
    audits, 117–19
    grant contracts, 116–17
    work papers, 121–23
Butler, John, 53
Butterfield Park District Board, 136

Cable Communications Policy Act (1984), 9
CACI International Inc., 162
California, 142, 145–46
Californian, 155
California Peace and Freedom Party
    (PFP), 105
Calumet Park Elementary School District, 147
Camden County tax commissioner, 144–45
Campbell, Duncan, 19
Campbell, James, 101
Campbell, John, 19
Campbell, Joseph, 55
Canham, Erwin "Spike" D., 50
Carnegie Commission, 128
Carrington, Edward, 19
Carter, Edward A., Jr., 106–7
Carter, Jimmy, 44
case law, of newspapers' challenges to
    government, 26–29
Case Western Reserve University
    (CWRU), 73
"Censorship at the Source" resolution, 50–51
censorship, Truman's executive order and,
    34–36, 50–51
Census Administration (Title 13), 12
census reports, 32
Center for Auto Safety, 114
Center for Citizens Media, 158
Center for Democracy and Technology, 158
Center for Media and Democracy, 158
Center for National Security Studies
    (CNSS), 77–78

Center for Responsive Politics, 159
Center for Survey Research, 157
Center for the Study of Responsive Law, 79
Centers for Disease Control and
    Prevention (CDC), 39, 127, 155
Central Intelligence Agency (CIA), ix
    California Peace and Freedom Party
        index of, 105
    and Center for National Security
        Studies, 77–78
    denial of records access by, 85
    documents on individuals by, 107
    FOIA queries to, 79
    on Freedom of Information Act
        revision, 65
    information released by, 100
    misleading testimony by, 129
    and Rosemary Awards, 164
Challenger (spacecraft), 93, 117, 118
Chamber of Commerce for the United
    States, 62
Charns, Alexander, 91
Cheney, Richard, 65, 81, 84
Chicago Daily Herald (newspaper), 140,
    147, 148
Chicago Public Art Program, 129
Chicago Tribune (newspaper), 127
Children's Online Privacy Protection Act
    (2000), 9
China, 104, 114
Christian Science Monitor (newspaper), 50
Chrysler automobile, 120
CIA. See Central Intelligence Agency (CIA)
CIA's War at Home, The (Mackenzie), 89
citizen action initiatives, 153–54
Citizens Alliance for Responsible
    Development, 128
Citizens for Responsibility and Ethics, 158
Civil Rights Division, Justice Department, 100
Civil Service Commission, 50
Clark, Charles E., 18

Clary Lakes Recreation Association
    (CLRA), 135
classification of information, 33–34, 45–48, 49
classified information
    under Bush administration, 83–84
    as classification category, 47
    reclassification of CIA documents, 88
    on stolen laptops, 161
    on strategic weapons, 162–63
Cleavinger, Howard C., 24, 51
Cleveland Plain Dealer (newspaper), 155–56
Clinton, Bill, 44, 72–73, 85, 119, 122
Cobb County Superior Court, 135
Cointelpro, 108
Colby, W.E., 65
colonial America, 18–20, 164–65
Colorado, 140–41
Colson, Charles, 128
Columbia University Press, 52
Columbine High School shooting, records
    on, 140–41
Commerce Department, 93–94
commercial information, 70
Committee in Solidarity with the People
    of El Salvador (Cispes), 92
Committee on Government Reform and
    Oversight, 73
Common Cause Magazine (magazine), 83
Communications Act (1934), 3
Community Relations Service, Justice
    Department, 100
Computer Security Act (1987), 46–47, 70
computers, information on. See electronic
    information
Congress
    on executive agency secrecy, 60–61
    and government withholding of
        information, 54–58
    public access to information policy, 15
    sharing of information between
        executive branch and, 41–43

congressional documents
   and depository library program, 9–11
   Housekeeping Statute on, 41–42
Congressional Research Service reports, 158
Congressional Wire, 159
Congresspedia.org, 158
Connecticut, 142–43, 144
Connecticut Local Politics, 158–59
Constitution, the, 9, 42
construction documents, 138–39
consumer groups, 96
consumer guides, 114–16
Consumer Product Safety (Title 15), 12
contaminated drinking water wells, story
   on, 56–57
Continental Congress, 9
Cooley, Thomas M., 8–9
Cooper, Kent, 52
Copeland, David, 18
corporate documents, 135
Corporation for Public Broadcasting, 128
corporations. See business community
Cosby, William, 20
Counterintelligence Program, 108
Courier-Journal (newspaper), 156
court news, crime and, 18
*Credit Scores and Credit Reports: How the
   System Really Works, What You Can Do*
   (Hendricks), 115–16
Crewdson, John, 94
crime, court news and, 18
criminal/police investigative records,
   140–42
Cross, Harold L., 50, 51–52, 54, 57, 58, 61
Crowley, Raymond L., 24
Cuban missile crisis (1962), 90
Cunningham, Randall "Duke," 118
Curry, Paul, 146
"curtain of secrecy," 58
Czechoslovakia, 110
Daily Business News, 155

Daily Chronicle (newspaper), 51
Daley, Richard J., 101–2
Dancs, Anita, 120
data-mining projects, government, 2–3
Davis, Scott, 135
Dawson, William, 54
Dean, Deborah Gore, 119
Declaration of Independence, 9
Defense Contract Audit Agency, 117–18
Defense Criminal Investigative Service, 116
Defense Manpower Data Center, 94
DelMonte, John J., 35
Demetracopoulos, Elias P., 107
Denver, Colorado, 141
Denver Post (newspaper), 141
Department of Agriculture, 3, 68, 121, 127
Department of Children and Family
   Services, 136
Department of Commerce, 3, 65
Department of Cultural Affairs, 129
Department of Defense (DOD)
   biological warfare testing by, 126–27
   and Black Hawk helicopters, 118
   failure of information control by, 3
   FOIA requests made to, 94–95
   post-September 11th access to infor-
     mation on, 75
   public access to information of, 16, 23
Department of Energy (DOE), 3, 75, 125, 126
Department of Health and Human
   Services (HHS)
   failure of information control by, 3
   FOIA costs to, 68
   FOIA-released documents from, 128
   post-September access to information
     on, 75
Department of Health, Education, and
   Welfare, 65
Department of Homeland Security, 3, 48, 76
Department of Housing and Urban
   Development (HUD), 68, 95–96, 102, 119

Department of Inland Fisheries and
Wildlife, 37
Department of Interior, 3
Department of Justice (DOJ)
FOIA costs to, 68
FOIA support by, 151
and Freedom of Information Act
implementation, 63, 66, 71
on Freedom of Information Act
revision, 65
Office of Information Law and Policy, 66
public access to information of, 16
*Department of Justice v. Reporters Committee
for Freedom of the Press* (1989), 70
Department of Labor, Employment
Benefits Security Administration, 124
Department of Social and Health Services
(DSHS), 140
Department of State
failure of information control by, 3
FOIA costs to, 68
FOIA queries to, 79
U.S. Information Agency, 100
Department of Transportation, 3
Department of Treasury, 3, 65, 68, 75
Department of Veteran Affairs, 2, 3
Depository Library Act (DLA), 10–11
depository library program, 9–11, 166
Desert Falls Country Club (Palm Desert,
California), 96
Detroit Free Press (newspaper), 39
Detroit News (newspaper), 155
Dever, Paul A., 35
Devlin, James, 35
Diana, Princess, x, 99
DiCarlo, Jacqueline, 146
digital records, 1–2
Diuguid, Lewis H., 108–9
document shredding, 1
DOE. See Department of Energy (DOE)
Doshisha University (Japan), 105

Douglas, William O., 91, 103
Drivers' Privacy Protection Act (1994), 9
Drug Enforcement Agency (DEA), 129
Duncan, Joseph W., 116
DuPage Election Commission, 148

Early, Jack, 113
Early, Robert P., 24
E.I. DuPont de Nemours & Company, 125
Eisenhower, Dwight D., 28
executive order No. 10501 by, 52–53
executive privilege used by, 44
and Housekeeping Statute amendment, 61
and Truman's executive order, 52
electric company reports, 137
Electronic Communications Privacy Act
(1986), 9
Electronic Freedom of Information Act
(EFOIA), 73
Electronic Freedom of Information Act
Amendments (1996), 9
electronic information
CIA, 88
FBI, 92
and Freedom of Information Act
compliance, 72, 83
and information technology advances, 1
privacy issues with, 71
and problems associated with FOIA, 80
protection of unclassified, 70
public access to, 1–2
e-mail, access to, 142, 143
English Common Law tradition, 8
English, Elaine, 80
Enright, Kevin A., 142
Enron Corporation, 122
Environmental Protection Agency (EPA),
1, 75, 78, 94, 113
EPA v. Mink (1973), 65
Epsy, Mike, 121

Erskine, Thomas, 21
Ervin, Walter C., 138
Evanzz, Karl, 101
executive agencies
 and Administrative Procedures Act
  (APA), 45, 60
 classification authority of, 53
 contractors handling FOIA work in, 162
 electronic information supplied by,
  71–72
 FOIA officers in, 151, 162
 Freedom of Information Act compliance by .See Freedom of
  Information Act (FOIA) compliance
 Freedom of Information Act requests
  made to, 83–96
 and Housekeeping Statute amendment, 60–61
 information requested by, 78
 information technologies investments
  by, 3
 obtaining information from quality of
  life, 124–28
 public access to information of .See
  public access to information
 secrecy of information by, 53, 60–61
 self-studies by, 119–21
 withholding of information by,
  60–61, 64
 see also individual agency names
executive branch
 executive privilege and, 42–45
 handling of congressional documents
  by, 41–42
 judicial branch on information privilege of, 43–44
 sharing of information between the
  legislature and, 41–42, 57–58
 withholding of U.S. Army reports, 53–54
Executive Order 10290, 22, 49, 50–51
Executive Order 10501, 52–53

executive privilege, 42–45, 49, 53–54,
 55–56
Exemption 7, 64, 65, 66, 67, 70–71
Exxon Mobil, 134
Exxon Valdez Oil Spill Trustee Council, 134

Fair Credit Reporting Act (1970), 9
Family Educational Rights and Privacy
 Act (1974), 9
Farrimond, Michael, 138
Faulkner, William, 161
FBI. See Federal Bureau of Investigation
 (FBI)
*FBI and Martin Luther King, Jr.: From
 "Solo" to Memphis, The* (Garrow), 100
FDA. See Food and Drug Administration
 (FDA)
Federal Alcohol Administration, 23
Federal Aviation Administration (FAA),
 116, 120
Federal Bureau of Investigation (FBI)
 and Alabama church bombing, 38–39
 and Center for National Security
  Studies, 77–78
 documents on individuals by, 107
 FOIA queries to, 79, 89–93, 97, 105–6
 and Frank Varelli, 107
 information released by, 100
 on laptop theft, 161
 Socialist Workers Party index of, 105
 surveillance by, ix–x, 100–1
 use of national security letters by, 161
Federal Department of Justice, 23
Federal Energy Regulatory Commission,
 75, 84
Federal Information Energy Act (2002), 3
Federal Internal Revenue, 23
federal property acquisition laws, 145
Federal Register, 75–76
Federation of American Scientists' Project
 on Government Secrecy, 162

Fernald, Ohio, 125

Ferroggiaro, William, 162

Fifth Amendment, 8

financial records, access to, 143–45

Fire at Sea (Gallagher), 108

First Amendment, 8, 26

First Amendment Foundation (Georgia), 157

FirstGov.gov, 33

Fleischer, Ari, 122

Fleming, Donald, 141

Florida, 139, 144, 155

Foerstel, Herbert N., 90

Food and Drug Administration (FDA), 113, 124, 125

Ford, Gerald, 44, 65–66

Foreign Aid Program, 55

Fortas, Abe, 91, 102, 104

Fort Lauderdale, Florida, 156

Fourteenth Amendment, 8

Fourth Amendment, 8

"fourth estate," 21

Fox River Grove Elementary school (Illinois), 147

Franke, Otto, 108–9

Frankfurter, Felix, 98, 104

Freedom of Access Act (FOAA) (Maine), 37

Freedom of Information (Brucker), 21

Freedom of Information Act (FOIA), 7, 59–76

  consumer reports made available through, 114–16

  court cases involving, 66–67

  definition of "information" cited in, 12, 13

  events leading up to, 49–58, 60–62

  exemptions in, 64, 65

  failures of, 166

  greatest beneficiaries of, 78–79

  groups focusing on administration of, 77–78

  and homeland security, 75–76

  law suits involving, 63, 66

  measuring success of, 164–65, 166–70

  passage of, 4, 62–63

  reporting on government activities, 32

  revisions in (1974), 64–66

  stories generated by use of, ix–x

Freedom of Information Act (FOIA) compliance, 79

  and classification standards, 83–85

  costs associated with, 68, 69–70, 80

  early history of, 63–64

  in the 1980s, 68–74

  problems with, 79–81

  in the twenty-first century, 74–75

Freedom of Information Act (FOIA) requests

  appeals strategies, 85

  audits, 117–21

  to the Central Intelligence Agency, 85, 86–88

  denials of, 39, 83–85

  disappointing and angry endings to, 108–11

  to federal agencies, 93–96

  on federal agency contracts with specialists, 116–17

  to the Federal Bureau of Investigation, 89–93

  on the Holocaust, 95

  on individuals, 97–111

  to NASA, 83, 93

  need for less, 167–68

  and privacy issues, 169

  to quality of life government agencies, 124–28

  types of requesters, 78

  using states' government access laws, 134–49

  on Vietnam War, 95

  for work papers, 121–23

Freedom of Information Act (FOIA),
support for
with annual awards, 154–56
citizen action initiatives, 153–54
by organizations, 151–52, 153
with projects and grants, 156–59
Freedom of Information Committee
(Associated Press Managing Editors), 24
Freedom of Information Foundation of
Texas, 157–58
Freedom of Information Reform Act
(1986), 67–68
Freedom or Secrecy (Wiggins), 26, 28, 163
"Freenet," 73
Free Press (newspaper), 155

gag laws, 27
Gallagher, Thomas, 108
Gallo, Robert C., 94
Gannon, Tom, 136
Garrow, David J., 88, 100
General Accounting Office (GAO), 32,
68, 74, 117–18
General Services Administration (GSA), 68, 78
geographic information system database,
142–43
Georgia, 135, 144–45, 146–47, 157
Georgia First Amendment Foundation,
157
Gingrich, Newt, 118
Glenn, John, 118
Glomar Explorer (ship), 87–88
"*Glomar response,*" 87–88
Go Tell It ont he Mountain (Baldwin), 100
government
computer security rating of, 3
database mishandling by, 2–3
and private sector model, 166–70
public need for news about, 18–21
relationship between journalism and, ix, x
relationship with news media, 4–5, 17–18

see also business of government; executive agencies
Government Accounting Office (GAO),
3, 32, 55, 68, 69, 74
government activity reports, 9, 173
government agencies. See executive
agencies
government housekeeping, 39, 41–48
Administrative Procedures Act (APA), 45
and congressional access to information, 41–42
executive privilege, 42–45
information security classification
system, 45–48
government information
and Associated Press Managing
Editors (APME), 34–36
available on the Internet, 73–74
classification system for, 33–34,
45–48, 49
collection of telephone call activities,
2–3
control of .See information control
depository library program, 9–11
early laws on public access to, 7–8
government reports, 32–33
on individuals, 97–111
legal definitions of, 11–14
legislative language defining, 11–14
loss of, 2, 161–62
news-gathering norms on accessing, 31–32
obtained from Americans, 7
overprotection of, 161–62
public access to .See public access to
information
reclassification of, 83–85, 88, 162–63
right to know principles, 28–29
secrecy of, 53, 60–61, 162–63
sharing of information between
executive branch and legislative
branch, 41–43

withholding .See information, with-
holding
see also classified information
Government Printing Office (GPO), 33
government reports, 32–33
Government Services Administration
(GSA), 33
grant contracts, 116–17
grants, FOIA support and, 156–59
Greene, Robert W., 32
Greenwich, Connecticut, 142–43
Gregory, Roger L., 39
Grumbles, Benjamin H., 94
Guantanamo Bay prison, 123, 155
Guantanamo camps, prisoner abuse in, 29
Gwinnett school system, 147

Hackler, Victor, 24
Haitians, 104–5
Hampton, Lionel, 102
Hanford Reservation (Washington),
125–26
Hangartner, Rick, 138–39
Hanssen, Robert, 103
harassment complaint records, access to, 140
harassment, public records used for, 146
Harbury, Jennifer, 109
Hardy, David T., 88, 92
Hardy, Porter, Jr., 55, 56
Harlan, John, 104
Hartford Courant (newspaper), 144
Harvard Law Review (journal), 9, 22
Hatch, Orrin, 67
Health Insurance Portability and
Accountability Act (1996), 9
Helms, Richard, 106
Hendricks, Evan, 115–16
Hennings, Thomas C., Jr., 61, 62
Henry, Patrick, 58
Hermando County, Florida, 144
Hersh, Seymour, 110

HHS. See Department of Health and
Human Services (HHS)
Himelfarb, Sheldon, 110
Hoar, Ralph, 120
Hollywood Communists, 101
Holocaust, the, 95
homeland security, 47, 75–76
Homeland Security Office. See
Department of Homeland Security
Hoover Commission, 53, 61
Hoover, J. Edgar, ix
files on others by, 101–2
gossip-filled files kept by, 98–99, 101–2
and Justice Warren, 91–92
hospital board members, 139
Houk, Robert W., 33
House Armed Services Investigating
Subcommittee, 55
House Committee on Government
Operations, 54–55
housekeeping. See government housekeep-
ing
Housekeeping Act, 41–42, 54, 55, 61–62,
78, 166
House of Representatives
Armed Services Committee, 163
Judiciary Committee, 161
House Subcommittee on Foreign
Operations and Government
Information, 64
House Subcommittee on Government
Management, Information and
Technology, 73
Howell, Vicki, 139
Hoyt, Clark, 164
HUD (Department of Housing and
Urban Development). See Department
of Housing and Urban Development
(HUD)
Hudson River, 127
Hutchins Commission, 21

Idaho, 135–36
identity theft, 161
Illinois, 136, 147, 148
Immigration and Naturalization Service, 104
immigration investigations, 104–5
Indiana, 133, 137, 154
Indiana Coalition of Open Government
    (ICOG), 157
Indianapolis Convention & Visitors
    Association, 137
Indiana University, 157
information
    defined in government statutes,
        11–12
    defining, 12, 14–16
    digitization of, 1–2
    laws asking Americans for, 7
    see also government information; pub-
        lic information
information access. See public access to
    information
"information anxiety," 1–2
information control, 4
    gag laws, 27
    government disclosure to news media,
        50–52
    reasons for, 8–9
    and right to know, 28–29
    secrecy of federal agencies, 53
    and taxation 27
    see also executive privilege; informa-
        tion, withholding
information scientists, defining "informa-
    tion," 14, 15
Information Security Oversight, 76
information technology, effect of, 1
information, withholding
    after September 11th attacks, 75–76
    on airline cargo regulations, 48
    APME resolution on, 50–51
    on B-36 plane crash, 51

    under Bush administration, 83–85,
        121–23
    on Communist infiltration, 53–54
    examples of, 55–57
    by executive agencies, 60–61, 64
    by the FBI, 89–90
    work of House Committee on
        Government Operations on, 54–55
insurance records, 138
Interagency Security Classification
    Appeals Panel, 85
Internal Revenue Code (Title 26), 12–13
Internet, the
    CIA searches on, 88
    FBI public files on, 92
    FOIA websites on, 153
    government information available on,
        73–74
    grant support for government infor-
        mation websites on, 158–59
    growth in, 73
Investigative Reporters and Editors Inc.
    (IRE), 153, 154
*Investigative Reporting for Print and
    Broadcast* (Gaines), 32
investigatory reports, 142
Iowa, 141
Iran, American hostages in, 106
Iraq, 29
Iraq war, 120

Jackson, Robert, 104
Janklow, Bill, 154–55
Jay's Treaty, 43
Jefferson, Thomas, 19–20, 42, 43–44, 164–65
John Doe Agency v. John Doe Corp. (1989),
    70–71
Johnson, Lyndon B., 44, 59
journalism. See news media
journalism education, 31–32
Journals (U.S. Congress), 9

258 | *Index*

J. Roderick MacArthur Foundation, 105–6
*Judas Factor: The Plot to Kill Malcolm X,
    The* (Evanzz), 101
judicial branch, 43–44
Judicial Watch, 93
Judiciary Committee's Subcommittee on
    Administrative Practice and Procedure, 62
Justice Management Division, 121

Kansas City, Missouri, 155
Kansas Court of Appeals, 38
Kassel, Tim, 147
Kelley, Clarence M., 101, 105
Kelley, Kitty, 99
Kemp, Jack F., 95, 96, 119
Kennedy, Edward, 66
Kennedy, John F., 44, 90
Kennedy, Robert F., 102
Kentucky, 137, 143, 148–49
Kern, Robert Lee, 141–42
Khrushchev, Nikita, 90
Kimball, Rex, 92
King, Martin Luther, Jr., x, 100
Kino Community Hospital (Arizona), 143
Kinzer, Stephen, 88
Kirkley, Donald Jr., 162
Kissinger, Henry, 79, 113–14
Klaper, Sarah, 148
Klopf, Ruth, 148
Knight, Frank A., 24
Kobort, Scott, 148
Korean War soldiers, 127
Kormbluh, Peter, 103
Krusten, Maarja, 163
Kyle, Kimber, 139

Labor Department's Employment Benefits
    Security Administration, 124–25
Lacrosse Tribune (newspaper), 36
Laird, Melvin R., 163
Lamy, Brian D., 137

Lankford, Richard E., 55
Lano, Angelo J., 92–93
laptop computers, theft of, 2, 161
LaRouche, Lyndon, 115
laws. See legislation
lawsuits
    for access to information, 78
    filed by prison inmates, 129
    for noncompliance to the Freedom of
        Information Act, 63, 66
Lawyers Committee for Human Rights,
    104
Lay, Kenneth, 122
Lay, Larry, 139
Leff, Lisa, 109–10
legal definitions of "information," 11–14
legislation
    privacy laws, 9
    public access to, 7–8
    see also state access laws; specific titles
        of legislation
legislature, the
    executive branch sharing information
        with, 57–58
    military officers working for, 118–19
Leonard, Thomas C., 20–21
Levison, Stanley, 100
Library Awareness Program, 90–91
Library Company of Philadelphia, 9
light rail transit system (Seattle), 138–39
Lippmann, Walter, 21
Lister, Walter, 24
London Magazine (magazine), 25–26
Long, Edward V., 62
Long, Gordon B., 148
Los Angeles Times (newspaper), 87
Louisiana, 38, 142, 148
Louisville Courier-Journal & Times
    (newspaper), 24, 50
Lynch, Mark, 79
Lynch, Mary K., 148

Machlup, Fritz, 14
Mackenzie, Angus, 89–90
MacLeish, Archibald, 161
MacNeil, Robert, 128
Madigan, Lisa, 115
Madison County, Kentucky, 137
Mahan, Daniel C., 92–93
Maheu, Robin, 144
Maine, 37–39
Maine Dairy and Nutrition Council, 37
Malcolm X, 101
Mallory, Alfonso, 135
Maplight.org, 158
Marion Brechner Citizen's Action Project
    (MBCAP), 151, 153–54
Marks, John, 86–87
Marshall, John, 43–44
Martinez, Mel, 121
Martin, Shannon, ix–x
Maryville Academy, 136
Massachusetts Institute of Technology
    (MIT), 90
Mattes, John, 95
McCaffrey, Barry, 110
McCarthy, Joseph, 53, 54
McConnell Center for Political
    Leadership, 156
McCormick, Joseph, 84–85
McDonnell, Robert J., 108
McDougal, James, 119
McGovern, George, 98–99
McGrain v. Daughtery (1927), 49
McNeil Technologies, 162
medical center finance reports, 145
Megabux Index, 159
Melibee (Chaucer), 12
mentally ill, Washington Post story on, 127
Merry Wives of Windsor, The (Shakespeare), 8
*Messenger: The Rise and Fall of Elijah
    Muhammad, The* (Evanzz), 101
Michigan, 142

Michigan Department of Corrections, 142
Mid-Continent Life Insurance Company, 138
military censorship, 36
military officers, working for legislative
    officers, 118–19
Military Sea Transportation Service, 55
military, the. See U.S. Army
Miller, Gordon, 15
Miller, Tom, 141–42
Mincberg, Elliot M., 162
mind control experiments, 86–87
Mink, EPA v. (1973), 65
Minnesota, Near v. (1931), 27
Missouri, 148
Missouri Group, 31
MKULTRA behavior experiments, 87
Monsanto, 113
Monteleone, Lenny, 148
Moore, K. Michael, 121
Moore, Miles, 39
Moore, Nancy, 140
Morro Castle (ship), 108
Moss, John E., 50, 51–52, 62–63, 79, 166
Murphy, Frank, 104
Mutual Security Act (1959), 56

Nader, Ralph, 78
Nagy-Talavera, Nicholas M., 107–8
National Aeronautics and Space
    Administration (NASA), 55, 83, 117–18
National Archives and Records
    Administration (NARA), 88, 95, 162
National Child Search Assistance Act
    (1990), 156
National Council on the Arts, 129
National Endowment for the Arts (NEA), 129
National Freedom of Information
    Coalition (NFOIC), 151, 153, 156–58
National Guard, the, 139
National Highway Traffic Safety
    Administration (NHTSA), 39, 119

National Imagery and Mapping Agency, 75

National Institutes of Health (NIH), 94, 128

National Newspaper Association, 153

National Parks, 16

National Security Agency (NSA), 2, 3, 95, 99, 115

National Security Archive, 78, 91, 102–3, 163–64

National Security Archive Research Center, 114

national security interests, 8

national security letters, 161

National Transportation Safety Board, 94

National Transportation Safety Board (NTSB), 94. 116, 120

National Transportation Services, 16

Naval Gun Factory, 55

Near v. Minnesota (1931), 27

Negroponte, John D., 123

Nevada, 145

Nevada Supreme Court, 145

New Hampshire, 133, 137

New Jersey, 145, 154, 155

New London Day (newspaper), 24

New Orleans, Louisiana, 156

News for All: America's Coming-of-Age with the Press (Leonard), 20

news media

    annual awards for FOIA-based news, 154–56

    in colonial news media, 18–20

    and Freedom of Information Act compliance, 72

    goals for an unfettered press, 164–65

    government non-disclosure to, 50–52

    news gathering by, 31–34

    and number of FOIA queries, 78

    public need for government news in, 18–21

    relationship between government and, ix, x, 4–5, 17–18

    responsibilities of, 31

    and twentieth century newspapers, 21–23

    on war efforts, 28–29

    see also newspapers

Newspaper Association of America, 153

newspapers

    championing access to government information, 23–26

    colonial, 18–19

    government attempts at information control, 26–29

    and private sector model, 165

    role of, in American society, 20–21

    taxation of, 26

    twentieth century, 21–23

    see also individual newspaper names

News Reporting and Writing (Missouri Group), 31

Newton, "Red," 35

Newton, V.M., Jr., 24

New York (state), 138

New York Herald Tribune (newspaper), 52

New York Sun (newspaper), 28

New York Times (newspaper)

    Centers for Disease Control story in, 39

    FBI stories in, 91, 92

    and Glomar Explorer story, 87

    HUD story in, 96

    and NASA, 93

    and Pentagon Papers, 27

New York Weekly Journal (magazine), 20

NFOIC. See National Freedom of Information Coalition (NFOIC)

Nicastro, Frank N., 144

Ninth Amendment, 8

Nixon, Richard M., 27, 44, 128

    see also Watergate scandal

nonprofit corporations, 137

non-public information, 13

Noriega, Manuel, 99

Norquist, Grover, 103

North Carolina, 36, 133
North, Oliver L., x, 99, 102–3
Northwest Pipeline Company, 38
not-for-profit corporation records, 138
Nuclear Regulator Commission (NRC), 85
nuclear wastes, 125, 126
Nureyev, Rudolf, 90

Oak Ridge, Tennessee, 125
Oberdorfer, Louis, 91
O'Brien, Kevin, 73
Occupational Safety and Health
 Administration, 125
"O & C" files, 98–99
O'Connor, Kathleen, 140
Office of Evaluation in the International
 Cooperation Administration (ICA), 55
Office of Information Law and Privacy, 66
Office of Management and Budget
 (OMB)
  Circular No. A-130, 33
  on Freedom of Information Act revision, 65
  on withholding of government
   information, 75
Ohio, 125, 133
oil pipeline spill, 116
Oklahoma, 138
Oklahoma City bombing, 110–11
Omar, Mullah, 164
OMB. See Office of Management and
 Budget (OMB)
Open Community Open Document
 Review System (OCODR), 158
Open Public Records Act, 145
OpenTheGovernment.org, 154
Oregon, 38
O'Reilly, James T., 113
organizations
  grant-giving and receiving by, 156–59
  supporting the FOIA, 151–52, 153–54
Ortiz, Dianna, 109

Over the Counter Pills That Don't Work
 (Public Citizen Health Research
 Group), 115
Owens, Howard T., Jr., 143
Oxford English Dictionary, 12, 13
Pacific Project, the, 127
Paducah, Kentucky uranium-handling
 plant, 126
Palm Beach, Florida, 155
"paper curtain," 58
Paperwork Reduction Act (1980), 33
Parade (magazine), 87
Park, Tongsun, 102
Patent Office, 113
Pate, William C., 145–46
Pawtucket, Rhode Island, 35
payment-in-kind (PIK), 121
Pennsylvania Avenue Development
 Corporation, 117
Pentagon Papers, 27
Pentagon's Defense Contract Audit
 Agency, 117–18
Pentagon, the, 127
People for the American Way, 162
People's Right to Know, The (Cross), 51–52
Perdue, Frank, 109–10
personnel records, 139–40
Peurifoy, John, 88
Phillippi, Harriet Ann, 87
physically ill, Washington Post story on, 127
Pierce, Samuel R., Jr., 96, 102, 119
Pike Nationa Forest, 56
Plato, 15
Political Science and Politics (Archibald), 166
Pope, James S., 24–25, 50, 52, 54, 57
Posada, Luis Carriles, 103–4
Post (newspaper), 155
Postal Reorganization Act (1970), 39
Potomac Alliance, 85
Press of Atlantic City (newspaper), 156
press, the. See newspapers

Prichard, Edward, Jr., 99
Printing Act (1895), 10
prisoners of war (POWs), 127
prison inmates
    access to records by, 141–42, 142
    award-winning stories on, 155
    lawsuits filed by, 129
    mind control experiments on, 87
Privacy Act (1974), 8, 9
privacy issues
    collection of telephone call activities, 2–3
    in conflict with the Freedom of
        Information Act (FOIA), 70–71
    see also right to privacy
privacy laws, 9
Privacy Protection Act (1980), 9
private sector model, 165–70
product safety, 114–15
Project on Government Oversight, 159
Projects Jennifer, 87
Public Access Counselor's (PAC) office, 157
public access to information
    Administrative Procedures Act, 45, 60, 61
    and Associated Press Managing
        Editors (APME), 34–36
    congressional policy on, 15
    early history of, 78
    House Committee on Government
        Operations on, 54–55
    and information classification catego-
        ries, 33–34
    on the Internet, 73–74
    lessening restrictions on, 167–68, 169–70
    newspapers championing, 23–26
    privacy issues vs., 70–71, 168–69
    and privacy rights of citizens, 22
    reasons for denying, 8
    and representative democracy, 166–67
    right to privacy vs., 168–69
    and September 11th attacks, 16
    and state government, 36–39

Public Citizen Foundation, 78
Public Citizen Health Research Group, 115
public information
    defined in the Freedom of
        Information Act (FOIA), 13
    information exempt from, 4
    and technological change, 1–2
public, need for government news by the,
    18–21
public records databases, 116
"Public Schools and the Open Records
    Act in Georgia," 157
Public Service Company of New
    Hampshire, 137
publishing office, government, 10
*Puzzle Palace: A Report on American's Most
    Secret Agency, The* (Bramford), 115
Pyke, Marni, 148

quasi-agency and agency reports, 134–39

radioactive emissions, 125–26
Radio-Television News Directors
    Association, 153
Rainer, David, 145
Rank, Everett G., Jr., 121
rap sheets, 70, 71
Ratner, Michael, 103
Rauzon, Mark. J., 127
Ray, Michael, 104–5
ReadTheBill.org, 159
Reagan-Bush Campaign Committee, 94, 95
Reagan, Nancy, 99
Reagan, Ronald, 44, 46–47, 70
reclassification, of government informa-
    tion, 88, 162–63
Reed, Stanley, 104
Reporters Committee for Freedom of the
    Press, 78
*Reporters Committee for Freedom of the
    Press, Department of Justice v.* (1989), 70

*Reporter's Handbook: an Investigator's
  Guide to Documents and Techniques,* 32
Reporting Public Affairs (Schulte), 32
research data, 135–36
Resolution Trust Corporation, 119
Reston, Virginia, 116
Richardson, Bill, 126
Richland, Washington, 126
Riddell, Charles W., 137
Riddleberger, James W., 56
right to be let alone, 9
Right to Financial Privacy Act (1978), 9
right to know principles
    APME resolution on, 50–51
    ASNE report on, 52
    first congressional session debating
        on, 59–60
    Jefferson on, 164–65
    and a representative democracy, 166–67
    tested, 28–29
*Right to Know: The Rise of the World Press,
  The* (Williams), 31
right to privacy
    and access to government news, 22
    balancing public's social concerns
        with, 8
    circumstances violating, 168–69
    denying public access to government
        information based on, 8
    nineteenth century articles
        supporting, 8–9
Roberts, John G., Jr., 162
Roberts, John Jr., 122
Rocky Mountain Arsenal, 56
Rolling Stone (magazine), 87
Roman Empire, 18
Room Eight, 159
Rosemary Awards, 163–64
Rosenberg atomic spy case, 91
Roundup (herbicide), 113
Rouse, James A., 141

Rubin, Robert E., 122
Rumsfeld, Donald, 65

Sabghir, Jonathan M., 144
Saccio, Leonard J., 55
Safavian, David H., 103
"Safeguarding Official Information In the
    Interests of the Defense of the United
    States," 52–53
Salisbury, G.H., 24
"Samuri Shuttle" episode, 83
sanctions for violations, 145–46
Sandburg, Carl, 161
Sanderson, Shannon, 147
San Diego Community College District, 142
San Diego Port District, 145–46
San Diego Union-Tribune (newspaper), 142
Sarto, Bill, 140
Saunderson, Lisa, 136
Savannah River Plant, 125
Scalia, Antonin, 65
Schack, Larry, 146
Schardt, Arlie W., 106
Schlesinger, Stephen, 88
Schmitt, Robert Patrick, Jr., 93
scholarship awards, award-winning story
    on, 156
school board meeting documents, 148
school construction contracts, 147–48
school lunches, contaminants in, 127
school/student records, 146–48
Schroeder, Patricia, 118–19
Schuh, Mary, 143–44
Schulte, Henry H., 32
Schwartz, Bernard, 57–58
Scott, William L., 117
Scripps Howard News Service, 156
*Search for the "Manchurian Candidate":
    The CIA and Mind Control, The*
    (Marks), 86–87
Seattle, Washington, 138–39

"Secrecy Report Card," 154
Securities and Exchange Commission, 102
security of government documents, 33–34
self-studies, federal agency, 119–21
"Semantic Quirks in Studies of
  Information" (Machlup), 14
Senate Bill 2190, 22
Senate Committee on the Judiciary, 68
Senate Judiciary Report, 60
Senate Select Committee on Intelligence
  Activities, 89
Senate Subcommittee on Government
  Organizations for Space Activities, 55
sensitive but unclassified information, 47–48
sensitive security information (SSI), 47–48
September 11th terrorist attacks
    information classification categories
        after, 47
    telephone records collection following, 3
    withholding of information following,
        75–76
sewer connection fees, 144
sex offenders, access to information on, 141
Shakespeare, William, 8
Sheffield, Ron, 136
sheriff department records, 140–41
shredders, 1
Sigma Delta Chi, 50, 53
Sinatra, Frank, 101
*Small-On Safety: The Designed-in Dangers of
  the Volkswagen* (Center for Auto Safety), 114
Snellville Middle School (Georgia), 147
Snyder, Murray, 56
Socialist Workers Party, 105
Social Security and Veterans
  Administration, 139
social services records, 140
Society for Public Access Computing, 73
Society of Professional Journalists, 72, 78, 153
soil safety, 135
Solway, Diane, 90

South Carolina, 38
Southern Tier Economic Development
  Inc. (STED), 138
Southwestern Bell Telephone, 38
Soviet nuclear submarine, 87–88
Soviet Union, 9
Spanish-American War (1898), 28
*Spying on Americans: Political Surveillance
  from Hoover to the Huston Plan*
  (Theoharis), 89
Stamp Act (1765), 26
Star (newspaper), 155
Starsky, Morris, 108
Starzel, Frank J., 25–26
state access laws
    agency and quasi-agency reports, 134–39
    board membership and personnel
        records, 139–40
    criminal/police investigative records, 140–42
    evidence of, 38–39
    financial records, 143–45
    generalizations among, 133–34
    Maine's Freedom of Access Act
        (FOAA), 37–38
    Public Records Act Citation, 131–33
    sanctions for violations, 145–46
    student/school records, 146–48
    variation among, 36–37
    voting records, 148–49
state agency reports, 134–39
State Commissioner of Labor and
  Industries, 35
state laws, on taxation of newspapers, 26
St. Charles water treatment facility, 128
Steinhardt, Barry, 2
Stevenson, Adlai, 98–99
Stewart, Potter, 91, 104
Stiers, Mike, 141
St. Petersburg Times (newspaper), 144
St. Tammany Parish School Board meeting, 148
student/school records, 146–48

student test records, 147
St. Vincent Millay, Edna, 161
Sullivan, William, 98
Summers, Lawrence H., 122
Sunlight Foundation, 158–59
Sun-Sentinel (newspaper), 156
Sunshine in Government Initiative, 153
Supreme Court of Connecticut, 142, 143
surveillance
    by the FBI, 89, 90–91, 100–1
    and Hoover's files, 98–99, 101–2
    of the not-so-famous, 104–8
    in public buildings, 169
*Surveillance in the Stacks: The FBI's Library
    Awareness Program* (Foerstel), 90
Symington, Stuart, 55

*Talking at the Gates: A Life of James
    Baldwin* (Campbell), 101
Tampa Morning Tribune (newspaper), 24, 35
tax commission office (Georgia), 144–45
taxes
    access to information on, 143–45
    and newspapers, 26
Taxpayers for Common Sense (TCS), 158
Taylor, Denise, 144–45
telephone call activities, and invasion of
    privacy, 2–3
Telephone Consumer Protection Act (1991), 9
Tenet, George, 85
Tennessee, 133–34
Texas, 157–58
Texas Air National Guard, 162
Theoharis, Athan, 89, 98, 102
"The Right to Privacy" (Warren/Brandeis), 9
Third Amendment, 8
This Is Not An Assault (Hardy/Kimball),
    92
Thomas, Joel, 139
Times-Picayune (newspaper), 156
Tocqueville, Alexis de, 165

Transportation Security Administration
    (TSA), 47, 48, 85
Treatise on the Law of Torts, A (Cooley), 8–9
Trentadue, Jesse, 110–11
Trentadue, Kenneth, 110–11
Truman, Harry S., 34, 36, 45–46
Twin Falls, Idaho, 135–36
Uniform Relocation Assistance and Real
    Property Acquisition Policy Act, 145
Union Carbide Corporation, 125, 126
Union of Concerned Scientists, 90
United Technologies, 118
university basketball, 148
University of Florida, 154
University of Louisville, 156
University of Missouri, 153
uranium-handling plant
U.S. Advisory Commission on
    Information, 50
U.S. Agency for International
    Development, 117
U.S. Army, 53, 95, 100, 106–7, 120
U.S. government. See government
U.S. Holocaust Museum, 95
U.S. Information Agency of the
    Department of State, 100
U.S. Marshall Service, 120
U.S. News & World Report (magazine), 79,
    87–88, 98, 124
U.S. Supreme Court
    favoring privacy over information
        access, 70–71
    on information provided by govern-
        ment officials out of office, 79
    on "right of privacy," 8
    wiretapping of justices in, 104
    see also individual Supreme Court cases
Valdez oil spill, 134–35
Vanocur, Sander, 128
Varelli, Frank, 107
Velasquez, Efrain Bamaca, 109

"velvet curtain," 58

Veterans Administration (VA), 68

veterans hospitals, award-winning story on, 155–56

Video Privacy Protection Act (1988), 9

Vietnam War, media reporting on, 29

Vinson, Fred, 99, 104

Vosburgh, William W., Jr., 24–25

voter assistance forms, 148–49

voting records, 148–49

Waco, Texas, 92

Wade, Mitchell J., 118

Wade, Troy E., 125

Wade Walker Park (Georgia), 135

Wall Street Journal (newspaper), 134–35

Waltzing With a Dictator: The Marcoses and the Making of American Policy (Bonner), 102

Ward Line, 108

war efforts, reporting, 28–29

Warren, Earl, ix, 91–92

Warren, Samuel D., 9, 22

Washington (state), 38, 138–39, 140

Washington Evening Star (newspaper), 98

Washington, George, 4, 42, 43, 78, 166

Washington Post (newspaper)

    on data-mining projects, 3

    Environmental Protection Agency article in, 94

    FBI story in, 92–93

    Guantanamo Bay prison story in, 123

    and Pentagon Papers, 27

    use of Freedom of Information Act requests by, 94, 127

    Watergate question addressed in, 163

waste sites, accidents at, 125–26

Watchdog.org, 159

Waterbury Republican & American (newspaper), 24–25

Watergate scandal, 27, 92–93, 163

weapons, importing of assault, 114

Weiner, Bob, 110

Welch, Jewel E., 142

Westin, Alan, 80

Westinghouse Electric Corporation, 125

Whilden, Evan H., 114

Whitaker, Stephen, 142–43

Whitewater Development Corporation, 119

Who Owns Information: From Privacy to Public Access (Branscomb), 2

Wiener, John, 97

Wiggins, James Russell, 23, 163, 169

    APME activity by, 24, 50, 51

    efforts to change classification system, 52

    involvement in House Committee on Government Operations, 54

    on need for access to information, 25–26

    on the right to know, 28

Wilkie, Wendell, 98

Williams, Francis, 31

Wilson, Cindi, 147

Wilson, Edwin P., 129

Wilson, Steve, 143

Winter Haven Hospital, 139

wiretapping, 104

Woods, Rose Mary, 163–64

Woodward, Bob, 92–93

work papers, 121–23, 162

World Trade Center attacks, 111

World Trade Center, contaminants and, 127

World War II, 95

Wurman, Richard, 1

"XYZ Affair," 43

Yatani, Choichiro, 105

Young, Edwin, 51

Zachary Police Department, 142

Zenger, Peter, 20

Mediating American History

SERIES EDITOR: DAVID COPELAND

Realizing the important role that the media have played in American history, this series provides a venue for a diverse range of works that deal with the mass media and its relationship to society. This new series is aimed at both scholars and students. New book proposals are welcomed.

For additional information about this series or for the submission of manuscripts, please contact:

Mary Savigar, Acquisitions Editor
Peter Lang Publishing, Inc.
29 Broadway, 18th floor
New York, New York 10006
Mary.Savigar@plang.com

To order other books in this series, please contact our Customer Service Department:

(800) 770-LANG (within the U.S.)
(212) 647-7706 (outside the U.S.)
(212) 647-7707 FAX

Or browse by series:

WWW.PETERLANG.COM